Detention before Trial

A STUDY OF CRIMINAL CASES TRIED IN THE TORONTO MAGISTRATES' COURTS

Martin L. Friedland

UNIVERSITY OF TORONTO PRESS

To my Family

Preface

THIS WORK was undertaken as part of the Programme in Criminal Studies, which is financed by a special grant provided by the Law Society of Upper Canada, at the Osgoode Hall Law School. The work began three years ago as an academic study of one of the most neglected areas in the administration of justice in Canada, detention before trial. Since then, many individuals, groups, and levels of government in Canada have shown genuine concern with the problems involved in this area.

Dean H. Allan Leal, Q.C., and Professor J. D. Morton, Q.C., formerly the Director of the Programme in Criminal Studies, now Regius Professor of Laws, Trinity College, Dublin, supported the study from its inception. The resources of Osgoode Hall were always readily available.

My greatest debt is owed to Professor Caleb Foote of the Faculty of Law, University of Pennsylvania, for the guidance and encouragement he has given over the past three years.

Four former students, Philip Alter, Barry Brown, Charles Gardner, and Melvin Morassutti, each spent a summer helping to collect and process the data; their assistance was invaluable. In addition, approximately 30 other law students helped in collating the data.

Dr. J. W. Mohr, Research Associate, The Forensic Clinic, Toronto, willingly assisted the writer in the non-legal world of statistics and research techniques. Mr. Hugh Allen, then a statistician with the Ontario Research Foundation, also assisted by advising on statistical methods. Mr. Jack T. Duggan, formerly of the UNIVAC Division of Remington Rand Limited, advised on the possibilities and limitations of computers and assisted with the processing of the data.

Co-operation and support was received from all levels of government and from those involved in the administration of justice: from the Attorney General's Department, in particular Mr. W. B. Common, Q.C., formerly Deputy Attorney General, and Mr. A. A. Russell, Q.C., Inspector of Legal Offices; from the Toronto magistrates and justices of the peace, in particular, His Worship Magistrate Elmore, Q.C., formerly the Chief Magistrate of Metropolitan Toronto, and Kenneth L. Gimblett, Justice of the Peace; from the Metropolitan Toronto Police, in particular, Chief James P. Mackey, Inspector R. M. Gibson, Inspector G. Russell, and Sergeants George McGowan and D. J. Pringle; from the Toronto Crown attorneys, in particular, Mr. H. H. Bull, Q.C.; from the Administrator of the Toronto Magistrates' Courts, Mr. R. W. Ruggles and other persons connected at the time of the study with the administrative side of the Toronto Magistrates' Courts, Messrs. R. M. Bowles, W. Huber, E. N. Gilbert, S. A. Newell, W. Patterson, H. V. Spong, D. Willard and S. A. Williamson; and from the Dominion Bureau of Statistics, in particular, Messrs. W. A. Magill and D. Cassidy.

I am grateful also to Professor H. W. Arthurs of Osgoode Hall, Professor H. Krever of the Faculty of Law, University of Toronto, and Mr. E. Patrick Hartt, Q.C., who read the manuscript and made many helpful suggestions; to Mr. George A. Johnston, Q.C., and Miss Rosemary McCormick of the Great Library, Osgoode Hall, for their help in obtaining material; to Miss Nancy J. Bramston for her careful secretarial work; and to the Director and editors of the University of Toronto Press for the care with which they went over the manuscript. Finally, I wish to thank my dear wife Judy not only for her patience and understanding, but also for her help and encouragement.

Osgoode Hall Law School
March 1965

M. L. FRIEDLAND

Contents

Figures

Tables

Detention before Trial

1. Introduction

DETENTION BEFORE TRIAL has been one of the most neglected areas in the whole administration of criminal justice.[1] In the past, attention has been focussed almost exclusively on detention *after* trial (i.e., sentencing), which touches the lives of significantly fewer persons than detention *before* trial. There has been no previous examination of our bail system, with the result that no one has had an accurate idea of the utility or effectiveness of its operation.

The purpose of the present study is to begin to fill this void by documenting statistically the extent and nature of custody before trial in the Toronto Magistrates' Courts, the courts where the overwhelming majority of persons charged with criminal offences (over 95 per cent of the indictable and all summary offences) in Toronto are tried. Some of the specific areas investigated are: the use of the summons; the extent to

[1]Recognition of the importance of the period before trial has been growing in the past few years in the United States. Comprehensive bibliographies can be found in *Bail in the United States: A Bibliography* (1964), compiled by Dorothy C. Tompkins, Institute of Governmental Studies, University of California; and in Freed and Wald, *Bail in the United States: 1964*. In spite of Arthur Beeley's important study in 1927, *The Bail System in Chicago*, there was little interest in the problems of bail until students from the University of Pennsylvania Law School, under the direction of Professor Caleb Foote, investigated the administration of bail in Philadelphia in 1954 ("Compelling Appearance in Court: Administration of Bail in Philadelphia" (1954) 102 *U. Pa. L. Rev.* 1031) and later, in New York ("A Study of the Administration of Bail in New York City" (1958) 106 *U. Pa. L. Rev.* 693). In addition to the interest generated by the University of Pennsylvania studies, the growing concern in recent years has arisen for a number of reasons: the United States Supreme Court's over-all concern with problems arising from the indigency of the accused; The Manhattan Bail Project, undertaken by the Vera Foundation in 1961 (described *infra*, chapter 4); the *Report of the Attorney General's Committee on Poverty and the Administration of Federal Criminal Justice* (1963); and the National Conference on Bail and Criminal Justice, co-sponsored by the Department of Justice and the Vera Foundation (described in (1964) 48 *J. Am. Jud. Soc.* 6).

For comparative material on practices in certain other jurisdictions, see "A Symposium: Conditional Release Pending Trial" (1960) 108 *U. Pa. L. Rev.* 290 (Scotland, Japan, Norway, and France); address by Botein J. before the National Conference on Bail and Criminal Justice, May 27, 1964 (Italy, Sweden, and Denmark); Husain, *Law of Bails in India and Pakistan* (Karachi, 1961).

which accused persons are detained in custody both before and after the first court appearance; the first court appearance; bail-setting practices and the ability to raise bail; the activities of professional bondsmen; the enforcement of penalties for absconding; and the relationship between custody and the outcome of the trial.

Many of the results of the study will surprise even those familiar with the practices in our courts. No agency now collects the type of data presented here, without which it is difficult to see more than a small part of the total operations of the administration of justice. Although the study is directed primarily at practices in Toronto, many of these practices can be found in other cities throughout Canada.

No attempt will be made to provide a detailed historical survey of the law of bail: this has been done by others.[2] Suffice it to say that the word "bail" comes from the ancient French word "baillier" (to deliver) and, as Lord Devlin has stated: "The right to be bailed is . . . as old as the law of England itself. . . ."[3]

The Collection and Presentation of the Data

The study comprises all the offences under the Criminal Code (a total of almost 6,000 cases) tried in the Toronto Magistrates' Courts over the six-month period from the beginning of September 1961 to the end of February 1962.[4] Before presentation here, the data had to be found (as we shall see, not always an easy task), recorded, categorized, coded, key-punched, processed electronically, and, finally, analysed.

Only criminal cases which were eventually concluded in the magistrates' courts were considered; cases tried in the higher courts and preliminary enquiries in the magistrates' courts were excluded. Individually the latter may be of at least equal importance with the cases studied here; quantitatively, however, they represent but a small proportion of the total number of Criminal Code cases tried in our courts. Provincial offences and municipal by-law violations have also been excluded.[5] Our

---

[2]See, e.g., De Haas, *Antiquities of Bail: Origin and Historical Development in Criminal Cases to the Year 1275* (New York, 1940); De Haas, "Concepts of the Nature of Bail in English and American Criminal Law" (1946) 6 *U. of T. L. J.* 385; Pollock and Maitland, *History of the English Law* (2d ed., 1923), II at p. 584 *et seq.*; Petersdorff, *Law of Bail* (1824); Holmes, *The Common Law* (Howe ed.) at pp. 197–98; Maitland, *The Constitutional History of England* (paperback edition: Cambridge, 1961) at p. 314 *et seq.*; Qasem, "Bail and Personal Liberty" (1952) 30 *Can. B. Rev.* 378; Egan, "Bail in Criminal Law" [1959] *Crim. L. Rev.* 705; note, "Bail: An Ancient Practice Reexamined" (1961) 70 *Yale L. J.* 966.

[3]*The Criminal Prosecution in England* (1960) at p. 75 citing Stephens, *History of the Criminal Law* (1883), I, at p. 233.

[4]During this period these courts were numbered A, B, C, D, E, and G.

[5]No doubt revealing data could be uncovered by a thorough study of the pro-

attention is concentrated here solely on violations of the federal Criminal Code and the federal Narcotic Control Act.[6]

A six-month period of time was chosen in order to obtain a large, but manageable, number of cases. There appears to be no sound reason to believe that the practice in the period from September 1961 to February 1962 is not reasonably representative of that in the Toronto courts over the past number of years. Indeed, with the increasing overcrowding in the magistrates' courts, the situation may now be worse.

A retrospective study of past cases, rather than a prospective study of cases as they arose, was undertaken not only because the records available made a retrospective study a practical possibility, but also because knowledge that a prospective study was in progress would tend to influence those being observed.[7] Moreover, a prospective study presents a problem with respect to cases which have not yet been concluded at the end of the time set for the collection of the data.

Sampling techniques were not employed. The more the cases chosen for study approximate the total universe of possible cases, the more confidence one can have in the conclusions reached. In addition, the number of variables was sufficiently great to necessitate the study of a fairly large number of cases. Most important, sampling would not appeal to the lawyer-reader: lawyers who tend to be wary of statistics in any form like technical statistical expertise even less.

The collection of the data was an onerous task. Although the records for Toronto are probably better than those found in most large cities, the relevant data are still not conveniently located in one place. The following are sixteen of the various sets of records, kept in different places, which had to be examined in order to extract the data relevant for this study: annotated daily court lists; records showing the transit of prisoners to and from the Don jail; informations (the formal documents setting out the charges); microfilmed cash bail records; property bail bonds; cash bail books; police station night bail books; Don jail bail records; Dominion Bureau of Statistics' records on prosecutions for

---

vincial offences. For example, custody pending trial is the invariable practice for certain provincial crimes such as drunkenness: see The Liquor Control Act, R.S.O. 1960, c. 217, s. 80(2). On the other hand, the summons, rather than arrest, is employed almost exclusively for offences against The Highway Traffic Act, R.S.O. 1960, c. 172.

[6]Stat. Can., 1960–61, c. 35: at the time of the study known as the Opium and Narcotic Drug Act, R.S.C. 1952, c. 201. The British North America Act, 1867, provides that the federal government has legislative jurisdiction over criminal law and procedure and that the provinces have jurisdiction over the administration of justice and the constitution of the courts.

[7]The writer is informed that those familiar with the physical sciences will recognize the similarity between this and the Heisenberg Uncertainty Principle.

skipping bail; records with respect to previous convictions which are sent to the Dominion Bureau of Statistics; Metropolitan Toronto Police Criminal Investigation Bureau's records of previous convictions; police station books showing data on all persons charged with offences; estreat material kept by the Clerk of the Peace; files kept in the probation office with respect to pre-sentence reports; bench warrant records; and Supreme Court data on applications to vary bail. Accumulating data from a number of different sources provided a good means of rechecking data already recorded because the same information on certain matters was often noted in several different places. If reference is required to at least 16 different sources to obtain a clear picture of the early stages of the criminal process, it is understandable why it is difficult to appreciate fully what has been happening in our courts.

The basic source of information and the one relied on initially to make up the cards for this study was the annotated daily court lists. It was primarily the existence of these lists that made a retrospective study possible. A mimeographed list of all new and remanded court cases is prepared every morning by the police. These lists, which would have been valuable as a starting point even if unannotated, include such data as age and date of arrest of all persons appearing in court that day. Extensive marginal notations by the police on the master copy immeasurably increased their value. A police officer, stationed in each court, makes notes on the appropriate list with respect to such matters as custody and bail, thus enabling the police to control accurately the large flow of prisoners between the police stations, the Don jail, and the City Hall. These records must necessarily be accurate. By carefully tracing the court appearances of accused persons through these lists the basic data required for the study was obtained. Simply to transfer this information onto cards took two months of full-time work for three researchers. This information was then supplemented by data obtained from the other sources noted previously.

After compilation, the material was coded according to categories established for this study. The raw data were translated into symbols which could be punched onto data-processing cards; approximately 30 law students assisted in this aspect of the project. Categories were established in advance for all variable factors in order to keep the data processing within manageable bounds. They were not set up, however, until a reasonably thorough working knowledge of the data had been obtained. One of the considerations used in setting up the categories was the possibility of comparing our results with those found in previous studies in other jurisdictions.

The coded material was then key-punched, verified, and processed electronically by the UNIVAC Division of Remington Rand Limited.

In many respects the analysis of the data presented the greatest challenge. An almost indispensable technique was to set out in advance various hypotheses which could be tested. Approximately 60 hypotheses were so tested, although they have not been set out in presenting the data. Unless such hypotheses are established, the material tends to become an overwhelming mass of directionless data. The figures were generally sufficiently telling to permit conclusions to be drawn.

Much of the presentation of the data is descriptive. However, attempts are made throughout the study to prove statistically the existence of causal relationships. For example, in chapter 6 an attempt is made to establish a statistical relationship between the outcome of the trial and custody before trial. It was recognized that this could be done only by the comparison of like cases. Accordingly, the data were usually broken down as fully as possible into such variables as offence and previous record. There were limitations to this, however, because the final figures were often too small to be meaningful. One particular stabilizing technique, used whenever possible, was to equate cases where bail was set initially at $500. This amount was chosen because more cases had bail set at this sum than at any other figure. No controlled experiments could be attempted; unlike medical scientists, lawyers cannot use guinea pigs and it is rare for courts to become involved in permitting the establishment of control groups.[8]

In addition to the analysis of the 6,000 cases, certain limited substudies were undertaken: for example, data on the time of the accused's arrest were gathered from a single large police station. It should also be pointed out that, because all percentages have been rounded off to the nearest full figure, the total may not always add up to exactly 100 per cent. Further, there will sometimes be a slight discrepancy between the total number of cases in the tables because, although each breakdown included a category of "not clear" cases, these have not been set out in the tables.

A Brief Description of the Early Stages of the Criminal Process

The reader who is unfamiliar with Canadian criminal procedure may appreciate at the outset a capsule summary of what happens to a person

[8]In New York City the courts did permit the establishment of a control group for a study of release on one's own recognizance by the Vera Foundation (discussed in chapter 4). It was discontinued, however, after it became apparent that the persons in the control group (who were not recommended for release on their own recognizance) were being treated unfairly by having to raise bail.

charged with a criminal offence. A person accused of an offence against the Criminal Code may be either summoned or arrested with or without a warrant. For a summons or an arrest with a warrant the complainant would first have gone before a justice of the peace to initiate proceedings; an arrest without a warrant requires no judicial authorization. An arrested accused is taken to one of the many police division stations in Toronto, "booked," lodged in a cell, and, for indictable offences, fingerprinted and photographed. He is liable to be questioned at any time while in police custody. Unless he is released on bail by a justice of the peace or brought almost directly to the City Hall courts, he will remain in police custody until transferred to the City Hall some time around 7.00 A.M. the next morning. He will then remain in the City Hall cells until his case is first dealt with, some time after 10.00 A.M., by a magistrate.[9] If he pleads guilty, the case will usually be disposed of at the first court appearance. If he pleads not guilty, the case will usually be remanded for one week and bail may be set or the accused released on his own recognizance. A remanded accused who has been denied bail or who has not yet been able to raise it will be transferred to the Don jail, to remain there until his next court appearance or until bail is raised.

All offences under the Criminal Code can be categorized according to the procedure employed for trying the case: "summary" (an offence which can be tried by the summary conviction procedure) or "indictable" (an offence which can be tried by indictment) or both, for certain offences, with the Crown having the choice of procedure. Unlike England and the United States, Canada has abolished the distinction between a felony and a misdemeanour. In the summary cases, which are less serious than the indictable ones, the magistrate tries the accused according to a procedure set out in Part 24 of the Code. An indictable offence may be one of three types: offences over which the magistrate has absolute jurisdiction;[10] offences over which the magistrate has jurisdiction only with the consent of the accused;[11] and, finally, cases such as murder, manslaughter, and rape, over which the magistrate has no jurisdiction. The present study analyses only those cases which were tried by a magistrate.

[9]All magistrates are justices of the peace, but not all justices are magistrates. The magistrate can try cases of indictable offences. The justice can hold a preliminary hearing for indictable offences, try summary offences, and perform such functions as issuing summonses and warrants of arrest, and granting bail.

[10]Because these offences cannot be tried by indictment it is, of course, anomalous to call them indictable offences.

[11]If this consent is not given, a preliminary hearing is held by the magistrate to see if the case is substantial enough to warrant committal for trial to a higher court.

2. The Summons

QUESTIONS CONCERNING BAIL AND CUSTODY arise only if the accused is arrested rather than summoned. It is, therefore, a necessary preliminary to inquire into the extent to which the Toronto police employ the summons procedure and the desirability of extending its use.

I. THE USE OF THE SUMMONS

A. In Toronto

The overwhelming majority of accused persons in Toronto charged with offences against the Criminal Code are arrested rather than summoned. In slightly over 92 per cent of the 6,000 cases examined in this study the accused was arrested. There was an insignificant variation between the use of the summons for indictable and non-indictable offences; in both, arrests were made in approximately 92 per cent of the cases.[1] The statistical report of the Metropolitan Toronto Police Department for the year 1961 also shows a 92 per cent rate of arrests for Criminal Code offences.[2] According to the Toronto police reports, the arrest figures for earlier years were: 1958, 97 per cent; 1959, 96 per cent; and 1960, 91 per cent. Between 1958 and 1960 there was a significant trend towards an increased use of the summons; this trend did not continue, however, in 1961. The report for 1962 does not show a breakdown between summonses and arrests. This change may be because the Dominion Bureau of Statistics does not seek this information for their publications and police forces now seek to conform to the requirements of the Bureau.[3]

[1]Arrests were made in 91.6 per cent of the indictable offences and in 92.1 per cent of the non-indictable. Young offenders are summoned with even less frequency than older offenders: for example, in the present study it was found that less than 5 per cent of those 16 and 17 years of age were summoned. Women tend to be summoned more frequently than men: 7.5 per cent of the males and 12 per cent of the females were summoned.

[2]*Statistical Report of the Metropolitan Toronto Police Department, 1961.*

[3]See the *Dominion Bureau of Statistics, Uniform Crime Reporting Manual,* 1962.

On August 23, 1961, one week before the start of the six-month period studied in this work, a notice was circulated through the police force directing its members to make more liberal use of the summons procedure "in dealing with persons charged with offences under the Liquor Control Act or the Disorderly House section of the criminal law." This notice was probably the result of an incident at a coffee house in Toronto in which the police were subjected to criticism for arresting "found-ins" unnecessarily. This incident and the resultant directive indicate that at the beginning of the period studied the police were conscious of the existence and, in some cases at least, the desirability of the summons procedure. It may well be, however, that the limited scope of the recommendation in the directive may have led some police officers to believe that increased use of the summons should be limited to those cases mentioned in the directive.

Private prosecutions (i.e., prosecutions in which the police do not become involved) are included in the above data (for both the published police statistics and the present study); if they were omitted, the percentage of arrests would undoubtedly be even higher. This is because private prosecutors show an understandable reluctance to arrest without a warrant; they feel the need of judicial sanction for their acts and, in order to initiate proceedings, will appear before a justice of the peace who will, in most such cases, issue a summons rather than a warrant of arrest. Private prosecutions, therefore, tend to increase the number of summonses issued. If offences outside the Criminal Code were included in the study the figures would show an increased use of the summons, mainly because most driving offences, which are provincial "crimes" and constitute the largest category of offences, are dealt with by means of the summons. On the other hand, for some offences outside the Criminal Code the summons is rarely employed. For example, out of 58,657 persons charged with the provincial offence of "being drunk in a public place"[4] in the years 1959–61 inclusive, not a single person was brought to court by means of a summons.[5]

B. Comparison with other Canadian Cities

It is difficult to compare the figures for Toronto with those for other Canadian cities.[6] Police reports were obtained from many of the larger

[4]The Liquor Control Act, R.S.O. 1960, c. 217, s. 80(2).
[5]See the Toronto Police Statistics for the years 1959–61.
[6]Professor Orfield stated in 1947 that the summons is "widely used in Canada." Orfield, *Criminal Procedure from Arrest to Appeal* (1947) at p. 33. See, to the same effect, Moreland, *Modern Criminal Procedure* (1959) at p. 9. Although this may be true in other areas in Canada, it would not seem applicable to the present

Canadian cities, yet a complete breakdown between summonses and arrests for Criminal Code offences was not shown separately in any of the published statistics examined.[7] Regrettably, as was pointed out above, Toronto discontinued the practice of breaking down its figures in 1962.

The most revealing comparison found is with Criminal Code driving offences in Vancouver. In 1961, Vancouver employed the summons for 34 per cent of these cases.[8] Toronto, on the other hand, summoned only 7 per cent of the offenders in this classification.[9] Thus there is almost a 5:1 ratio between Vancouver and Toronto in the use of the summons for Criminal Code driving offences. Restricted as the comparison may be, it would seem to suggest that there is no real necessity for the apparent reluctance in Toronto to use summonses rather than arrests—at least in respect of driving offences.

C. Comparison with England

In contrast with the practice in Toronto is the widespread use of the summons in England, where approximately 35 per cent of those charged with indictable offences are summoned.[10] Thus, in relation to the total number of persons charged with indictable offences, the summons was employed in England during 1961 in over four times as many cases as in Toronto. There are, of course, variations between categories of offences in England; for example, 51 per cent of all persons charged with indictable offences against the person were summoned in 1961

---

practice in Toronto. An accurate comparison can be based only on further research.

[7]The Medicine Hat police force compiled a report in answer to the writer's request. The figures involved were probably too small to give rise to any firm conclusions. There was a somewhat surprising jump in the use of the summons from 13 per cent in 1960 to 24 per cent in 1961.

Unpublished figures for the city of St. John, New Brunswick, appear to indicate that the summons is used there in fewer cases than in Toronto. In 1962, for example, excluding motor vehicle cases, the summons was used in only about 3 per cent of the criminal cases.

[8]Out of a total of 1,426 charges, 476 were summoned. The 1962 figure for Vancouver is slightly lower, 29 per cent.

[9]Out of a total of 6,339 charges, 470 were summoned.

[10]The figure is set at "about thirty per cent" in *Kenny's Outlines of Criminal Law* (17th ed.) at p. 541. However, recent statistics from the annual publication, *Criminal Statistics, England and Wales*, show that the figure should be higher: 1958, 35 per cent; 1959, 35 per cent; 1960, 34 per cent; 1961, 35 per cent. Even for the offence of intoxication, for which no persons are summoned in Toronto the English police summoned 5 per cent in 1961. In France, Germany, and Italy the summons is apparently used even more widely than in England: see Orfield, *op. cit. supra* note 6, at p. 33.

(51 per cent in 1960), whereas 23 per cent of those charged with offences against the person with violence were summoned (21 per cent in 1960).

It is difficult to compare summary offences in Canada with those in England. The English statistics on non-indictable offences include offences which are not Criminal Code violations in Canada and, therefore, were not included in this study (for example, offences involving drunkenness and traffic violations, which are provincial offences in Canada). However, a rough estimate was made by analysing only those non-indictable offences in England which are roughly comparable to Criminal Code offences in Canada. It was found that the summons was used in about 50 per cent of these cases. (It will be recalled that the summons was employed in only 8 per cent of the summary conviction cases in Toronto.) If the figures for these particular offences were to be included with the English figures on indictable offences, the percentage of cases in which the summons was employed would be increased from 35 to 40 per cent and the discrepancy in practice between England and Toronto in the use of the summons would be even greater.[11] It is difficult to believe that the discrepancy between the use of the summons in England and Canada can be attributed solely to factors other than a conscious and deliberate policy of using the summons.

Any comparison between national figures and those for a large metropolitan area, such as Toronto, must take into account possible differences between urban and rural practice. The figures for the large urban centres in England may be somewhat lower than the national figures, but there is no reason to believe they are significantly different.[12] There is no suggestion in the literature that the general procedures for compelling the accused's appearance in court differ in various sections of the country, nor is there any indication that the summons is infrequently used in the larger cities. The national figures for England show a percentage of summonses sufficiently high to allow for the possibility that all persons in non-urban areas were summoned yet still show a reasonably extensive use of the summons in urban areas.

[11]As in Canada, the summons is normally not initially employed in vagrancy-type offences (1961 England, 5 per cent; 1961 Toronto, .05 per cent), or traffic offences involving drunkenness (1961 England, 10 per cent; 1961 Toronto, 2 per cent). On the other hand, the summons is widely used in England for the offence of malicious damage (1961, 80 per cent), whereas in Toronto it is not (1961, 5 per cent).

[12]The Home Office was unable to supply the writer with figures for any large urban centres.

A comparison of certain specific offences presents a more striking picture of the difference between practice in England and Toronto. Those of forgery and uttering, indecent exposure, indecent assault on a male, and criminal negligence in the operation of a motor vehicle will be examined.

Forgery and Uttering. In England, 44 per cent of all persons charged with the felony of forgery and uttering were summoned in 1961.[13] In the same year, not one person out of 123 prosecuted in Toronto for forgery and uttering was summoned. Data for other years in Toronto and England show a similar pattern.[14] Because forgery is not normally an offence which the police officer discovers in the course of its perpetration, the Toronto data strongly support the view that arrest is a routine procedure followed by the police, rather than a necessary practice dictated by the nature of the offence.

Indecent Exposure. Whereas in England 59 per cent of those charged with the non-indictable offence of indecent exposure during 1961 were summoned, in Toronto only 3 per cent were summoned.[15] Legally, an arrest without a warrant cannot be made in Canada for the summary conviction offence of indecent exposure unless the accused is found committing the offence.[16] Arrest without a warrant should probably not occur often; the police officer would not normally find the accused indecently exposing himself but would act on the basis of a call from a member of the public. Because arrest without a warrant would thus not normally be legal, in light of the English figures, and because the officer would have to appear before a justice of the peace to initiate proceedings, one might expect a greater use of the summons for this offence than in fact occurs in Toronto. A combination of two equally undesirable procedures would appear to account for the extremely limited use of the summons for this offence: police officers are arresting accused persons for indecent exposure without a warrant, even though they do not find the accused committing the offence; and police officers as a matter of course are obtaining warrants of arrest rather than

[13]The misdemeanour of forgery has been excluded.

[14]Toronto Police Statistics: 1958, 5 out of 84 (6 per cent); 1959, 1 out of 33 (3 per cent); 1960, 1 out of 101 (1 per cent); percentage for years 1958–61 inclusive is 3. English Statistics: 1958, 47 per cent; 1959, 46 per cent; 1960, 43 per cent; percentage for years 1958–61 is 45.

[15]This figure was obtained from the present study. The Toronto Police Statistics do not isolate this offence.

[16]See ss. 158 and 435(b) of the Criminal Code. See generally, G. A. Martin, "Powers of Arrest," *in* Sowle (ed.), *Police Power and Individual Freedom* (1962) at p. 37 *et seq.*

summonses from justices of the peace. The former reason would appear to be the dominant one.[17]

Indecent Assault on a Male. Summonses were issued in 1961 in 38 per cent of the cases where persons were charged with homosexuality in England; in Toronto during the same period the summons was used in only 3 per cent of these cases.[18]

Criminal Negligence in the Operation of a Motor Vehicle. An exact comparison with England is not possible because the scope of the offences involving criminal negligence in the operation of a motor vehicle is not precisely the same. However, a useful comparison can be made between the English offence of causing death by dangerous driving, for which in 1961 93 per cent of those charged were summoned, and the Canadian offences involving criminal negligence in the operation of a motor vehicle, for which, out of a total of 48 persons charged in 1961, not a single person was summoned. Out of 418 persons charged with criminal negligence in the operation of a motor vehicle in Toronto during the years 1958–61 inclusive, only four persons were summoned, less than 1 per cent.[19]

II. DESIRABILITY OF USING THE SUMMONS

The foregoing discussion is sufficient to demonstrate that the summons is infrequently employed in Toronto. This is clearly undesirable in light of the many sound arguments in favour of limiting the process of arrest to those cases in which it is a reasonable necessity. In 1931 the Wickersham Report on law enforcement in the United States concluded: "Indiscriminate exercise of the power of arrest is one of the most reprehensible features of American criminal justice."[20] Although

[17]It often happens that the police arrive at the scene in answer to a complaint but do not actually see the offence taking place. The common practice in such a case is to arrest the accused without a warrant, even though it is illegal to do so.

[18]Toronto Police Statistics: 1958, 0 out of 39; 1959, 0 out of 29; 1960, 1 out of 34 (3 per cent); 1961, 1 out of 35 (3 per cent); percentage for the years 1958–61 inclusive, 1.5. English statistics: (the offences of buggery, attempt to commit buggery, and indecency between males were combined to arrive at these figures): 1958, 38 per cent; 1959, 38 per cent; 1960, 42 per cent.

[19]Toronto Police Statistics: 1958, 0 out of 122; 1959, 0 out of 140; 1960, 4 out of 108 (4 per cent); 1961, 0 out of 48. English statistics: 1958, 88 per cent; 1959, 89 per cent; 1960, 90 per cent; 1961, 93 per cent. The Vancouver figures are much higher than those for Toronto, although the numbers involved are not sufficiently large to enable any definite conclusions to be drawn: 1960, 8 out of 25 (32 per cent); 1961, 21 out of 29 (72 per cent); 1962, 2 out of 13 (15 per cent).

[20]*National Commission on Law Observance and Enforcement, Report on Criminal Procedure* (1931) at p. 14. For other critical views see, e.g., Beeley, *The Bail System in Chicago* (1927); Orfield, *op. cit. supra* note 6, at pp. 31–33;

the situation in Toronto would seem to be less serious than that existing in most large American cities,[21] the previous section indicates that the observation of the Wickersham Committee still has relevance to Toronto today.

Historically, the procedure of arrest was understandable. At common law all felons were arrested.[22] This was necessary at a time when many offences were considered serious enough to warrant the death penalty and when there were no police forces or efficient means of tracking down a suspected criminal in order to serve or ensure compliance with the summons. Society's view of the gravity of many of these offences has altered and, in addition, effective means of bringing offenders to justice have been devised; these changes militate against continued indiscriminate use of the power of arrest.[23] It should not be forgotten that at one time arrest was the normal method of bringing a defendant before the court in a civil case. In this area persuasion has been substituted for force as it should be where possible in criminal cases.

The English *Report of the Royal Commission on Police Powers and Procedure*, 1929, suggested that "the arrest of an offender is always to be avoided if a summons will suffice."[24] No elaboration of this

Perkins, *Cases on Criminal Law and Procedure* (2d ed., 1959) at pp. 899–901; Tappan, *Crime, Justice and Correction* (1960) at p. 329.

[21]Professor Caleb Foote, who examined police department reports in over a dozen American cities, states: "The only American police report examined which indicated any use whatsoever of the summons for any other than minor or regulatory offences was that of Cincinnati, which in 1955 used the summons in 351 cases involving Class I crimes [the most serious offences], compared with 2,465 arrests." Foote, "Safeguards in the Law of Arrest" (1957) 52 *N. W. U. L. Rev.* 16 at pp. 32–33. See also Puttkammer, *Administration of Criminal Law* (1953) at p. 71. For the legal restrictions on the power to issue summonses in American jurisdictions, see *infra* note 36.

In the United States *Report of the Attorney General's Committee on Poverty and the Administration of Federal Criminal Justice* (1963), in which four federal districts were studied (Table V, p. 136) that the summons was used in 1961 in the following percentage of cases (the number of cases is in parentheses): Northern District California (San Francisco), 29 per cent (316); Northern District California (Sacramento), 7 per cent (25); Northern District Illinois, 7 per cent (46); District of Connecticut, 36 per cent (96). Because these figures are not broken down into offences it is not possible to compare accurately the use of the summons in the federal courts with its use in Toronto. Cf. a later survey by Freed and Wald, *Bail in the United States: 1964* at p. 71: "A nationwide survey disclosed that a few districts use the summons a great deal. In the Northern District of California, 257 summonses were issued in 1963 compared with 364 warrants."

[22]See Warner, "Modern Trends in the American Law of Arrest" (1943) 21 *Can. B. Rev.* 192 at p. 211; Pollock and Maitland, *The History of English Law* (2d ed., 1923), II at pp. 582–83.

[23]See generally, Perkins, *op. cit. supra* note 20, at pp. 857–58, 899–901, 909.

[24]Cmd. 3297 at p. 51.

statement was deemed necessary; it was treated as axiomatic. The basic policy that a summons, if reasonably effective, is preferable to an arrest is unquestioned in the English literature.[25] In view of contrary practice in Toronto, some discussion of the relative merits of the summons procedure is necessary.

When an accused is summoned, rather than arrested, all the harmful consequences of custody pending trial are automatically eliminated: the possible effect of custody on the outcome of the trial and on the sentence of the accused if he is not released pending trial; the higher incidence of guilty pleas for those kept in custody; the possibility of improper treatment while in custody; the possible delay and inconvenience in attempting to raise bail; the opportunity for the accused to become enmeshed with illegal bondsmen and unscrupulous lawyers; and generally all the personal considerations, such as loss of employment, decreased income and protection for the accused's family, and anxiety of relatives and friends. Regardless of how many improvements are made in the bail system to ensure speedy release and proper custodial conditions pending release, it would be most unrealistic to expect that all the harmful aspects of custody would be eliminated. There must necessarily be some delay between the time of arrest and subsequent release. This delay and its concomitant hardships can be eliminated through greater use of the summons.

Greater use of the summons would cut down the cost of the administration of justice. In terms of the total number of man-hours required the arrest procedure may not differ significantly from that for the summons. Although an arrest requires more officers to guard the accused and transport him first to the police station and then to the courts, the issuance of a summons necessitates an appearance before a justice of the peace to have the summons sworn and one or possibly more than one trip is required to serve the summons. In addition, the use of the summons may result in a lower number of guilty pleas at the first court appearance.[26] Additional investigation, the routine work of contacting witnesses, and a greater number of court appearances by the officer are then required. Moreover, should the accused not appear in answer to the summons, the officer must first prove that it was served before

---

[25]A leading English police officers' manual, *Moriarty's Police Law* (16th ed., 1961) at p. 42 states: "Proceedings by summons is the usual method of making persons amenable for offences. . . ." See also Devlin, *The Criminal Prosecution in England* (1960) at pp. 69–70; Fitzgerald, *Criminal Law and Punishment* (1962) at p. 147; Stephen, *A History of the Criminal Law of England* (1883), I at p. 191.

[26]See chapter 3.III.B.

a bench warrant will be issued.[27] There are, however, other substantial costs involved. The more that the arrest procedure is used, the greater will be the capital cost of constructing and maintaining police lockups. The accused who is arrested and detained and thereby cut off from his source of income may not be able to support his family or finance his defence. These costs tend to fall on the shoulders of society. In terms of cost, then, it would appear that the summons is probably less expensive than arrest.[28] If certain time-saving procedures, for example, summonses issued by the police, were used, the financial balance would tip more clearly in favour of the summons.

English law has always maintained that the physical integrity of the body and freedom from confinement are of paramount importance. Summoning an accused saves him from the indignity of being physically taken away by the police. Unless the application of even the most minimal force is reasonably necessary it should not, of course, be applied.

Unnecessary arrests weaken the whole fabric of the administration of justice. They further community disorder and create bad will between the public and the police force. Many of the cases involving police violence, resisting arrest, and assault on police officers arise out of situations in which the police are legally but needlessly using the arrest procedure. The administration of criminal law directly affects a substantial proportion of the community.[29] Not only will the accused react unfavourably to what he feels to be abusive procedures, but his friends

[27]S. 441(6) of the Criminal Code. For an example of the difficulties that can be encountered in proving service, see *Regina* v. *Peel Construction Co. Ltd.* [1964] 2 C.C.C. 196 (Ont. S.C.).

[28]Whatever the case may be for the economy of using the summons in lieu of arrest, it almost certainly would be cheaper if the summons were used after arrest in lieu of detention. See chapter 3.IV.D.(iii).

[29]Excluding juveniles and detentions that are not noted by the police as arrests, approximately 45,000 *persons* were arrested by the police in 1961 in Toronto. This figure includes Criminal Code and provincial offences. Many of these persons will, however, have appeared in court more than once during the year. Nevertheless, the figure certainly indicates that a reasonably large proportion of the population of Toronto is being arrested each year. It is not correct to assume that the number of first offenders within this group is small. There are no reliable statistics on the number of first offenders who appear before the courts. Those compiled by the Dominion Bureau of Statistics are unreliable because they never show a person convicted on a multiple-count indictment as a first offender, even though it may have been the first time he had ever been in a court: see the review by this writer of "Statistics of Criminal and other Offences, 1960" (1963) 41 *Can. B. Rev.* 475. The present study suggests that the number of first offenders may be much larger than is generally suspected. No record is kept by the police of offences punishable on summary conviction, but for indictable offences the data showed that out of 2,619 persons charged with indictable offences, 1,416 (54 per cent) had no previous convictions for indictable offences.

and relatives also will tend to lose respect for those who use unduly harsh and primitive techniques for compelling appearance in court. By arbitrarily arresting all accused persons the police cannot hope to enlist public sympathy and support.[30]

It is not suggested that the use of the summons is necessarily desirable for compelling the accused's appearance in court when he is charged with one of the very serious offences such as murder, rape, or robbery.[31] The initial decision in these cases as to whether the accused should be free pending trial should be made by someone other than the arresting officer. However, these offences make up but a small proportion of the total number of charges: in 1961 they comprised under 3 per cent of the total prosecutions for offences against the Criminal Code. The overwhelming majority of cases involve lesser charges such as assault, impaired driving, and petty theft. It is for these lesser offences that greater use of the summons is advocated.[32] Many of the persons who are charged with these offences have no previous convictions for indictable offences. The present study shows that over half (54 per cent) of those who are arrested for indictable offences have no such record. Thus it is not the hard-core criminal offenders or those charged with heinous crimes with whom the police are normally dealing.

III. Effectiveness of the Summons in Compelling the Accused's Appearance

Is the summons procedure effective in ensuring the appearance of the accused in court? The summons has been widely employed in England with no suggestion of a sufficient lack of response to it to warrant a change of practice.[33] The summons cannot, of course, be as effective

[30]See Hall, "Law of Arrest in Relation to Social Problems" (1936) 3 *U. of Ch. L. Rev.* 345 at pp. 372–73: the elimination of "abusive practices by police" is "the essential prerequisite to the enlistment of public support, and hence to efficient detection and arrest."

[31]The summons is rarely used in England for these offences. In 1961 not a single person charged with murder was summoned, and only 3.7 per cent of those charged with burglary were summoned. For the offence of rape 13 per cent were summoned, a surprisingly high figure, yet well below the over-all English figure of 35 per cent. Giles, the author of a popular paperback, *The Criminal Law* (Pelican Books, revised 1961), states (at p. 78): "A summons against a burglar, for instance, would be a singular rarity."

[32]See Freed and Wald, *op. cit. supra* note 21, at p. 71.

[33]A survey conducted in the American federal courts did not turn up any dissatisfaction with the result of using the summons: see Freed and Wald, *op. cit. supra* note 21, at p. 71: "Over 60 districts used the summons or informal letters for misdemeanors or violations of regulatory statutes. No district reported any default problem. All defaults on summonses in the federal system in 1963 totalled 44."

as arrest and complete custody before trial. However, a comparison with other techniques which allow the accused his freedom pending trial will give a more practical picture of its effectiveness.

In the absence of any controlled experiment, the first step is to see whether accused persons who are summoned appear at the first court appearance in proportionately as many cases as those who are arrested and then released on bail from the police station. Figures obtained in the present study show that the summons compares favourably with arrest and subsequent bail as a means of securing the appearance of the accused in court. Out of 460 cases in which a summons was used initially, in only six was it necessary for the magistrate to issue a bench warrant at the time set for the first court appearance: i.e., the accused appeared at the first court appearance in 98.7 per cent of the cases in which he initially was summoned. This percentage is the same as that for those arrested and then released on bail from the police station.[34] An exact comparison between the effectiveness of the summons and that of arrest and subsequent bail is difficult to make. Even if the persons in each category were comparable risks, the length of time between the initiation of proceedings and appearance in court differs in each case. An arrested accused is usually bailed to appear in court the next morning whereas a summons is normally returnable at a much later date. Therefore, the factors which may affect the accused's appearance will necessarily differ.

The fact that the summons is effective may be in part because those who are summoned tend to be better risks than those who are arrested. A strong indication of this is reflected in the finding of the present study that a high percentage (perhaps 90 per cent) of those summoned had no previous convictions for indictable offences.[35] In comparison, 78 per cent of those arrested and bailed before the first court appearance and 50 per cent of those kept in custody until the first court appearance had no previous convictions. On the other hand, a person's previous record is not by itself conclusive evidence that such a person is a bad risk and, in any event, the data show that there were a number of summoned persons (approximately 5 per cent or more) who had three or more previous convictions for indictable offences. In addition, the procedure

[34]Out of 608 persons released on bail from the police station, eight did not show up the next morning at the first court appearance: i.e., 98.7 per cent did appear.

[35]The reason why this figure cannot be given with certainty is that there were approximately 10 per cent in the "not clear" category in the information supplied by the Metropolitan Toronto Police. It was apparently more difficult for the police to state with certainty whether a person had previous convictions in the summons than in the arrest cases.

followed by the police is often determined by such fortuitous factors as whether the complainant wants the police to summon the accused rather than arrest him, or whether there is a police car available to take the accused to the station. In these cases there is little or no investigation of the accused's background; it cannot, therefore, be said that the police have consciously summoned only the better risks.

Even if a closer analysis should disclose that the summons is less effective than arrest and subsequent bail, any indication of its effectiveness approximating the percentage found in this study would be sufficient justification for alleviating the rigours of arrest by an increased use of the summons.

IV. Legal Factors Affecting the Use of the Summons

A. *Legal Restrictions on the Use of the Summons*

Canadian law, in contrast to that in most American jurisdictions,[36] imposes no legal restriction on the use of the summons to compel the

[36]Few American jurisdictions permit the use of the summons instead of arrest. Perkins states: "In the relatively few jurisdictions in which [the summons] procedure is recognized by state law, it is limited to misdemeanors (and usually to certain specified misdemeanors, determined by type or penalty), to violations of municipal ordinances, to offences by juveniles, or to some combination of these." See Perkins, *op. cit. supra* note 20, at p. 900. When the police citation is included as a form of summons the percentage of American jurisdictions permitting the summons in lieu of arrest is a little over 50. In Freed and Wald, *op. cit. supra* note 21, it is stated at p. 71: "Although approximately 28 states and the federal courts have statutory provisions for judicially issued summonses in lieu of warrants, or for police citations in lieu of sight arrests, their use is presently limited largely to traffic offences and violations of municipal codes and county ordinances." It appears that most American commentators advocate the removal of these limitations: see Orfield, *op. cit. supra* note 6, at pp. 31–33. Wider use of the summons is permitted by s. 12 of the American Law Institute's Code of Criminal Procedure (1930) and by s. 9 of the Uniform Arrest Act (prepared by the Interstate Commission on Crime and published in 1941): see Warner, *op. cit. supra* note 22 and Rule 4(a) of *The Federal Rules of Criminal Procedure*, which gives the discretion to the prosecutor: "Upon the request of the attorney for the government a summons instead of a warrant shall issue." (In addition, Federal Rule 9 permits a summons on the recommendation of the Judge.) The Uniform Arrest Act and the A.L.I. *Code of Criminal Procedure* limit the use of the summons to misdemeanors. The latter provides:

"12 (1) Where the complaint is for the commission of an offense which the magistrate is empowered to try summarily he shall issue a summons instead of a warrant of arrest, unless he has reasonable ground to believe that the person against whom the complaint was made will not appear upon a summons, in which case he shall issue a warrant of arrest.

"(2) Where the complaint is for a misdemeanor, which the magistrate is not empowered to try summarily, he shall issue a summons instead of a warrant of arrest, if he has reasonable ground to believe that the person against whom

appearance of the accused in court.[37] Section 440(1) of the Criminal Code provides: "A justice who receives an information shall . . . issue, where he considers that a case for so doing is made out, a summons or warrant, as the case may be, to compel the accused to attend before him."[38]

It is clear law that a justice should not issue a warrant of arrest when a summons would be sufficient. Lord Devlin stated the accepted legal view as follows: "a warrant will not be issued in any case where a summons to attend court and answer the charge there would in the opinion of the magistrate be sufficient."[39]

These legal rules might reasonably lead one to expect that the summons is widely used in practice. The writer has asked many Toronto

---

the complaint was made will appear upon a summons." It is somewhat surprising that these sections do not permit the use of the summons for felonies. Apparently it was thought that the punishment for a felony "is usually sufficiently severe to make the substitution of summons for arrest inexpedient." See Warner, *op. cit. supra* note 22, at p. 211; Moreland, *op. cit. supra* note 6, at p. 9. The *Tentative Final Draft of the Proposed Illinois Code of Criminal Procedure*, 1963 (effective January 1, 1964) allows for the issuance of a summons in lieu of arrest for *all* offences: Article § 43–14(a) states: "When authorized to issue a warrant of arrest a court may in lieu thereof issue a summons."

[37]If the accused elects trial by a higher court and is committed for trial, he cannot be summoned to stand trial. He can, however, enter into his own recognizance without sureties or without any deposit. It is stated in Bird, *A Manual on Arrest for Peace Officers* (1963) at p. 42, that an officer executing a disorderly house search warrant must arrest the occupants: "The provision [s. 171(1)] seems mandatory; no permissiveness can be found, indicating that although some of the offences being committed are punishable upon summary conviction the use of a summons to the defendant is prohibited." This is surely not correct; the search warrant merely authorizes an arrest but does not make it mandatory.

[38]For the comparable English legislation, see the Magistrates' Courts Act, 1952, c. 55, s. 1. The original predecessor of this section was (1848) 11 and 12 Vict., c. 42, s. 1.

[39]*The Criminal Prosecution in England* (1960) at p. 70. See also (1885) 49 *J.P.* at p. 228: "A warrant ought never to be issued when a summons will be equally effectual in procuring the appearance of the person charged, except, perhaps, when the charge is of a very serious nature." The Canadian law is the same: see *Regina* v. *Wentworth Magistrate's Court, Ex parte Reeves* [1964] 2 O.R. 316 at p. 318 *per* McRuer C.J.H.C.: "A warrant ought not to be issued where it is clear that a summons would be effective and it is not to be overlooked that if an accused fails to obey the summons a warrant may always be issued. It is no trivial or formal discretion that the Justice of the Peace exercises under s. 440 of the *Cr. Code*." See also, Martin, "The Preliminary Hearing: Canadian Practice" (1937) *J. of Cr. L.* (Eng.) at pp. 109, 110; *Seager's Magistrates' Manual* (2d ed., 1907) at p. 247; *Tremeear's Criminal Code* (5th ed., 1944) at p. 724; *Carruthers* v. *Beisiegel* (1908) 8 W.L.R. 255 (Alberta S.C.); *Regina* v. *Fox* (1958) 27 C.R. 132 (Ont. C.A.). *Cf. Watters* v. *Pacific Delivery Service Ltd.* [1964] 2 C.C.C. 62 at p. 67 (B.C.S.C.); *Romegialli* v. *Marceau* [1964] 2 C.C.C. 87 at p. 88 (Ont. C.A.).

lawyers to give their opinion as to the frequency of the use of the summons in Toronto. Almost without exception, the estimate has been significantly higher than the true picture; even experienced criminal lawyers have placed the figure at 30 or 40 per cent. By concentrating on the law one can easily be misled; the law in practice is far removed from the law in theory.

B. Shifting Responsibility from the Justice of the Peace to the Police

Traditionally, criminal law has interposed the independent scrutiny of a justice of the peace between the police and the accused as a safeguard against unwarranted arrests. An examination of existing practice discloses that this judicial function has been shifted to the very body that society is concerned with controlling—the police. As a result, the summons has been used infrequently.

For the safeguard to operate, the police officer must appear before a justice of the peace who must exercise his independent discretion as to whether to issue a summons or a warrant of arrest. Even if it is assumed that justices properly exercise their discretion, the fact that almost all police arrests are made without the police officer appearing before a justice of the peace makes this potential safeguard almost non-existent. The arrest records for the month of November 1961 of a large division station in Toronto[40] show that out of a total of 380 arrests for offences against the Criminal Code, only 24 were with a warrant, i.e., 94 per cent of all the accused persons who were arrested were arrested without a warrant.[41] There is no reason to suspect that a complete analysis of all arrests throughout Metropolitan Toronto over a longer period would yield results substantially different. Thus, over 90 per cent of all arrests in Toronto are made without a warrant.[42] It may

[40]At the time of the study this station was known as Number 1 Division Station on College Street.

[41]This figure does not include cases in which outstanding warrants were executed on a person in custody who was initially arrested without a warrant. The statistical section of the Metropolitan Toronto Police Department supplied the writer with figures which show a slightly higher percentage of warrants, but their figures include warrants executed against persons already in custody. The figures on the offence of indecent exposure (infra, note 15) support the figure of 94 per cent.

[42]Cf. Report of the Royal Commission of Inquiry Respecting the Arrest and Detention of Rabbi Norbert Leiner by the Metropolitan Toronto Police Force, 1962, reprinted, in part, in Bird, op. cit. supra note 37, at p. 122: "The normal arrest is done by the issue of a warrant. . . ." In England arrests without a warrant occur in approximately 90 per cent of the indictable cases, although it must be remembered that the proportion of arrests to total prosecutions is much lower in England because of the greater use of the summons: see Kenny's Outlines of Criminal Law at pp. 535, 541. Warner states, op. cit. supra note 22, at p. 197, that "in most American cities police prosecutions are not usually initiated by the

well be that the over-all percentage would be higher because Number 1 Division Station is apparently used more frequently by detectives for booking prisoners arrested by them with warrants than other stations. If private prosecutions are excluded, the percentage of persons arrested without a warrant would tend to be even greater because, as was previously pointed out, private individuals rarely arrest on their own initiative without appearing before a justice of the peace.

Warrants of arrest, in practice, are normally limited to cases in which the accused cannot be found and so cannot be arrested without a warrant. Warrants thus provide a formal record of persons who are wanted by the police. A warrant may also be used when there is a possibility that the person arrested might later sue for false arrest and false imprisonment. At the present time, it is probably accurate to state that the police do not bother to obtain a warrant of arrest if, as a practical matter, they can arrest without one.

Canadian law has consistently granted to the police wider and wider powers of arrest without a warrant. Section 435 of the Code provides:

435. A peace officer may arrest without warrant
    (a) a person who has committed an indictable offence or who, on reasonable and probable grounds, he believes has committed or is about to commit an indictable offence or is about to commit suicide, or
    (b) a person, whom he finds committing a criminal offence.[43]

issuance of a warrant of arrest." In Philadelphia, 95 per cent of arrests for major crimes are without a warrant: see Foote, *op. cit. supra* note 21, at p. 20; note, "Philadelphia Police Practice and the Law of Arrest" (1952) 100 *U. Pa. L. Rev.* 1182, at pp. 1183–84. The Boston Police claim that in 1955 only 15 per cent of all arrests for major crimes against person or property were without a warrant. *Sed quaere.* See Foote, *op. cit. supra* note 21, at p. 21. See also Freed and Wald, *op. cit. supra* note 21, at p. 71: "Percentages of arrests made without warrants have been estimated by city officials or docket surveys as follows: Philadelphia, more than 97%; Phoenix—99%; Miami—93%." On the other hand, arrests without a warrant are apparently seldom employed in the Federal system. "In the federal system in February 1964, 2,620 warrants were reported compared to only 434 arrests without warrant." *Ibid.* at p. 71.

[43]S. 25 protects a peace officer "if he acts on reasonable and probable grounds." Whereas there is considerable doubt as to the rights of private individuals to arrest without a warrant (see Wright, *Cases on the Law of Torts* (3d ed., 1963) at pp. 138–40), it seems clear that a peace officer is protected from civil and criminal liability if he arrests an accused without a warrant when he has reasonable and probable grounds to believe either that an indictable offence has been committed by the accused or that he has found the accused committing any criminal offence. These powers are even wider than they might first appear to be because almost all offences may be proceeded with by indictment at the election of the Crown. For example, the offences of common assault (s. 231) and impaired driving (s. 223) may be treated as either offences punishable on summary conviction or as indictable offences. It would seem that for the purpose of arrest

Perhaps the best indication that can be given here as to the increasing power of the police to arrest without a warrant is to compare the position before and after the Code of 1953–54 for the four offences previously discussed. The old Code gave the police approximately the same right to arrest without a warrant on reasonable and probable grounds for the offences of forgery and uttering (s. 477 of the 1927 Code). Neither the old nor the new Code give the police the right to arrest without a warrant for indecent exposure (s. 205 of the 1927 Code) unless the accused is found committing the offence. Thus far, then, the position is the same. For the other two offences of indecent assault on a male (s. 292 of the 1927 Code) and criminal negligence in the operation of a motor vehicle (s. 285 of the 1927 Code) the old Code gave the police no right to arrest without a warrant unless the accused was found committing the offence, whereas under the new Code the accused can be arrested if the police act on reasonable and probable grounds that the offence was committed by the accused. In other words, in the old Code the police could arrest without a warrant for one out of the four offences discussed; in the new Code they may do so for three out of the four offences.

It is not suggested that this increased power is undesirable: the police should have wide powers to arrest without a warrant in cases where there is no opportunity to procure a warrant and immediate action is necessary.[44] Indeed, there is some indication that their present powers are not wide enough. For example, as we have seen, the police cannot arrest an accused person without a warrant for the summary conviction offence of indecent exposure (s. 158) unless the accused is found committing the offence (see s. 435). The Statistical Section of the Metropolitan Toronto Police Department supplied the following information: out of 178 persons arrested for indecent exposure between January 1 and September 30, 1963, only eight were with a warrant, i.e., over 95 per cent were without a warrant. It is highly unlikely that the police found the accused actually indecently exposing himself in over 95 per cent of the cases where the accused was arrested. It would seem to be more desirable to give the police the power to arrest without a warrant in cases where the identity of the accused cannot be established than to force them to act illegally. The effect of giving the police the power

---

these offences can be treated as indictable, even though the Crown may later elect to proceed summarily. See *Regina* v. *Beaudette* (1957) 118 C.C.C. 295 (Ont. C.A.).

[44]See generally, Warner, *op. cit. supra* note 22, at pp. 203–4; Warner, "The Uniform Arrest Act" (1942) 28 *Va. L. Rev.* 315; Tappan, *op. cit. supra* note 20, at pp. 282–85; Coakley, "Restrictions in the Law of Arrest" (1957) 52 *N.W. U.L. Rev.* 2 and articles cited in footnote 1 therein.

to arrest without warrant in these cases, however, is further to shift the responsibility as to whether to summon or arrest from the justice of the peace to the police.

Some substitute technique must therefore be found to ensure that the police exercise their power of arrest reasonably. It is unsound to leave such an unfettered discretion solely in their hands. A discretion which cannot be challenged ceases to be a matter of discretion; it is naked power. Police officers are not neutral nor is it reasonable to expect them to be. They are protagonists in society's struggle against crime. In the eyes of many police officers all persons whom the police prosecute are guilty[45] and the experience of being arrested and spending time in custody pending trial is a punishment justly deserved.

C. Restrictions on Arrest: The Return of Responsibility to the Courts

Greater concern by magistrates might aid somewhat in ensuring that police exercise their powers responsibly. The courts in Toronto have, however, more or less completely abdicated their traditional role as society's watchdog over police practices.[46] The writer has personally heard both an English magistrate[47] and a New York judge ask the arresting officer at the first court appearance to justify his use of the arrest procedure. It would appear that Toronto magistrates rarely ask for this justification, in part no doubt because of the overcrowded court dockets. However, this form of judicial policing would not be a complete solution: Canadian courts are not willing to take the bold step of allowing improper police procedures to affect the outcome of the criminal trial (except in the area of involuntary confessions). Illegality at most gives rise to a civil cause of action against the arresting officer.[48]

Greater use of the summons and less abuse of the power of arrest would result if the power of the police to arrest without a warrant were curtailed, but, as has been previously pointed out, the power of arrest without warrant is necessary for the proper enforcement of the law. The solution is not to eliminate his power but to ensure that the police officer exercises it reasonably. Perhaps the most desirable solution is

[45]It is certainly proper for the officer making the arrest to hold this view. See, e.g., Lord Porter's statement in *John Lewis & Co. Ld.* v. *Tims* [1952] A.C. 676, at p. 691 (H. L.): "Those who arrest must be persuaded of the guilt of the accused. . . ."

[46]See generally, the *Report of the Royal Commission on the Police*, 1962, Cmnd. 1728 at p. 11 *et seq.*

[47]Cf. Sybille Bedford, *The Faces of Justice* (New York, 1961) at p. 69.

[48]See, e.g., *A.G. for Quebec* v. *Begin* [1955] S.C.R. 593; *R.* v. *McNamara* (1950) 99 C.C.C. 107 (Ont. C.A.); *R.* v. *Honan* (1912) 20 C.C.C. 10 (Ont. C.A.).

to make the police officer's right to arrest without a warrant dependent on his having reasonable grounds for believing that an arrest is necessary. At the present time there would appear to be no such limitation. Section 435 of the Criminal Code states: "A police officer may arrest without a warrant (a) a person . . . who, on reasonable and probable grounds, he believes has committed or is about to commit an indictable offence. . . ." "Reasonable and probable grounds" seem to relate only to the question whether an offence has been committed by the accused.[49] The abuse of process, inherent in an arrest made where other procedures would be equally effective, apparently is not encompassed. There are no reported civil cases where an accused has sought damages for such an arrest.[50]

A provision requiring that there be "reasonable and probable grounds" for the use of the arrest procedure would be consistent with the common law's distrust of an unfettered executive discretion. In many other areas such a provision is built into the Criminal Code.[51] The framers of the 1879 English Draft Code, the source of the Canadian Criminal Code, stated that it is "a principle of the common law that all powers, the exercise of which may do harm to others, must be exercised in a reasonable manner. . . ."[52]

The effectiveness of a prohibition against unnecessary arrest would, to a certain extent, hinge on the consequences attached to non-compliance. One effect of the suggested amendment to the code would be to leave a police officer who makes an unnecessary arrest open to a criminal charge of assault.[53] However, it would appear that the police are reluc-

[49] See ss. 25 and 435 of the Code. Even though it is possible to argue that s. 25, which protects persons acting under authority when they act on reasonable and probable grounds, relates to the process used, it is unnecessary to refer to s. 25 to justify an arrest under s. 435(a). The reasonableness of the process employed might apply in cases under s. 435(b) when the accused is in fact found committing a criminal offence. In such a case the police officer would have to justify his action under s. 25.

[50] The American Law Institute's *Restatement of the Law of Torts* (1934) I § 130 introduces the concept of reasonableness in relation to the time of making an arrest, although this limitation applies only to misdemeanors not involving a breach of the peace. *Cf.* the A.L.I.'s *Code of Criminal Procedure* s. 23 "An arrest may be made on any day and at any time of the day or night."

[51] See ss. 25 and 435 of the Code.

[52] *Report of the Royal Commission Appointed to Consider the Law Relating to Indictable Offences*, 1879, C. 2345, at p. 11.

[53] Under s. 231 of the Code. The officer would seek in vain for protection under s. 25 of the Code which states: "Every one who is required or authorized by law to do anything in the administration or enforcement of the law . . . (b) as a peace officer or public officer . . . is, if he acts on reasonable and probable grounds, justified in doing what he is required or authorized to do and in using as much force as is necessary for that purpose." In the case of unnecessary arrest

tant criminally to charge a fellow officer who has simply shown excessive zeal in the execution of his duty. Though many cases have been reported concerning civil actions against the police for arrest, there are very few instances where criminal action has been undertaken. Private prosecutions are, of course, possible, but rare.

A possible result of such a provision in the Criminal Code might be the creation of a civil right of action against an offending officer. It is probable that in this case breach of a statute would not create a civil cause of action.[54] Thus, legislation would be necessary. Constitutionally, the federal government cannot directly create a civil cause of action; the legislation would have to be enacted provincially.[55] Civil action, though never a complete check on police practices,[56] is a not ineffective means of ensuring due compliance with the law. It is only reasonable to expect the police officer in the execution of his duties to be aware of the threat of civil action and its consequent financial penalties. There are a number of actions now pending against the Metropolitan Toronto police and the writer has the impression that the Toronto police are sensitive to this form of sanction. Professor Livingston Hall's suggestion that the right of action be permitted against the municipality as well as the officer would appear to be desirable. As he points out, "A community which pays the bill will not long tolerate habitual lawlessness."[57]

Even assuming that relatively few criminal and civil actions result and that the threat of an immediate sanction is virtually non-existent, the mere fact that there is a prohibition against unnecessary arrest should have some salutary effect. Most police officers sincerely desire to operate in most instances within the scope of the legally permissible. In addition, a limitation on the power of arrest as suggested above would provide the public and the press with the opportunity to criticize unnecessary arrest as being illegal.[58] At present, it is not only difficult to frame any criticism in a striking manner, but it is also perhaps too much to expect that criticism which amounts to "mere advice" will be

the requirement of "reasonable and probable grounds" would deny him the protection of this section.

[54]If the courts were willing to recognize such a cause of action independently of the Criminal Code, the Code could be used as a yardstick of wrongfulness.

[55]See generally, Wright, *op. cit. supra* note 43, at pp. 138–40. See, e.g., *Transport Oil Ltd.* v. *Imperial Oil Ltd. and Cities Service Oil Co. Ltd.* [1935] O.R. 215, *Gordon* v. *Imperial Tobacco Sales Co. et al.* [1939] 2 D.L.R. 27, *Reg.* v. *O'Connor* [1965] 1 C.C.C. 20.

[56]See, e.g., Hall, *op. cit. supra* note 30; Foote, "Tort Remedies for Police Violations of Individual Rights" (1955) 39 *Minn. L. Rev.* 493.

[57]Hall, *op. cit. supra* note 30, at p. 373.

[58]See Hall, *op. cit. supra* note 30, at p. 373; Foote, *op. cit. supra* note 21, at p. 19.

heeded by the police to the same extent as criticism which alleges illegality.[59]

A further possible solution might be to exclude all confessions or even to dismiss the charge in cases where the accused has been unnecessarily arrested. As previously pointed out, it is clear law that an unreasonable arrest will not as a matter of law affect the criminal trial. To change this rule by legislation would necessitate a complete re-thinking of our rules of criminal procedure and evidence and will not, therefore, be further explored here.

It appears probable that a municipal *ombudsman* might effectively review the activities of the police, depending, of course, on the particular individual chosen and the fact-finding and research facilities at his disposal. In any event, such an independent official would probably operate as a better check on illegal police practices than a Police Commission which would appear to be inevitably too closely identified with the police and law enforcement generally.[60]

If police power to make arrests were regulated, the summons would no doubt be used more frequently. However, unless other changes are made there would still be many instances where as a practical matter it would not be unreasonable for the police to arrest rather than summon. The practical objections to the use of the summons will now be explored and attempts made to assess their validity and to find means of meeting them.

V. Practical Factors Affecting the Use of the Summons

A. Identification

(i) *Identity*. A major obstacle to the use of the summons is that the police officer may not be sure of the accused's identity. The problem of identity can easily be exaggerated. It cannot apply in every case in which the police officer does not know the accused personally. Identity is only of prime importance when the actual offender is not known to those who have sought the aid of the police or when the police officer finds the accused committing the offence and there is no reliable person capable of identifying him. Assuming identity to be a problem, if the accused refuses to establish his identity the solution is obvious: arrest him without a warrant (assuming that an arrest can be made without

[59]*Cf. Regina* v. *O'Connor* [1965] 1 C.C.C. 20 *per* Haines J.

[60]Presumably this question, which is too vast to be explored here, is being considered by the Royal Commission on Civil Rights in Ontario (the McRuer Commission). See generally the English *Report of the Royal Commission on the Police*, 1962, Cmnd. 1728.

a warrant in the particular case).[61] The real difficulty occurs when the accused purports to establish his identity, but the police officer suspects that he is not telling the truth. In such a case the police officer can seek additional proof of identity and if the accused refuses or fails to comply with the officer's request he can be arrested (again assuming that an arrest can be made without a warrant in the particular case). There are many ways of checking an accused's identity; for example, a friend, relative, or employer can describe the accused or identify his voice over the phone. Most accused persons would be willing to co-operate if it were to mean that they would not be arrested.

To discourage those who might not co-operate, legislation could make it an offence for a person to give a false name or address with intent to escape liability after he has been notified that he will be charged with a criminal offence.[62] Such a provision is not strictly necessary for the case where the accused flatly refuses to give his name because the power to arrest can be utilized in these cases. However, it is somewhat uncertain at present if an accused can be charged with the Criminal Code offence of obstruction when a false name is given.[63] Clarification of the law would be desirable.

Such a provision would not be a complete solution because, as Glanville Williams has pointed out, "It is little use piling up the offences committed by the anonymous culprit when the difficulty is to know how to get him into court for any of them."[64] Nevertheless, the very existence of this form of sanction would have some deterrent effect on many offenders, particularly if it became generally known that an offender giving a false name would be assiduously sought and prosecuted by the police.

Even if the accused is arrested because he cannot establish his identity to the satisfaction of the officer, there is no reason why, if other circumstances warrant it, he should not be released when the police become convinced of his true identity.

[61]For a discussion of the problems that can arise when there is no power to arrest without a warrant, see Williams, "Demanding Name and Address" (1950) 66 *L. Q. R.* 465.

[62]*Ibid.* at p. 477.

[63]S. 119(1) states: "Every one who wilfully attempts in any manner to obstruct, pervert or defeat the course of justice is guilty of an indictable offence and is liable to imprisonment for two years." A distinction could be drawn between the refusal to give his name, which would not be covered by s. 119 and actually misleading the police, which perhaps comes within it. On the other hand, a respectable argument can be advanced that if giving a false name is an offence then giving a false alibi, which apparently is not covered by the section, should be also. See Williams, *ibid.* at pp. 473–74.

[64]Williams, *op. cit. supra* note 61, at p. 477.

(ii) Formal Fingerprinting. Another major reason why the police arrest accused persons is that it is legally necessary to have the accused in custody in order compulsorily to obtain his fingerprints and photograph.[65] For a number of valid reasons good police practice requires that an accused be fingerprinted; this is necessary for the case the police are working on at the time as well as for future reference. Prints taken from an accused can be compared with any found at the scene of the crime for this or any future offence. In addition, with the aid of prints and photographs, the police are able to build up files of information on persons involved in certain types of offences: this catalogue of information *(modus operandi)* is a valuable aid in the solution of future crimes. In certain cases prints are useful in determining the previous criminal record of the accused.

The power forcibly to fingerprint accused persons is given in the Identification of Criminals Act of Canada,[66] which specifies that before the power can be exercised the accused must be "in lawful custody charged with . . . an indictable offence."[67] Because there is no legal sanction for compulsorily obtaining the accused's prints when he is not in custody, the police have no means of obtaining the prints of a person who has been summoned. It is not clear whether an accused person who has been summoned can later be arrested because he refuses to be fingerprinted voluntarily; the police probably do not have the power to arrest without a warrant in such a case, and it is more than doubtful whether it would be proper for a justice to issue a warrant of arrest on this basis alone when there is no indication that the accused will fail to show up for his trial.[68] The matter is sufficiently uncertain to

[65]See generally, Borins, "Police Investigation and the Rights of an Accused," *Law Society of Upper Canada Special Lectures 1963,* 59 at p. 70 *et seq.*

[66]R.S.C. 1952, c. 144. Authorization to take fingerprints is not found in the Act itself, but in the Regulations. The Act, first introduced at a time when the process of fingerprinting did not exist (1898, 61 Vict., c. 54) still has not been brought up to date. Rather, authority to fingerprint is incorporated into the Regulations under the Act. See *Statutory Orders and Regulations, Consolidation* (1955), II, p. 1855: "For the purposes of the Identification of Criminals Act, the measurements, processes or operation of fingerprinting and photography are hereby sanctioned."

[67]S. 2(a). See *Warnock* v. *Foster* [1936] 3 W.W.R. 625 at p. 632 (B.C.S.C.). The English provision also requires that the accused be in custody. See the Magistrates' Courts Act, 1952, s. 40. The English legislation provides that fingerprints taken by virtue of a court order must be destroyed if the accused is acquitted. Some American jurisdictions have similar provisions. See Lafave, "Detention for Investigation by the Police: An Analysis of Current Practices" [1962] *Wash. U. L. Q.* 331 at p. 359. For a general discussion of the use of fingerprints see Moffat, "Taking Finger Prints upon Arrest" (1926) 12 *A. B. A. J.* 175.

[68]See s. 444 of the Code.

warrant an amendment to the Act making it mandatory for a summoned accused to appear at a police station or at the court some time prior to his trial to be fingerprinted and photographed. The legislation could provide that a notice may be attached to a summons for an indictable offence requiring the accused to appear at a designated place within a predetermined period of time before his trial, and that if he fails to appear a warrant may be issued for his arrest.[69]

In most cases, the police would probably wish the period of time to be reasonably short, say, within 12 or 24 hours of delivery of the summons. Thus if the accused turns out to be a bad risk by not showing up to be printed, the police will at least be "hot on his trail." If he shows up to be printed, and a check of his fingerprints should disclose a previous record under a different name, the police are at liberty to apply to a justice of the peace for the issuance of a warrant of arrest to supersede the summons.[70] The justice would presumably take into account the fact that the accused did show up to be printed.

(iii) Informal Fingerprinting. Less hesitation to use the summons might result if the police were given the power to fingerprint the accused at the time of first contact without taking him into custody. This would require a further amendment to the Identification of Criminals Act.[71] Technically, "informal" fingerprinting could easily be accomplished. A police officer could carry a small fingerprinting apparatus in his pocket or in the police car, and take, for example, a thumb or fingerprint on the spot. The single print would not, of course, be adequate for permanent police records, but it could be used in some cases to establish the true identity of a defaulter as well as subsequently to prove him to be the person who failed to appear in answer to the summons.

Establishing the identity of a person from a single print is at present technically difficult, however. The police keep single print records only on those offenders whom they suspect might again come into contact with the law. Also, the classification system for the single print has not yet been as fully developed as that for the full set of prints, and checking a single print against the records can be a long and laborious task. Nevertheless, the system, though time-consuming, would enable the police, in much the same manner as they now establish the identity of a

[69]This procedure could be used both under the present system (where a justice of the peace must issue the summons) or under a system which allows police to issue summonses.

[70]Sec. 444(1) of the Code reads as follows: "A justice may issue a warrant in Form 7 for the arrest of the accused notwithstanding that a summons has already been issued to require the appearance of the accused."

[71]R.S.C. 1952, c. 144.

criminal from a single print found at the scene of the crime, to determine the identity of most habitual or professional criminals who fail to appear (a matter which is of prime concern to the police). In addition, work should be undertaken towards developing a procedure of classification which allows quick reference to the single print of all previous offenders.

Even if the above procedure proves abortive in the particular case and the identity of the accused cannot be established in advance, the single print is still of great value. If a defaulter is later apprehended the police have little means of proving that he is the individual on whom the summons was served beyond the recollection of the officer who served the summons. A single print taken at the time the summons is served would give the police the necessary means of proof. Though the present classification system makes a comparison between a single print and the thousands of single prints on file difficult, two prints allegedly from the same finger of the same man can easily be compared.

(iv) Previous Convictions and Outstanding Warrants. In many cases the police wish to check whether there are outstanding warrants against the accused and whether the accused has any previous convictions. An outstanding warrant will normally cause his immediate arrest. His previous record will have some influence on whether he is a sufficiently good risk to be summoned. It will also affect any application for bail and is vital for the purpose of sentencing. Normally checking a record is a simple operation; the police keep complete records at Headquarters and are extremely efficient in supplying the information desired. Checking an accused's record is a serious problem only when there is uncertainty about his identity. If the officer has established the accused's identity to his satisfaction there is no reason why he cannot ask the accused to remain with him for the brief period (often only three or four minutes) until he is able to check with police headquarters about his record. In most cases the possibility is negligible that the accused has a previous conviction recorded under a different name because, though a person may be arrested under an assumed name, by the time he has been convicted and sentenced his true name will have emerged, particularly if he has been in trouble with the police on more than one occasion before.

If the Toronto police have no file on an accused, a quick check will not, of course, disclose whether he has previous convictions in some other city. This information is obtained from the R.C.M.P. in Ottawa and usually requires from three to five days to obtain. However, it would certainly be unfair to arrest rather than to summon an accused who has no Toronto police file on the supposition that he *may* have a record elsewhere in Canada. He would then be put in the anomalous position of being possibly worse off than the person who *has* a Toronto record.

B. *Consequences of Failure to Obey a Summons*

The summons would probably be used in more cases if a penalty were provided for wilful failure to appear in obedience to its terms. Both the American Law Institute's *Code of Criminal Procedure*[72] and the Uniform Arrest Act[73] contain such a provision. Failure to appear in answer to a summons would not appear to be an offence in Canada. Even if disobedience could be considered contempt of court, magistrates would not have power summarily to commit the accused because the contempt would not have taken place "in the face of the court." The only possible provision which could be relied on by the prosecution is s. 108 of the Criminal Code (disobeying an order of the court) which provides: "Every one who, without lawful excuse, disobeys a lawful order made by a court of justice or by a person or body of persons authorized by any Act to make or give the order, other than an order for the payment of money is, unless some penalty or punishment or other mode of proceeding is expressly provided by law, guilty of an indictable offence and is liable to imprisonment for two years." However, it can be argued that some "other mode of proceeding is expressly provided by law": s. 444(2) of the Code provides for the issuance of a warrant of arrest when a summons is not obeyed. There are no cases reported in which the prosecution has attempted to prosecute under s. 108 for disobedience of a summons.

Though a magistrate may take the accused's disobedience of the summons into account in passing sentence, it would be unfair to the accused to impose a penalty greater than that warranted for the principal offence on the basis of conduct which is of itself not an offence and which may not properly be proved by the prosecution. Moreover, it is not possible either to impose a penalty for failure to appear if the charge is dismissed or to put the accused on probation for the principal offence and at the same time impose a penalty for disobedience to the summons.[74]

[72]S. 14: "If the person summoned fails, without good cause, to appear as commanded by the summons, he shall be considered in contempt of court, and may be punished by a fine of not more than twenty dollars. . . ."
[73]S. 9(2): "Wilful failure to appear in answer to the summons may be punished by a fine of not over one hundred dollars or imprisonment for not over thirty days." See Warner, *op. cit. supra* note 44, at p. 346. It will be noted that the penalty may be imposed even though a police officer issued the summons without the intervention of a justice of the peace.
[74]S. 638(1) of the Criminal Code permits the suspension of sentence "instead of sentencing him to punishment."

There being no effective technique at present to ensure compliance with the summons, apart from a subsequent arrest, legislation making it an offence wilfully to disobey a summons is desirable.[75] Such a provision would undoubtedly have some effect in ensuring obedience to the summons, though it would not, of course, be the main factor: fear of arrest would still be the principal deterrent against non-appearance.

A penalty should be available for a further reason beyond providing for an immediate effect on the accused; the administration of justice has a vital interest in demonstrating the solemnity of a court order and vindicating any affront to its dignity. As a New Brunswick Chief Justice stated: "[The court] must see that its orders are obeyed, and those who do not appreciate the binding force of the order of a Court must be made to understand that its commands cannot, at the desire, or at the whim of the party at whom they are directed, be flouted and set aside."[76]

It would be desirable to change the form of the summons so that its appearance would be commensurate with the gravity of a Criminal Code charge. At present the summons used in criminal cases is a singularly unimpressive document, not differing in appearance from the summons used for breach of The Highway Traffic Act or of a municipal parking by-law. Most people are readily familiar with these documents and are aware that disobedience of the initial traffic summons will result in a second summons being served, and not in an arrest being made. In the case of a Criminal Code summons, however, no second chance is given; a bench warrant for arrest is issued after the initial disobedience. A more forceful and impressive looking criminal summons would tend to prevent any misunderstandings. In addition, if failure to obey a summons were made an offence, this fact and its consequences should be clearly spelled out on the summons, as it is for provincial traffic offences.[77]

The Criminal Code at present gives the court power to commit for

[75]At present, the Criminal Code allows for substitutional service of a summons. S. 441(3) provides: "A summons shall be served by a peace officer who shall deliver it personally to the person to whom it is directed, or, if that person cannot conveniently be found, shall leave it for him at his last or usual place of abode with some inmate thereof who appears to be at least sixteen years of age." If consequences were to be attached to failure to obey a summons, it would be unfair to impose a penalty where the accused does not have actual notice of the summons. In fact, the existing practice of issuing a bench warrant for failure to appear is unfair where there has been substitutional service and no actual knowledge of the summons. Where substitutional service is not obeyed, the Code should provide for personal service on the accused, unless there is some proof that the summons was brought to his attention.

[76]R. v. Sharpe and Lingley; Ex Parte Sharpe (1921) 36 C.C.C. 1 at p. 4 per McKeown, C.J.K.B.D.

[77]Rev. Reg. Ont. 1960, Reg. 550.

contempt a *witness* who wilfully disobeys a summons.[78] In addition, an accused who has been released on recognizance can be charged under s. 125(c) of the Code with the offence of skipping bail. The extension of the principle to cases where an accused is summoned would not break new ground.[79]

C. Continuation of the "Illegal" Conduct

For the purpose of the present analysis "continuation" has been separated from "repetition," the distinguishing feature being the point of time at which the alleged conduct might recur. The difference is one of degree rather than of kind, and though many of the same arguments will be applicable to both, the possibility of repetition as a factor in detention before trial will not be discussed until later. If the possibility of continuation is not a valid consideration in a particular case for arresting rather than summoning the accused, then the possibility of an even later continuation or repetition of the conduct should be equally invalid.

It might at first seem that an arrest is reasonable whenever there is a possibility that the accused's conduct will be continued. A closer analysis shows that this theory, though a valid consideration in determining in some cases whether an accused should be arrested, is in many cases overstressed and in many others inapplicable.

At common law, private persons and police officers had the power to arrest without a warrant, apart from felonies, only for a "breach of the peace."[80] No authoritative definition of breach of the peace has been judicially attempted. Glanville Williams sums up the cases as follows: "Each of these instances involves some danger to the person, and it is submitted that this is the general meaning of a breach of the peace in

---

[78]S. 612. The witness is "liable to a fine of one hundred dollars or to imprisonment for ninety days or to both, and may be ordered to pay the costs that are incident to the service of any process under this Part and to his detention, if any." Under the old Code a summons was issued to a witness. The penalty provided by the 1927 Code was twenty dollars or one month or both. (S. 674(2).)

[79]An additional consequence that might be imposed would be to allow the magistrate to order that the accused pay the additional costs of compelling the accused's appearance in court after his failure to obey the summons, even if the ultimate decision concerning the charge is in his favour. At present, costs can be awarded against a person who disobeys a summons only for a summary conviction offence where a conviction is registered (s. 716 of the Criminal Code). This penalty could reasonably be extended to cover indictable offences and cases where no conviction has been registered.

[80]*Kenny's Outlines of Criminal Law* at p. 537. See Williams, "Arrest for Breach of the Peace" [1954] *Crim. L. Rev.* 578. The English law of arrest is exceptionally technical and no attempt will be made here to give a learned exposition of it.

criminal law. . . . If there is no threat to the person, it seems that a threat to property should generally be regarded as insufficient."[81] It would seem then that, historically, breach of the peace in essence involved some threat of physical harm to the person.

The limitation under common law of the use of arrest without a warrant, apart from the serious cases, to breaches of the peace implicitly recognizes that for many offences the danger of continuation is not sufficiently serious to warrant an arrest by the police without judicial sanction. The wider powers of arrest given to the Canadian police are not necessarily inconsistent with this approach; these powers are perhaps needed in Canada to overcome local problems in ensuring the appearance of the accused in court and should not be subverted to any other use.

To say that there is a possibility of the offence being continued implies that the original conduct constitutes a crime. The police, however, are not always correct in their interpretation of the law. In addition, such an implication usurps the function of the courts and places it in the hands of the police. Although this may be necessary in the severe cases where a breach of the peace is threatened, it becomes increasingly less desirable as the type of harm becomes less irreparable.[82] In many cases the harm caused by a continuation of the conduct is not sufficiently serious to justify an arrest without a warrant, and any illegal continuation of the conduct can effectively be dealt with by the court in its sentence. This is particularly true for those offences which directly involve only consenting parties such as prostitution, homosexuality, or gambling.

In many other cases, simple measures short of arrest could be adopted by the police to avoid the danger of a continuation of the conduct. An example is found in the offence of impaired driving. Out of 4,084 persons charged with impaired driving in 1961, only 23 were summoned (i.e., over 99.4 per cent were arrested)[83] and it seems probable that a good proportion of these 23 were summoned only because they were injured and undergoing hospital treatment. At first glance, this high

---

[81]Williams, *ibid.* at p. 579. *Kenny's Outlines of Criminal Law* takes a somewhat broader view of what constitutes a breach of the peace: at p. 537 it is stated, "But, as it seems to mean a 'breach of the Queen's peace' it should include every crime."

[82]The word "irreparable" is used advisedly: irreparable harm is the test used by courts of Equity on an interlocutory application for an injunction to decide whether conduct should be enjoined before trial.

[83]*Statistical Report of the Metropolitan Toronto Police Department, 1961.* The English figures for 1961 show that slightly more than 10 per cent were summoned for this offence. The Vancouver figures are just a little higher than those for Toronto: 6 out of 804 or under 1 per cent.

rate of arrest seems sound; summoning an impaired driver would simply allow him to continue to drive in the same condition. Yet a simple procedure could remove this danger without the necessity for an arrest: the police officer could ask the accused voluntarily to give up the possession of his car for a period of time. If he refused then, of course, he would be arrested. If the police had the power compulsorily to take the accused's vehicle for a certain period of time, say 12 hours, the accused's opportunity for driving would virtually be eliminated and this approach would be even more effective. Legislative authority would, of course, be required for such a step. At the present time, leaving aside the provision for impounding a vehicle after conviction,[84] the police have power only to detain a motor vehicle under The Highway Traffic Act if they *arrest* the accused without a warrant (s. 156). It is not immediately apparent why a similar power is not given when the accused is summoned (or for that matter when he is arrested with a warrant). The Act should also give the police the power to release the vehicle absolutely at any time.[85] The fact that persons were charged with the offence of driving while their ability was impaired rather than that of driving while intoxicated indicates that they could safely be sent home by taxi. In most cases of impaired driving there is no need for arrest, provided the danger of driving is eliminated.[86]

Another example can be found in the offence of assault. Merely because police intervention is required to break up a fight does not mean that an arrest is always necessary to prevent any continuation. The police have a common-law right temporarily to restrain a person's liberty to prevent a breach of the peace without actually making an arrest.[87] It may be sufficient in some cases for the police to stop the fight, wait a few minutes until the heat of passion has cooled, and ask the combatants to go on their respective ways. If they refuse, they would be arrested; if they comply, they would be summoned.

There is a further group of cases in which the opportunity to continue the crime does not exist or is at best negligible. Where the police are not present at the time of the commission of the crime, or where the crime has been completed (as in a charge of abortion against the person

[84]The Highway Traffic Act, R.S.O. 1960, c. 172, s. 157.

[85]S. 156 in its present form is not very clear; it appears to provide that the vehicle can be released only if security for its production at a later time is given. The writer is assuming that the section is constitutionally valid, an assumption which may be unwarranted. In practice the police rarely use s. 156 for driving offences. It is used mainly when an inspection of the car is required.

[86]The police often arrest impaired drivers in order to obtain evidence against them. The problems involved in this practice are discussed later.

[87]*Kenny's Outlines of Criminal Law* at p. 537.

aborted) there can be no possibility of continuation. Where property offences such as fraud or embezzlement have been perpetrated against a person, his notification of the alleged conduct will make the accused's opportunity to continue the conduct negligible.

It would appear, therefore, that the threat posed by a possible continuation of the conduct is not a significant factor in a great number of cases. Its validity as a consideration in determining whether a summons can safely be used should be limited to those cases where substantial harm is threatened by a breach of the peace, and, even in these cases, the harm can often be alleviated by measures short of arrest.

D. Convenience of the Arrest Process for the Police

(i) Difficulty in Summoning. As has been pointed out, the present system does not allow a police officer to summon on his own initiative, but requires him first to attend before a justice of the peace for the issuance of a summons. Thus, it is often easier for the officer to arrest than to obtain and serve a summons. If the officer wishes to obtain a summons on short notice he may find it difficult to locate a justice of the peace, particularly at night. If, on the other hand, the application for a summons is not made until a justice is readily available, it may prove to be troublesome and time-consuming to find and serve the accused. In addition, the police officer who serves a summons must either be in court at the first court appearance in order to prove that the summons was served, or he must prepare an affidavit to this effect and have it sworn before a justice of the peace.[88]

The most obvious way for the officer to avoid these inconveniences is simply to arrest the accused[89] or not to act at all. The present practice tends to favour those in the higher social classes; the officer who feels it is not proper to arrest this type of person for a minor offence and have him mix with criminals will often not bother to obtain a summons at a later time. A person not in as favourable a social position will often be arrested under the same circumstances. Selective enforcement of the law may often be desirable; whether the inconvenience of the officer is a proper standard to apply is another matter.

There is little point in requiring the police officer to obtain a summons from the justice of the peace; the issuing of a summons in Toronto is a routine, perfunctory job. It is doubtful whether there are many instances where a justice of the peace has refused to issue a process at the request

---

[88]S. 441(6) of the Criminal Code.

[89]See Warner, op. cit. supra note 22, at p. 211; Walter, "Some Proposals for Modernizing the Law of Arrest" (1951) 39 Cal. L. Rev. 96 at p. 108.

of the police, particularly when the police merely desire a summons. This supposed safeguard, designed for the preservation of liberty, has the opposite effect: it tends to force police officers to arrest accused persons. Little harm would result if the justice of the peace no longer played a role in the issuing of process to compel the accused's appearance in court.

It would simplify and increase the use of the summons to give police officers the power to summon an accused on the spot without resorting to an appearance before a justice of the peace. This is now possible for provincial driving offences,[90] and provision is made for this procedure in the American Uniform Arrest Act.[91] Although most commentators would limit summonses issued by the police to minor cases, it is not readily apparent why any limitation is necessary.[92] Perhaps the reason is a feeling that police officers should not be trusted with this power for anything but minor offences. Yet giving the police the power to issue summonses is "designed to further, rather than to restrain, personal liberty."[93] As a tactical matter the introduction of such a provision would be facilitated if the document were called, as in some American jurisdictions, a "Notice to Appear."[94] In this way illogical opposition to summonses issued by the police, on the basis that police powers would thus be undesirably extended by allegedly usurping the function of the judiciary, would be circumvented. If we are willing to entrust our police with the power to arrest without a warrant in a particular case, we surely should allow them to take the less drastic step of summoning the accused without prior judicial approval.[95] In any event, whether or not the police

[90]Summary Conviction Act, R.S.O. 1960, c. 387, s. 7.

[91]S. 9 provides: "In any case in which it is lawful for a peace officer to arrest without a warrant a person for a misdemeanor, he may, but need not, give him a written summons. . . ." See Warner, *op. cit. supra* note 44, at pp. 334–36; Warner, *op. cit. supra* note 22, at p. 211. Cf. the wording of s. 9 in Inbau and Sowle, *Cases and Comments on Criminal Justice* (1960) at p. 520. No such provision is made in the A.L.I. *Code of Criminal Procedure* or the *Federal Rules*. See Orfield, *op. cit. supra* note 6, at p. 33. See also Moreland, *op. cit. supra* note 6, at p. 10; Perkins, *op. cit. supra* note 20, at pp. 901–2. Moreland states (p. 9, note 22): "Legislative bodies have not taken kindly to the idea of allowing police officers to issue summonses on the spot for misdemeanors committed in their presence in other than traffic cases."

[92]See, e.g., Warner, "The Uniform Arrest Act," *op. cit. supra* note 44, at pp. 334–36; Moreland, *op. cit. supra* note 6, at p. 10.

[93]Warner, "The Uniform Arrest Act," *op. cit. supra* note 44, at p. 336.

[94]As in the *Tentative Final Draft of the Proposed Illinois Code of Criminal Procedure 1963*, article 43–15. In some jurisdictions they are referred to as "police citations." See Freed and Wald, *op. cit. supra* note 21, at p. 71.

[95]Article 43-15(a) of the *Tentative Final Draft of the Proposed Illinois Code of Criminal Procedure 1963* provides: "Whenever a peace officer is authorized to

are given the power to issue summonses for all offences, they should at least be given this power for offences punishable on summary conviction in cases where an arrest can be made without a warrant.

If it is considered that the intervention of the justice of the peace provides some necessary safeguard for the accused, the legislation could provide that the police officer should go before a justice as soon as it is reasonably convenient to have the information sworn. If the justice feels that there were no reasonable and probable grounds for issuing the summons, he could direct the officer to notify the accused that the summons is void. It is interesting to note that no provision is made in The Summary Convictions Act[96] for revoking a summons even though the Act provides in s. 7(8) that a traffic summons issued by a police officer is subsequently to be "sworn to before a justice." It would appear that the possibility of the justice not swearing the information never crossed the collective mind of the legislature.

Should the consequences of failure to obey a summons issued by the police be anything other than a warrant of arrest? It will be recalled that the suggestion was made earlier that a penalty should be provided in the case of a summons issued by a justice of the peace. The argument in favour of such a provision is less strong here because there is no judicial solemnity attached to the order. There are many cases under The Highway Traffic Act where failure to obey a police order is an offence,[97] however, and a penalty would make a summons issued by the police more effective by acting as a deterrent against non-appearance.

(ii) Advantages of Detention. The arrest and detention of accused persons makes the work of the police easier in at least two ways: the police have the opportunity of questioning the accused and obtaining a confession, and they know that, whether or not the accused is questioned, he is more likely to plead guilty the next morning if he is kept in custody rather than if he initially is summoned. Custody in order psychologically to induce guilty pleas is obviously not proper. Detention for questioning is the crux of the problem. If society considers that the police require wide powers of detention for questioning, then the law should be changed to recognize the practice openly and steps should be taken to keep it within bounds. As Professor Lafave has stated in his recent study of investigation practices by the police in the United States: "In any criminal justice system which recognizes *some* form of police detention, effective controls are necessary to insure that detentions occur only

---

arrest a person without a warrant he may instead issue to such person a notice to appear."
[96]R.S.O. 1960, c. 387.   [97]R.S.O. 1960, c. 172, ss. 14, 17, 35, 54, 55.

in the proper circumstances and that the investigations incident thereto are conducted fairly."[98] The hypocrisy of the present position is obvious: we decry coercion of prisoners, but do nothing to prevent police from arresting persons unnecessarily (and as will be seen in the following chapter, holding them in custody for considerable periods of time), a procedure which enables the police to engage in the very practices we condemn. One of the most striking examples of blatant hypocrisy is that we permit the police to arrest impaired drivers (who could in many cases, without danger, be sent home and summoned) in order to subject them to the breathalizer test. Although taking the test is voluntary, few are aware of this fact. The difficult problem as to whether the breathalizer test should be made compulsory is conveniently sidestepped by permitting the police to arrest virtually all impaired drivers.

Certain American jurisdictions have openly recognized a limited right of detention. For example, the new *Illinois Code of Criminal Procedure* recognizes detention for investigation but attempts to place limitations on its use. Article 43-3 of the Code provides as follows:

(a) A peace officer may under reasonable circumstances detain for investigation for a reasonable period of time any person whom he believes has committed, is committing, or is about to commit any offence, even though the nature of the offence may be unknown.

(b) A period of detention in excess of four hours shall be *prima facie* unreasonable. At the end of the detention period the person so detained shall be released or shall be arrested.

(c) The release of the person detained does not of itself render the detention unlawful.[99]

[98]Lafave, *op. cit. supra* note 67, at p. 385 *et seq.* See generally on police detention and questioning, Williams, "Questioning by the Police" [1960] *Crim. L. Rev.* 322; Smith, "Questioning by the Police: Further Points" [1960] *Crim. L. Rev.* 347; *Report of the Royal Commission on Police Powers and Procedure*, 1929, Cmd. 3297 at p. 60 *et seq.*

[99]*Tentative Final Draft of the Proposed Illinois Code of Criminal Procedure 1963.* See also the American Uniform Arrest Act which provides as follows in s. 2:

"(1) A peace officer may stop any person abroad whom he has reasonable ground to suspect is committing, has committed or is about to commit a crime, and may demand of him his name, address, business abroad and whither he is going.

"(2) Any person so questioned who fails to identify himself or explain his actions to the satisfaction of the officer stopping him may be detained and further questioned and investigated.

"(3) The total period of detention provided for by this section shall not exceed two hours. Such detention is not an arrest and shall not be recorded as an arrest in any official record. At the end of the detention period the person so detained shall be released unless arrested and charged with a crime."

Other techniques might be to exclude confessions by the accused which have not been mechanically recorded or which have not been made before a magistrate.[100] On this latter point Dean Roscoe Pound has stated:

> My proposition is that the remedy for the third degree and its derivatives is to satisfy the reasonable demands of the police and the prosecutors for an interrogation of suspected persons and thus do away with the excuse for extra-legal questionings. . . . I submit that there should be express provision for a legal examination of suspected or accused persons before a magistrate; that those to be examined should be allowed to have counsel present to safeguard their rights; that provision should be made for taking down the evidence so as to guarantee accuracy. As things are, it is not the least of the abuses of the system of extra-legal interrogation that there is a constant conflict of evidence as to what the accused said and as to the circumstances under which he said or was coerced into saying it.[101]

VI. Summary of Recommendations for Ensuring Greater Use of the Summons

Professor Puttkammer has stated that police officers do not use the summons because of "sheer inertia, the habit of doing things as they have all along been done" and "inefficiency." On the latter point he says: "If we have a hidebound inefficient force, we may expect it to use the method of arrest, because that at least is sure-fire: the police grab the fellow and hang on to him. It has the merit of simplicity. The summons calls for a greater degree of efficiency because it rests on the ability of the police department first to warn the offender that he is going to be called on and then to track him down if he does not appear."[102]

To impede the progress of inertia and overcome the force of habit it is necessary both to take steps to place obstacles in the path of unnecessary arrest and to adopt measures which facilitate the use of the summons. The following two sections summarize the principal recommendations made in this chapter towards these ends. In addition to these specific recommendations, it is important to heed the warning stated by the Committee on the Proposed Illinois Code of Criminal Procedure:

> The committee research and studies have revealed that as a practical matter any reasonable solution must depend upon increased standards of recruitment and training of police which will assure proper respect at all times for the basic rights of individuals, criminally-inclined or law-abiding; and

[100]See Williams, *op. cit. supra* note 98, at p. 341.
[101](1934) 24 *J. Cr. L. & C.* 1014 at p. 1017.
[102]Puttkammer, *op. cit. supra* note 21, at pp. 70–1.

increased education of the public generally to a better understanding of the practical problems of overall law enforcement, and the need for co-operation with the police for the protection of all.[103]

A. Obstacles to Unnecessary Arrest

The first step in placing reasonable barriers in the path of the arrest procedure is to create a public awareness of the existing situation. Criticism in the press, comment in Parliament, probing by an *Ombudsman*, and greater concern by magistrates would influence the police and might induce our legislatures, which have historically shown a lack of interest in the exercise of police powers, to take appropriate action.

As has been stated, a provision against unnecessary arrest is vital in order to check the unfettered power of arrest by the police which presently exists. It has been shown that the existing potential safeguard of individual liberty, the justice of the peace, is of insignificant practical value. The concept that power must be exercised on "reasonable and probable grounds" runs through the Criminal Code and its application to this aspect of the arrest procedure, while providing the necessary safeguard, would not significantly hinder efficient police action. At the present time, there is no legal or non-legal review of whether an arrest without warrant, as opposed to a summons, was the necessary or reasonable procedure.

Data on summons and arrest would allow for constant judicial and public vigilance over police practices. The Dominion Bureau of Statistics, as well as individual cities, should in their yearly published reports show a complete breakdown of prosecutions into those initiated by arrests and those initiated by summonses. In addition, the police officer who makes an arrest should be required to file a short written report to the court, explaining why he found an arrest to be necessary.

B. Facilitating the Use of the Summons

We have seen that there are at present some practical obstacles to the use of the summons which would make an arrest necessary and reasonable in many cases. In order to implement and give the desired effect to any prohibition against unnecessary arrest, legislation removing these obstacles would be required.

The police officer should be given the power to summon on his own initiative, without prior judicial approval. He should be able to fingerprint an accused without having him in custody, and to require the

[103]*Tentative Final Draft of the Proposed Illinois Code of Criminal Procedure 1963*, Committee Comments at p. 97.

accused to appear at court or at the police station some time prior to his first court appearance to be fingerprinted for the purpose of permanent police records. In addition, evasion of a summons should be made an offence, so that if an accused gives the officer a false name or fails to appear in answer to the summons he may then be criminally charged. This fact should be forcefully stated on the summons document. Further, to obviate the need for making an arrest with respect to driving offences, the police should be given the power to detain vehicles, even though the accused is not arrested. These measures would facilitate the use of the summons, making many arrests unnecessary and unreasonable and thereby allowing for some alleviation of the existing hardships of arrest.

3. Custody before the First Court Appearance

SOME OF THE HARMFUL CONSEQUENCES of an arrest can be mitigated if the accused has the opportunity of being quickly released from police custody. In this section an analysis will be made of the extent to which police custody pending the first court appearance is used in Toronto.

Unfortunately, this discussion must be limited to the records of cases where the accused was "booked" by the police (i.e., the arrest was officially recorded in the station records);[1] these were the only records that were officially available to the writer. There remains the vast area of detention for investigation of which no official records are kept and which could not therefore be statistically analysed. Brief field interrogation is practised widely in Toronto; compulsory detention in police stations for questioning would also appear to be fairly frequent. These arrests are not necessarily illegal—they are simply not recorded in the published police statistics or in the permanent station records that were available to the writer. The officer may well have had reasonable and probable grounds for initially arresting the accused, but did not book him when subsequent investigation showed the accused not guilty or produced insufficient evidence to proceed. Let it be stressed again that this study deals only with cases in which the accused was booked and officially lodged in the police cells.[2] Further research into cases where the accused is arrested and interrogated, but never charged, is necessary if one is to comprehend fully the true extent of police custody.

[1]"Booking" is used in some cases to refer to the approval given by the sergeant to proceed with a charge; in others, it refers to the actual recording of the name of the accused and relevant data in a record book kept in each police station. In most cases the word "booking" refers to both procedures which normally occur at approximately the same time. The writer is here using the term in the second sense, the recording of the data.

[2]For an excellent analysis of police detention for investigation in two American jurisdictions, see Lafave, "Detention for Investigation by the Police: An Analysis of Current Practices" [1962] *Wash. U. L. Q.* 331.

It will be recalled that in the present study approximately 92 per cent of all persons charged with criminal offences were initially arrested. The data in this chapter will show that of these 92 per cent who were arrested, only 12 per cent were bailed from the police stations. An additional 4 per cent were released on bail from the Don jail on Sunday afternoons. (Early Sunday morning all persons then in police custody are transferred to the Don jail, as the magistrates' courts do not sit on Sunday and the police stations do not have facilities for feeding persons in custody. The transfer to the Don jail is simply an administrative arrangement; the accused are still technically in the custody of the police. They are kept separate from persons at the Don jail awaiting trial who have already appeared in court.) In other words —and this is certainly one of the most significant facts to emerge from this study—84 per cent of all persons *arrested* for criminal offences remained in police custody until their first court appearance. If all charges under the Criminal Code, whether instituted by summons or arrest, are included, then 77 per cent of all persons *charged* with a criminal offence were kept in police custody until their first court appearance.

Some offenders, mainly those charged with driving offences, are released from the City Hall cells on their own recognizance (i.e., without security or sureties) immediately prior to their first court appearance. They are not included in the figure showing the number that were bailed prior to the first court appearance. This policy of release just before trial has been in operation for several years and may be due to a number of reasons. The major reason would appear to be that there is no direct route, without using the public corridors, from the cells to the court that handles the driving offences, and therefore to bring accused persons into court while in custody would not only require too many officers to lead each accused from the cells to court and to supervise him, but would also be publicly degrading for the accused. Another factor may be that this technique makes it more difficult for certain lawyers to "pick up" clients directly from the cells. Whatever the reason, the present procedure clearly shows that there is no real necessity to keep these accused in custody until they are transferred to the magistrates' courts. Release immediately before the first court appearance makes a farce out of the whole system. If the accused can be trusted to appear in court after they are released from the City Hall cells, they can also be trusted to appear in answer to a summons or after being released shortly after their arrest.

I. LENGTH OF TIME BEFORE THE FIRST COURT APPEARANCE

To enable a detailed analysis to be made of the amount of time spent in custody by accused persons before their first court appearance, the following study of the records of a single police station over a four-month period was undertaken. This analysis of all the arrests made under the Criminal Code in the largest division station in the Metropolitan area (at the time of the study referred to as Number 1 Station on College Street)[3] shows that the periods of time spent in police station lockups are far from insignificant.

A. For Those in Custody before the First Court Appearance

(i) Time of Booking. Figure 1 shows the total number of arrested persons who were booked during each hourly period. It is often said that most arrests occur during the early hours of the morning and therefore bail before the first court appearance that morning is not of paramount importance. The data do not indicate that this is the case; although there are a large number of bookings in the early hours of the morning, in less than 40 per cent of the total cases was the accused booked between midnight and 7.00 A.M. Approximately the same number was booked between 7.00 A.M. and 6.00 P.M. (355 persons) as between midnight and 7.00 A.M. (354 persons).[4]

(ii) Time of Arraignment. Magistrates' courts in Toronto sit from 10.00 A.M. until 1.00 P.M. from Monday through Saturday, with special courts sitting on weekday afternoons. This study shows that, although an accused person booked before 11.00 A.M. stands a good chance of appearing before the court that day, an accused person who is booked after 11.00 A.M. will not usually appear in court that day: he will have to wait until the following morning. A person booked after 5.00 P.M.

[3]The Metropolitan Toronto Police Station numbers have since been changed: Number 1 Division has become Number 52.

[4]The writer was informed that the division station analysed has a high rate of day-time arrests and so may not be typical of the general pattern throughout Metropolitan Toronto; for example, many of those arrested during the day for shop-lifting in the downtown department stores are dealt with by this division station. None the less, this does not decrease the necessity for ensuring that those arrested in the specific division analysed are not kept in custody for lengthy periods. Cf. Lafave, *op. cit. supra* note 2, at p. 336: "As to the actual arrests which are followed by detention for purposes of investigation, most of them (especially in the larger cities) are made in the early hours of the morning." This refers to "on suspicion" rather than what Professor Lafave terms "on the nose" arrests (i.e., the supposedly clear-cut cases). The practice in Toronto for this type of arrest is probably the same.

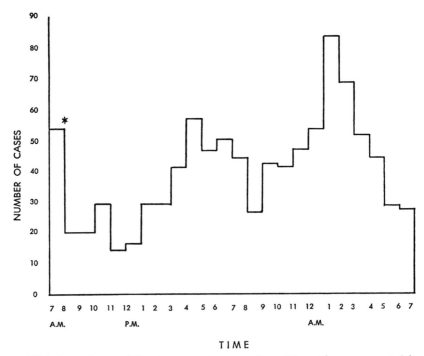

TIME

*This figure is out of line because a large number of found-ins was arrested in one raid.

FIG. 1. Time of booking accused persons (Number 1 Division Station).

never appears in court until the next morning. (In no case was a person who was booked after 7.00 A.M. Saturday morning brought before the court on Saturday.) Approximately 84 per cent (113 out of 134) of the persons booked between noon and 5.00 P.M. on weekdays did not appear in court until at least the following morning. If the cases between noon and midnight are studied, the figure rises to 94 per cent. (The references in this chapter to "appearance on the same *day*" are to a police day, as found in the police records, which begins at 7.00 A.M. one morning and runs until 7.00 A.M. the next.)

Figures 2 and 3, compiled from the analysis of the records in Number 1 Division Station, show when the accused appeared in court in relation to the time of booking. Those booked between 7.00 A.M. Saturday and 7.00 A.M. Monday have been excluded from Figure 2 in order to present a clearer picture of the regular day-to-day pattern. The upper level of the Figures shows how many persons were booked during each

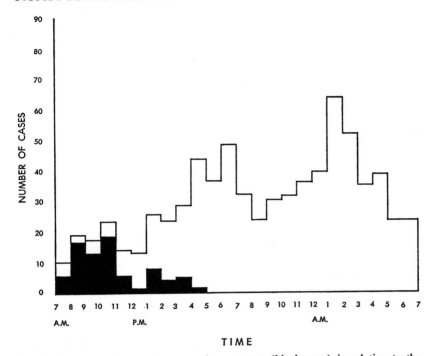

FIG. 2. Appearance in court on same day as arrest (black area) in relation to the total number of bookings (excluding weekend arrests).

hourly period. The lower level indicates how many of those arrested were brought before the court the same day.

Number 1 Division Station is geographically the closest station to the magistrates' courts at the City Hall and so distance is not an important factor in this analysis. If anything, because of the longer distances to court, accused persons at other division stations are probably less likely to make their initial court appearances on the same day as they are booked than are accused persons booked at Number 1 Division Station.

(iii) Twenty-four-hour Rule. It can be seen from Figure 3 that some accused persons were kept in custody for slightly longer than the 24-hour period specified in the Code. Section 438(2) provides:

A peace officer who receives delivery of and detains a person who has been arrested without warrant or who arrests a person with or without warrant shall, in accordance with the following provisions, take or cause that person to be taken before a justice to be dealt with according to law, namely,

(a) where a justice is available within a period of twenty-four hours after the person has been delivered to or has been arrested by the peace officer,

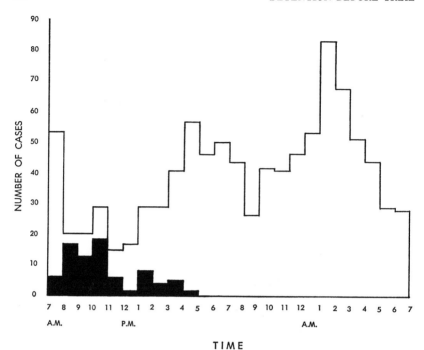

Fig. 3. Appearance in court on same day as arrest (black area) in relation to the
total number of bookings (including weekend arrests).

the person shall be taken before a justice before the expiration of that
period; and

(b) where a justice is not available within a period of twenty-four hours
after the person has been delivered to or has been arrested by the peace
officer, the person shall be taken before a justice as soon as possible.

It is true that when a person is arrested at, say, 8.00 A.M. a justice
is not available when the 24-hour period expires. However, the section
speaks of the availability of the justices "within a period of twenty-four
hours" and a justice is available in the morning and afternoon following
the arrest. There is, therefore, a legal obligation on the police to bring
these persons before the court on the day of their arrest.

Apart from these few cases, the Toronto police appeared to be fairly
careful in observing the 24-hour rule. Apart from weekend arrests, no
cases were found in which the accused was kept in police custody for
a substantial period over the 24-hour limit.

Unfortunately, information was obtainable only with respect to the
time of booking the prisoner, not with respect to the time of his ap-

prehension. It is not possible to say to what extent different results would be obtained if the time of apprehension were taken. That the figures would be changed to some extent is certain. In some cases the gap between the time of arrest and booking would not be great; in others, it might amount to a considerable period of time.[5] Interrogation normally takes place before the accused is booked and, if the accused is interrogated at police headquarters, he is usually fingerprinted and photographed before his arrest is noted in the records of the division station.

If the police have not completed such procedures as fingerprinting, the justice can remand the accused to the custody of the police for a brief period. Section 451(c)(ii) of the Criminal Code provides: "A justice . . . may remand an accused . . . (ii) orally, to the custody of a peace officer or other person, where the remand is for a period not exceeding three clear days." The writer has been informed that police in Montreal sometimes resort to this practice for the purpose of further interrogation. It is seldom, if ever, used in Toronto. Further investigation by the police is, however, permitted at the Don jail, where the accused is in the custody and under the supervision of penal authorities.

B. For Those Bailed before First Court Appearance

Mention has already been made of the fact that only about 12 per cent of all persons arrested were bailed from the police stations. The individual station records indicated that proportionately fewer persons were bailed from the division station chosen in this study than from other Toronto division stations. Nevertheless, the analysis of this single station which follows seems to show the general pattern of operation.

(i) Number Bailed. Out of 950 persons who were arrested and not immediately transferred to court, only 57 were bailed from the police station prior to their first court appearance; 94 per cent were held in custody until their first court appearance. Figure 4, broken down into the hours in which accused persons were booked, shows the number of accused who were bailed at some time prior to their first court appearance in relation to the total number of persons arrested. Those arrested between 7.00 A.M. and 5.00 P.M. who were brought into court on the same day are excluded (there were 81 and if they were included the paucity of the use of bail would be accentuated); weekend arrests are included.

[5]Collection of this data would be difficult but certainly not impossible. The actual time of arrest is noted in the officer's note-book as well as in the confidential instructions to the Crown prosecutor.

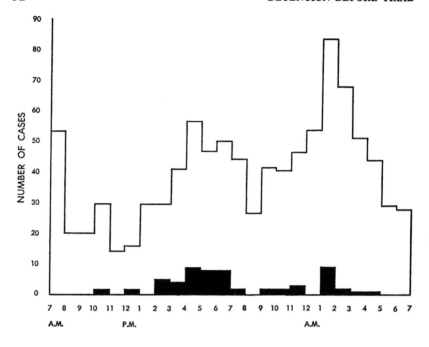

TIME

FIG. 4. Bail before first court appearance (black area) in relation to the total
number of bookings.

(ii) Delay before Release on Bail. In the cases where the accused
was released on bail from the Division Station, there was a general
pattern of delay before bail could be arranged. The average (mean) time
spent between booking and bail in Number 1 Division Station was
approximately four and a half hours. Of course, there were wide variations (perhaps not due simply to chance). The data show, for example,
that of the eight persons who were booked between the hours of 4.00
and 5.00 P.M., and released on bail, five had to wait until after 9.00 P.M.
before they were released; the other three, who were released within
one hour from the time of booking, were charged with bookmaking.

(iii) The Justice of the Peace. A short description of the role of the
justice of the peace in arranging bail will give some indication of why
procedures for release before arraignment are so inadequate in Toronto.
At present the police do not have the power to set or take bail; the
accused must wait until he is brought before a magistrate, or until a

justice of the peace visits the police station.[6] The power of a justice to bail an accused from the police station is not explicitly granted by the Criminal Code. Although it seems likely that a court would uphold the power because of its obvious desirability, this informal procedure might better be legitimized by a clear legislative provision.

Those arrested between 7.00 A.M. and 5.00 P.M. have almost no opportunity of being released on bail during this period if the police do not choose to bring the offender to the City Hall for a court appearance. No justice of the peace is assigned to visit the police stations during these hours. The one justice of the peace who is fully engaged with bail matters during the day is too busy with the routine bail work at the City Hall and at the Don jail to be able to devote additional time to bailing persons from the police stations. No doubt some accused persons are released on bail from the stations during this period, but only as a special favour from a justice of the peace.

No justice of the peace is officially available between 5.00 and 8.00 P.M. Between 8.00 P.M. and midnight two justices are "on duty" to cover all Metropolitan Toronto, which is divided into two areas for this purpose.[7] Each justice will normally make one tour of his part of the city during this period. The data from Number 1 Division Station indicate that the justice normally arrives there sometime between 9.30 and 10.30

[6]The argument can be made, although it does not appear to have been raised in any reported case, that there is no authority for a justice of the peace to release an accused person from the police cells at night because the justice in purporting to act under s. 451 of the Code is not sitting in open court. If, in fact, there is no jurisdiction in these cases, then the recognizance will not bind the accused, bail cannot be forfeited, and a prosecution for skipping bail will fail. It is true that the justice can exclude members of the public, but only where it appears "that the ends of justice will be best served by so doing" (s. 451(j))—hardly applicable to setting bail. It seems reasonably clear, for example, that a justice cannot remand an accused for a 30-day mental examination under s. 451(c) when not in open court. Why should the justice have jurisdiction to exercise any of the other powers in s. 451, including setting bail, when not in open court? *Tremeear's Criminal Code* (5th ed., 1944) states at p. 794 with reference to the 1927 Code: "There is no specific provision for bail before the opening of the inquiry in the case of arrest without warrant." In the case of arrests with a warrant, s. 664 of the 1927 Code made specific provision for bailing the accused before the opening of the preliminary inquiry. Accused arrested without a warrant were apparently bailed from the police station by virtue of s. 668 of the 1927 Code. Tremeear states at p. 747: "A common practice makes [s. 668] cover an enquiry immediately after the arrest as to the question of bail and the taking of bail before the magistrate if he can be got to attend at the gaol or police station for that purpose. . . ."

[7]See Haggart, "A Weekend of Abuse: It's Just Routine," *Toronto Daily Star*, Feb. 18, 1964, where it is pointed out that: " 'On duty' means they are at home and they give their phone numbers to the police stations. If the police phone, they are supposed to come. If the police don't phone, the JP's don't come."

P.M. This means that an accused arrested during the day and taken to Number 1 Station usually has to wait until late in the evening before he can be bailed.

From midnight until court opens in the morning, there is only one justice of the peace to handle all of Metropolitan Toronto. (There are two justices who share this responsibility, on alternate weeks.) Even if he were available at all times during the night it would be almost impossible for him adequately to cover all the division stations throughout Metropolitan Toronto. It should be noted that Metropolitan Toronto has a population of over 1,500,000 persons and covers an area of approximately 250 square miles. There are over 20 police division stations. In fact, the single justice is not always available.[8] For example, one of the justices who is expected to work from midnight until morning every second week also holds a full-time job at City Hall. This would mean that every second week he is expected to work 16 hours a day. In addition, though the justices use their own automobiles, they receive no gas allowance. They are subject to little or no supervision, and their salaries are not commensurate with the potential importance of their function.

One justice of the peace in Toronto claims that bail is a "privilege" and compares his function in arranging night bail with that of a bank: according to him the citizen has no *right* to expect the services of either during the night-time. The problem of arranging bail is particularly acute for those who are transferred to the Don jail on weekends. Whereas a justice is, theoretically, always on call at police stations, on Sundays he will visit the Don jail only during the hours of 1.00–3.00 P.M. Clerks at the Don jail can give an inquirer only a rough estimate of the amount at which bail will be set, and seldom mention the need for deeds or tax certificates for property bail (which often cannot be acquired on Sunday in any event). Thus when the person who wishes to put up bail comes down to the Don jail, he must, on the basis of a clerk's guess, have the exact amount at which bail is to be set or be out of luck. Also, many persons confuse the visiting hours of 2.00–4.00 P.M. with the justices' hours and some find when they arrive that they are too late.

Needless to say, the service offered by the justices is not entirely effective. The police tend to blame the justices for the fact that many accused persons who should be released are kept in custody overnight,

[8]The City of Philadelphia apparently recognizes the reluctance shown by magistrates to leave their homes at night and therefore provides for an accused person to be released when a "copy of the charge" is signed by a magistrate at his home. See Freed and Wald, *Bail in the United States: 1964* at p. 20.

and also for the fact that in cases where the accused is bailed there is usually a period of considerable delay before bail is granted.

(iv) Police Opposition. The justice will seldom set bail if the police object to the accused being released, and if the justice does set it in such a case, then it is usually at a very high amount.[9]

The police will oppose the release of an accused charged with an indictable offence until he has been taken to police headquarters to be printed and photographed. There is often considerable delay before an accused is transported to headquarters: two men must be taken off their other duties to bring the accused to headquarters, wait for him, and then return him to the police station. As a result, the police often wait until there is more than one accused. Surely there are ways of expediting the procedure to obtain prints and photographs of the accused.[10] The actual process of printing and searching the records takes very little time. One writer has stated: "Taking of fingerprints is a matter of a few moments, and because of the remarkably effective system of classification an expert can locate a card among thousands of records in less than three minutes."[11]

An additional reason for delay is that for some offences the police seem to follow a rule of thumb in refusing to allow the release of an accused for a certain length of time after his arrest. For example, it appears that the police will object to bail being granted to a person charged with impaired driving until he has been in custody at least three hours. If the accused is still drunk this makes good sense, of course, but as a fixed rule it is improper. By the time the three-hour period has passed the accused may have missed the visit of the justice of the peace. One reason put forward by the police for the three-hour rule is that an earlier release would enable defence counsel to argue that "the accused could not have been very impaired if the police released him." Under existing practice there is some validity in the position of the police. A magistrate who is accustomed to impaired drivers being kept in custody for at least three hours might raise his eyebrows, so to

[9]See Galligan, "Advising an Arrested Client," *Law Society of Upper Canada Special Lectures 1963* at p. 44. The same practice was found to exist in Detroit. See Lafave, *op. cit. supra* note 2, at p. 338. See also *Re Sommervill's Prohibition Application* (1962) 38 W.W.R. 344 (Sask. Q.B.).

[10]Because of the shortage of manpower, the police have recently (since the present study was undertaken) begun to change their practice in this respect. They now send out two fingerprinting experts with their apparatus to make the rounds of the police stations.

[11]Moffat, "Taking Finger Prints upon Arrest" (1926) 12 *A. B. A. J.* 175 at p. 176. See also "The Baumes Bills: A Beginning in the Reorganization of Criminal Procedure in New York" (1926) 26 *Col. L. Rev.* 752 at p. 753.

speak, if the accused were released sooner. However, if in general impaired drivers were released as soon as practicable, this point would lose its force.

(v) Night Bail. The above procedural considerations impeding release are minor when compared with the problem of raising bail at night. If bail is set at $200 for a particular offender, the accused or his friends must obtain this sum or the bondsman by producing the required title documents must be able to convince the justice that he has real property worth that amount. Very few persons are in a position to produce such a sum of money in the evening. Cheques will not be accepted by the justices, and by the time that the accused is booked, the banks and lending institutions are closed. Even if he is booked during the day-time the banks will usually be closed before the justice has told the accused what amount of bail is required.

There are also practical difficulties in putting up real property at night. Justices of the peace will usually not take real property unless the accused has the required title documents and tax certificates. In many cases these documents are in a safety deposit box or in a lawyer's file. In addition, the justice will sometimes require a registrar's abstract of title and a valuator's report. These, of course, cannot be obtained at night. Some justices at times employ their own personal rule of thumb which tends to keep down the number of persons bailed; for example, one rule is that property bail will not be accepted if there are two mortgages on the property. Further, professional bondsmen or persons who loan money for bail are not active in the evening. When the other "rules" are added (for example, that a wife cannot put up for her accused husband property which is jointly owned by the wife and the accused), it is not difficult to understand why so few persons are released on bail at night. Assuming that some form of security in advance is desirable, such highly restrictive "rules" are unnecessary. For example, few difficulties would be encountered, particularly for the minor offences, in permitting the justice to accept a personal cheque from the surety. If the cheque is not honoured in the morning the accused could be re-arrested and proceedings brought against the bondsman. It is highly unlikely that a cheque would be issued to a justice of the peace knowing that it would not be honoured.

C. For all Arrested Persons

Figure 5 shows more clearly the extent of police custody of accused persons in Toronto. The data from Figures 3 and 4 are combined to show the total amount of time spent in custody before the first court

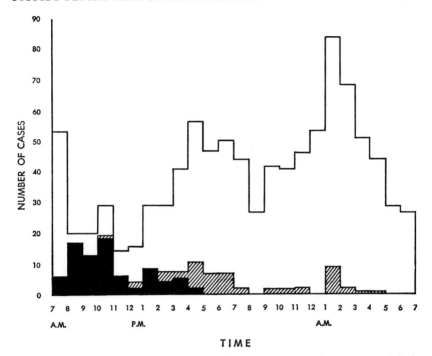

FIG. 5. Bail (shaded area) and appearance in court on same day as arrest (black area) in relation to the total number of bookings. White area indicates cases remaining in police custody until transferred to City Hall cells or Don jail (on Sundays) next morning.

appearance in relation to the total number of bookings. From the data from Number 1 Division Station for all cases, it appears that over 80 per cent of all those booked between 7.00 A.M. and midnight are kept in police custody over 10 hours before their first court appearances and many are in custody for periods substantially greater. It is obvious then that most accused persons in Toronto spend lengthy periods of time in police custody.[12]

II. Conditions in the Lockups

In the light of the length of time spent in custody by many accused before their first court appearance, the physical conditions of the police

[12]Cf. Williams, "Questioning by the Police: Some Practical Considerations" [1960] *Crim. L. Rev.* 325 at p. 340: "Under the English practice, the police only have a few hours in which to question the arrested suspect before bringing him before a magistrate."

lockup are of interest. Regrettably, Toronto in many respects faces the same unhappy situation existing in many American jurisdictions.[13]

No attempt will be made to discuss in detail the conditions in police lockups; the subject would provide scope for a further study.[14] Although the lockups appear to be clean, they are certainly not designed for comfort; neither mattresses nor blankets are provided in the men's cells. There are no regular meals. If an offender has his own money he can sometimes persuade an officer to bring him a sandwich from a nearby restaurant. Apparently there is a fund which the police may use to provide meals for those who cannot afford to buy their own; but the fund is seldom used. Although it is generally accepted by the police forces that an accused is entitled to contact a lawyer or a relative after he is arrested, there is often a considerable delay before he may do so. Many officers, out of a supposed kindness to lawyers, do not permit the accused to telephone a lawyer late at night or early in the morning. There are also many who feel that the accused, if permitted to use the phone at all, is entitled to make only one telephone call, whether completed or not. Of course, the law is clear that an accused has the right to contact his lawyer.[15] There is a highly punitive atmosphere in the police lockups. To a certain extent it may be attributed to the fact that a large proportion of persons in them are common drunks who constantly and loudly shout for their "rights" and are just as frequently ignored. In the

[13]See Freed and Wald, *op. cit. supra* note 8, at p. 44.

[14]The John Howard Society of Chicago formerly published a detailed annual report on the conditions in police lockups in Chicago which have had a significant effect on their improvement. The writer is indebted to Mr. A. M. Kirkpatrick, Executive Director of the John Howard Society of Ontario, and co-author of the 1952 Chicago report, for making these reports available.

[15]See *Koechlin* v. *Waugh and Hamilton* (1957) 118 C.C.C. 24 (Ont. C.A.); *Regina* v. *Gray* (1962) 132 C.C.C. 337 (B.C. Mag. Ct.); Galligan, *op. cit. supra* note 9, at p. 36. See also the extract from the *Report into the Arrest and Detention of Wright and Griffin* per Roach J.A. set out at p. 57 of the *Law Society of Upper Canada Special Lectures 1963*; the *Report of the Royal Commission on Police Powers and Procedure*, 1929, Cmd. 3297 at p. 68 stated that an accused should be able to consult his legal advisers "immediately on arrival at the Police station." The "one call" philosophy seems to include even those calls which are not completed: see *Regina* v. *O'Connor* [1965] 1 C.C.C. 20 at p. 28 *per* Haines J.: "These things of course are as unacceptable as their apparent notion that persons in custody are permitted only one phone call, completed or otherwise." See also Haggart, *op. cit. supra* note 7. It is interesting to note the non-committal statement by Staff Inspector Bird of the Ontario Provincial Police in Bird, *A Manual on Arrest for Peace Officers* (1963) at pp. 93–94: "A problem which often confronts those in charge of lock-ups is what rights must be allowed to accused persons to contact a solicitor, or relatives and friends. In municipal areas it is probable that a policy has grown over the years that restricts, and yet allows, this type of contact to be made."

eyes of the police everyone in the lockup tends to be on the level of the drunk. A lack of facilities often does not permit the police to separate the young person in custody from the older offenders, with whom he is allowed to mingle freely. In some stations the only effective, but obviously undesirable, method of segregating the young offender is to put him in what amounts to an isolation cell. Conditions in the lockups are certainly worse than those provided for persons who have been found guilty and have been sentenced to jail. An accused arrested on Saturday is transferred for the weekend to the Don jail where the physical conditions are no better and the admitting procedures are more degrading.

A vivid description of the treatment that may be suffered by an impaired driver was given by Ron Haggart in his column, "A Weekend of Abuse: It's Just Routine."[16] The accused (identified as "B" here) was arrested on a Saturday night and was taken to the Don jail the next morning.

. . . B. had been to a Saturday night corn roast in Woodbridge with his wife and 11-year-old daughter. He was stopped by a constable in a yellow traffic cruiser just after midnight and taken to a police station on Sheppard Ave. in North York.

His wife phoned a relative of hers who owns a store. She knew he would have a lot of money at home with him over the weekend. He came down with about $1,000 in his pocket.

The police at the station said B's bail would probably be $100, which turned out to be correct, so the store-owner gave B. $100 in cash and enough for cab fare, and went home.

From about 2 a.m. on Sunday morning to some time after 1 p.m. on Sunday afternoon, B had $100 in his pocket. But in all that time, he couldn't get out of jail.

He was locked in a cell where he slept on a sheet of steel. He was put in handcuffs and herded into a paddy-wagon and taken to the Don jail, where he got the rubby-dub's breakfast of bread and pea soup. . . .

B. stripped off his clothes, was given a shower, and what is euphemistically called a skin frisk. They found no heroin in his anus. Friends who came to help him at the Don jail on Sunday morning were sent away by a faceless voice speaking over a public address system through the locked outside door.

"Get your hands off those bars," a guard barked at him in the Don jail.

"I want to phone my wife—what time is it?" B. asked.

The guard was hilarious: "What're you worrying about, you ain't goin' no place."

B. was allowed to make the classic 'one phone call' from the police station on Sheppard Ave. He phoned home for his wife and got no answer. At that moment, Mrs. B. was either in another part of the station, or on her way

16Haggart, *op. cit. supra* note 7. See also Haggart, "The Law is the Same for Everyone," *Toronto Daily Star*, Dec. 9, 1964.

home from it. B. didn't know his wife had been to the station, but that was his 'one' phone call,' and he couldn't make another until he got out of the Don jail on Sunday afternoon.

. . . B. is a sheet metal mechanic at [D] aircraft, where he's worked for 13 years. He has three children, a car (which was locked up in an auto pound) and he has been the president of his union. . . .

III. POSSIBLE EFFECTS OF CUSTODY BEFORE THE FIRST COURT APPEARANCE

The time spent in police custody before the first court appearance is a most critical period. Mr. Justice Douglas of the United States Supreme Court has said that "what takes place in the secret confines of the police station may be more critical than what takes place at the trial."[17] Three main effects of such custody will be discussed in this section: the opportunity it affords for improper police practices, its effect on the accused's plea, and the relationship between custody and the retention of counsel.

A. Improper Police Practices

Although improper police practices are universally rejected as indefensible, they still find their way into use in all large cities, including Toronto. No general statistical study of improper treatment of accused persons in custody before trial can be made; it is extremely difficult to document the third degree, physical or psychological. It would seem that the longer a person is exposed to the police behind the locked doors of the police station (very often without the benefit of counsel) the greater is the opportunity for improper practice by the police.[18]

B. Guilty Pleas

The reader will recall that 84 per cent of all persons arrested for criminal offences were kept in custody until their first court appearance. It seems reasonable that these extended periods increase the likelihood that the accused will plead guilty at the first court appearance. Persons who spend lengthy periods of time in police custody will be more inclined to plead guilty than persons who originally were summoned. Many reasons for this can be suggested: the possibility in fact and in the mind of the accused that if he pleads guilty he will not have to spend a further

---

[17]A dissenting opinion in *Crooker* v. *California* (1957) 357 U.S. 433 at pp. 444–45.

[18]See Honsberger, "The Power of Arrest and the Duties and Rights of Citizens and Police," *Law Society of Upper Canada Special Lectures 1963* at pp. 9–11: "It follows that the longer the prisoner is detained before he appears in court, the less authentic will be the public trial." See also MacInnes, "The Criminal Society" in *The Police and the Public* (1962, ed. Rolph) at pp. 101–2.

period of time in custody;[19] the desire to be released from a distasteful experience; the effect of suggestions by the police and fellow accused that it is better to plead guilty; and the use of highly developed police interrogation methods, both proper and improper.[20]

The cases studied tend to bear out the above assumption, although the differences in the data are perhaps not as significant as one might have expected. Approximately 40 per cent of those who appeared in court in custody pleaded guilty at the first court appearance, while slightly less than 30 per cent of those who were summoned or who were bailed before their first court appearance did so. When broken down into summary and indictable offences the figures of those who pleaded guilty at the first court appearance were as shown in Table I.[21]

TABLE I

GUILTY PLEAS AT FIRST COURT APPEARANCE

Offence	Bailed and Summoned (per cent)	Custody (per cent)
Summary	31	41
Indictable	27	40
Total	29.8	40.4

These figures do not "prove" any causal relationship; they merely show that the common sense view of this effect of custody is borne out by a study of the data.

It has been suggested that the courts would be unable to cope with the increased number of not guilty pleas which might result from decreasing the number of persons who come into court in custody. Aside from the conceptual invalidity of this argument, the fact that 30 per cent of the "non-custody" cases pleaded guilty indicates that the increased burden on the courts would not be as great as might be suspected.

[19]See note, "Bail: An Ancient Practice Reexamined" (1961) 70 *Yale L. J.* 966 at pp. 969–70, note 27, where it is noted that "many accuseds plead guilty in order to avoid the delay and frustration that await a decision to contest." See also Douglas, "Vagrancy and Arrest on Suspicion" (1960) 70 *Yale L. J.* 1 at p. 4.

[20]For a discussion of the practical aspects of police interrogation, see Inbau and Reid, *Criminal Interrogation and Confessions* (1962).

[21]Cases in which the charge against the accused was withdrawn at the first court appearance are not included in the figures. If guilty pleas after the first court appearance were included, the number of guilty pleas would, of course, be much higher. See *infra* chapter 5.II.B.

C. Difficulties in Retaining Counsel

Over 95 per cent of all persons who appeared in court in custody and pleaded guilty at their first court appearance did not have a lawyer.[22] Many of these are people who cannot afford services of a legal counsel but must rely on free legal aid. Yet the legal aid system, as it now operates, bypasses persons in custody who plead guilty at the first court appearance. The accused often does not know of legal aid and has little opportunity of finding out about it while in custody. No systematic attempt has been made to provide legal advice to accused persons prior to their first court appearance.

Those who can afford regular counsel are often denied this right by police adherence to the "one call" rule. Further, the facilities provided for interviews with counsel in the lockups and City Hall cells are poor and not conducive to a proper conference between solicitor and client.

The difficulty and inability to consult counsel is the most vital of the deleterious effects of such custody. The individual who can obtain no legal advice before his arraignment is susceptible to improper police practice, is more likely to plead guilty, and less likely to develop any legitimate defence he may have. Investigation and the location of witnesses may be hampered or even made impossible by the passage of time.[23] "Indeed, the pre-trial period is so full of hazards for the accused that, if unaided by competent legal advice, he may lose any legitimate defence he may have long before he is arraigned and put on trial."[24]

IV. POSSIBLE SOLUTIONS

There are a number of possible solutions that might assist in ensuring a speedy release for persons taken into custody by the police. At this point only the procedural solutions to the difficulties of arranging bail before the first court appearance will be discussed. The conceptual aspects of setting bail will be discussed in chapter 10.

A. Increasing the Effectiveness of the Justice of the Peace

As has been pointed out above, the present system of having a justice of the peace set and take bail at police stations often delays the release

[22]The percentages for both summary and indictable offences were approximately the same: summary, 95.9 (680 out of 709); indictable, 95.3 (750 out of 795).

[23]As the Special Committee of the Association of the Bar of the City of New York and the National Legal Aid and Defender Association of the United States stated in *Equal Justice for the Accused* (1959) at p. 60: "The earlier any investigation is initiated the more effective it is likely to be."

[24]"Criminal Procedure—Right to Counsel Prior to Trial," 44 *Ky. L. J.* at pp. 103–4 (cited in *Crooker* v. *California* (1957) 357 U.S. 433 at pp. 445–46). See also *Escobedo* v. *State* (1964) 378 U.S. 478.

of accused persons. There are presently an insufficient number of justices to cover adequately the large metropolitan area. This problem, particularly acute at night, is compounded by a rigid insistence that cash or real property be put up for bail purposes. An obvious possible solution is to increase the number of justices available for setting and taking bail. Yet such measures would be inadequate to cope effectively with the problem. Providing sufficient justices to service a large metropolitan area efficiently may prove to be impractical; no one would suggest that there should be a justice of the peace in every police station. There is little opportunity for public and judicial control of the actions of a justice who does his work in the privacy of the police station and keeps no official records. Often the decision of the justice does not represent an independent judicial opinion because of his ready amenability to police suggestions on the question of bail. It is for these reasons that, in addition to steps being taken to improve the efficiency and effectiveness of the justices of the peace, alternative methods of setting and taking bail must be devised.

B. Arraignment Court

A simple solution to the problems inherent in total reliance on the justice of the peace is to have one magistrate act as a court of first appearance to take the guilty pleas (assuming that it is desirable to permit a guilty plea in these circumstances) and to remand all the other cases to a later date after setting bail. If such a court were available, accused persons could be brought before it at any time during the day. The magistrate setting bail and remanding the accused in an open court probably would not be as inclined to accept automatically police opinion on questions concerning bail as would a justice of the peace operating outside the scope of public scrutiny. Appearance in arraignment court would also provide the accused with an effective and early opportunity to contact a legal adviser, relative, or friend.

Most accused persons arrested during the day-time were not brought before the court the same day, in part because some police officers consider that the 24-hour period mentioned in the Code permits them to hold a person for up to 24 hours. However, s. 438, set out earlier, is not permissive but simply sets an outside limit on the length of time that a person may be kept; thus the common-law rule that a person should not be kept for an unreasonable length of time still applies.[25]

[25]S. 438 was introduced in the 1953–54 Code. S. 652 of the 1927 Code was the only section of the previous Code remotely comparable, but it applied only to loitering at night. It provided that "no person who has been so apprehended shall be detained after noon of the following day without being brought before a justice." Thus, prior to the 1953–54 Code, resort to the common law was necessary.

What is a reasonable length of time will, of course, depend on the circumstances, but it would appear to be unreasonable to hold a person after the routine paper work and investigation have been completed if there is a magistrate's court sitting at that time.

In the leading case of *Lewis* v. *Tims*,[26] Lord Porter stated that the proper test is "whether, in all the circumstances, the accused person has been brought before a justice of the peace within a reasonable time, it being always remembered that that time should be as short as is reasonably practicable."[27] This would also appear to be the Canadian law. If it were not so interpreted, then what was obviously meant as a restriction on the power to hold would be turned into a permission to hold. The letter of the Code would be more clearly consonant with the common law if (as has been done in some American states) the phrase "without unreasonable delay" were added to s. 438.[28]

The reason generally given by the police for not bringing an accused before the court on the day of the arrest is that magistrates tend to look with disfavour on officers who make their difficult task even more difficult by disrupting the hearing of cases. There is probably much truth in this. The magistrates finish with the remands and guilty pleas within half an hour to an hour after the courts open at 10.00 A.M. and wish to devote the remainder of the time to the trial of contested cases. A special arraignment court would remove this difficulty.

C. Night Court

There is no sound reason why an arraignment court should not sit after 5.00 P.M.; the later the court were to sit, the more useful it would be. Many large American cities have instituted a night court.[29]

[26][1952] A.C. 676 at pp. 691–92 (H.L.).

[27]Section 38(4) of the English Magistrates' Courts Act, 1952, c. 55 states: "Where a person is taken into custody for an offence without a warrant and is retained in custody, he shall be brought before a magistrates' court as soon as practicable." See generally, the *Report of the Royal Commission on Police Powers and Procedure*, 1929, Cmd. 3297 at p. 54. See also Fitzgerald, *Criminal Law and Punishment* (1962) at p. 179: "A police officer who arrests a man without warrant is bound to bring him before the magistrates as soon as possible." American law is the same. Bohlen and Shulman in "Effect of Subsequent Misconduct upon a Lawful Arrest" (1928) 28 *Col. L. Rev.* 841 at p. 852 have stated: "The cases are unanimous in holding that one who has made a privileged arrest must use due diligence to present his prisoner promptly before a proper tribunal." See also Orfield, *Criminal Procedure from Arrest to Appeal* (1947) at pp. 37–39.

[28]See Lafave, *op. cit. supra* note 2, at p. 333 for examples of American legislation. The Alaska Act states: "without unnecessary delay, and in any event within twenty-four hours." Alaska Comp. Laws Ann. § 66-5-34 (Supp. 1958).

[29]For example, a night court for misdemeanours operates until midnight in New York City. See Freed and Wald, *op. cit. supra* note 8, at p. 20.

D. Giving the Police the Power to Release an Arrested Person

(i) Bail by the Police. Though an arraignment court would remove many of the drawbacks of the present system, in many cases a certain delay would be inevitable. To allow an accused the opportunity to be bailed at the earliest possible moment, the police should be entitled to set and accept bail in criminal cases when the accused is in police custody. If the police initially have the power to decide whether to arrest without a warrant or to apply for a summons, it is absurd that the police should not also have the power to release the person whom they have arrested.[30] The police at present possess this power when the accused is in custody charged with a provincial offence. Section 15(1) of The Summary Convictions Act of Ontario provides:

Where a person who is charged with an offence to which this Act applies is taken into custody either with or without the warrant of a Justice and is brought into a police station at any time during the day or night, the police officer in charge of the station, if he thinks the case a proper one, may take bail without fee from such person by recognizance conditioned for his appearance within two days before the Magistrate or other justice at the time and place therein mentioned.[31]

In many respects they perform this function now in criminal cases; a justice of the peace will rarely disregard the wishes of the police in deciding whether to set bail before the first court appearance or, in most cases, the general amount of security required if bail is to be set. Whether or not the police have the power to set bail, they should clearly have the

---

[30]The law does not apply evenly throughout Canada. Most provinces are policed by the Royal Canadian Mounted Police and senior R.C.M.P. officers are justices of the peace. However, it is not clear whether their power is widely used. See s. 17 of the R.C.M.P. Act, 1959, Stat. Can., c. 54, s. 17(2) which provides: "Every Superintendent and every other officer designated by the Governor in Council is *ex officio* a justice of the peace." The Ontario Police Act, R.S.O. 1960, c. 298, s. 41, makes only the Commissioner of Police a magistrate.

It is interesting to note that it used to be common in Toronto for the police to set and accept bail at night and then have the documents sworn by the justice of the peace the following morning. The practice was stopped about eight years ago, apparently because there was no legislative authorization for it.

[31]R.S.O. 1960, c. 387. A similar provision was first introduced into Ontario law in 1896 by (1896) 59 Vict., Stat. Ont., c. 27, s. 1, An Act to authorize Police Constables to take Bail.

Although there is no statutory authorization for the practice, some police departments permit the accused to post bail without taking him into custody. See Bird, *op. cit. supra* note 15, at p. 105, who states that it is used without statutory authorization "when it is obvious, or reasonably so, that the offender from the other province or country will not return in answer to a mailed summons and the constable does not have the authority to arrest without warrant."

power to accept bail that has already been set by a justice. Rule 68(1) of the English Magistrates' Courts Rules, 1952, provides:

Where a magistrates' court having jurisdiction to take a recognisance from any person has fixed the amount in which he and his sureties, if any, are to be bound, the recognisances may be entered into before any justice of the peace, or before the clerk of any magistrates' court, or before any police officer not below the rank of inspector, or before the officer in charge of any police station or, if the person to be bound is in a prison or other place of detention, before the governor or keeper of the prison or place.[32]

(a) Arrest without a warrant. The English police possess wide powers of bailing accused persons who are arrested without a warrant. Section 38(1) of the Magistrates' Courts Act, 1952, provides:

On a person's being taken into custody for an offence without a warrant, a police officer not below the rank of inspector, or the police officer in charge of the police station to which the person is brought, may, and, if it will not be practicable to bring him before a magistrates' court within twenty-four hours after his being taken into custody, shall, inquire into the case and, unless the offence appears to the officer to be a serious one, release him on his entering into a recognizance, with or without sureties, for a reasonable amount, conditioned for his appearance before a magistrates' court at the time and place named in the recognizance.

The police in England therefore may bail any accused unless the offence appears to the officer to be a serious one, and *must* do so if the accused cannot be brought before a magistrates' court within 24 hours. Considerable leeway is provided by the qualification that bail is mandatory in such a case only if the offence is not a serious one. In any event, the section at least takes care of the obvious cases where the police have no objection to releasing the accused.[33] Such a provision is necessary

[32]See the Magistrates' Courts Act, 1952, ss. 95 and 105 for the statutory authorization for the rule.

[33]A somewhat analogous power is provided by s. 10 of the American Uniform Arrest Act (see Inbau and Sowle, *Cases and Comments on Criminal Justice* (1960) at p. 520): "Any officer in charge of a police department or any officer authorized by him may release instead of taking before a magistrate any person who has been arrested without a warrant by an officer of his department. . . . B. When such person was arrested for a misdemeanor and has signed an agreement to appear in court at a time designated, if the officer is satisfied that such person is a resident of the state and will appear in court at the time designated." However, this is not bail. No forfeiture (or even a penalty) is envisaged if the accused does not appear. See generally, Warner, "Modern Trends in the American Law of Arrest" (1943) 21 *Can. B. Rev.* 192 at p. 212; Warner, "The Uniform Arrest Act" (1942) 28 *Va. L. Rev.* 315 at pp. 336–39, 346. It has been stated that bail by a police officer would be unconstitutional in the United States: see Puttkammer, *Administration of the Criminal Law*, at p. 103 (cf. p. 67). Although this would appear to be so if the courts were completely ousted from their traditional role in setting bail, it

in Canada. As Lord Goddard C.J. stated, in discussing this procedure for a case of shop-lifting, "Now that a police officer has statutory powers to grant bail, he will do so, except in cases of gravity or where for good reason he may think it would be unsafe to grant bail. In an ordinary case of a crime of this sort, a police officer is as efficacious, for the protection of the subject, as a justice. . . ."[34]

The earliest statutory provision in England granting the police the power to set bail in these cases was in the Metropolitan Police Act of 1821.[35] Section 28 permitted "the constable or headborough attending at any watchhouse between the hours of eight in the afternoon and six in the forenoon, to take bail by recognizances, without fee or reward, from any person who shall be brought into his custody within the said hours, without the warrant of a justice, charged with any petty misdemeanor. . . ." In earlier periods of English history it would appear that the sheriff, a non-judicial officer, had the power of releasing accused persons on bail.[36]

Section 38(2) of the English Magistrates' Courts Act 1952 also permits the police to bail an accused, arrested without a warrant conditioned for his appearance at a police station at a later time, when it appears that "the inquiry into the case cannot be completed forthwith." This is related to the English practice of the "delayed charge" which would appear to be widely employed in Canada in practice, if not in theory.[37] This procedure of interim release could usefully be employed

---

would not appear to be unconstitutional if the police had this power in addition to the judiciary, particularly with respect to the period between arrest and court appearance. Such a power could act only to the accused's advantage. A few states have such a provision. See Orfield, *op. cit. supra* note 27, at p. 38.

[34]*Tims* v. *John Lewis & Co. Ld.* [1951] 2 K.B. 459 at p. 468 (C.A.).

[35]1 & 2 George 4, c. 218. See Petersdorff, *Law of Bail* (1824) at pp. 502–3. The Summary Jurisdiction Act of 1879, c. 49, widened this power to its present limit. The *Report of the Royal Commission on Police Powers and Procedure*, 1929, Cmd. 3297 stated at p. 53: "We consider that station officers should use this power of releasing on bail as freely as the circumstances will allow."

See also s. 13 of the Children and Young Persons Act, 1933, which provides that an accused who is arrested without a warrant for certain offences against children and young persons must be bailed unless to do so would tend to defeat the ends of justice, or to cause injury or danger to the child or young person against whom the offence is alleged to have been committed. S. 32 of the same act provides that a person under the age of seventeen arrested with or without a warrant must be released on bail unless the charge is very serious; or it is necessary in the accused's interest to remove him from association with any reputed criminal or prostitute; or the officer has reason to believe that his release would defeat the ends of justice.

[36]See Petersdorff *op. cit supra* note 35, at pp. 500–1.

[37]The status of the "delayed charge" is somewhat uncertain. The *Report of the Royal Commission on Police Powers and Procedure*, 1929, Cmd. 3297 assumed

here in cases where the police require further time to decide whether to proceed with the charge or require the accused's presence at a later time, for example, for an identification parade, but have no objection to the accused meanwhile being released. Without such a power the police will keep the accused in custody.

(b) Arrest with a warrant. It will be noted that the English provision applies only when the accused is arrested without a warrant.[38] When the accused is arrested with a warrant the justice who issued the warrant will often accomplish the same end by endorsing the warrant with a direction that the accused shall on arrest be released on raising a specified amount of bail which can be accepted by the officer in charge of the station.[39] This procedure, known as "backing the warrant for bail"[40] is presently not possible in Canada; only a justice of the peace can set bail, and only a justice can perform the purely administrative act of filling out the bail bond. Legislation could be introduced to permit the justice to endorse the warrant for bail and to authorize the police to accept bail in such a case. The most convenient solution, however, would be to allow the police to set bail even though the accused was arrested with a warrant. The Summary Convictions Act of Ontario presently gives the police this power in the area of so-called "provincial crimes."[41] A legal purist might argue that such a power interferes with

---

that it was a valid concept: see p. 53 *et seq.* The report also appears to assume that an accused cannot be released after he is formally charged and "booked." See also note, "Detained for Questioning" [1959] *Crim. L. Rev.* 79.

The concept of the delayed charge was generally thought to have been laid to rest by the House of Lords in *Christie* v. *Leachinsky* [1947] A.C. 573. In *John Lewis & Co. Ld.* v. *Tims* [1952] A.C. 676 at p. 691 (H.L.) Lord Porter stated: "Those who arrest must be persuaded of the guilt of the accused; they cannot bolster up their assurance or the strength of the case by seeking further evidence and detaining the man arrested meanwhile or taking him to some spot where they can or may find further evidence." See Brownlie, "Police Questioning, Custody and Caution" [1960] *Crim. L. Rev.* 298 at pp. 313, 324; Williams, *op. cit. supra* note 12, at p. 330. Yet the concept has recently been resurrected in the latest formulation of the *Judges' Rules*, Home Office Circular No. 31/1964, reproduced in [1964] 1 All E.R. at pp. 237–39. More will be said later on the question whether the police can voluntarily release an accused without legislative authorization.

[38]Cf. s. 32 of the Children and Young Persons Act, 1933.

[39]Magistrates' Courts Act, 1952, c. 55, s. 93.

[40]See Qasem, "Bail and Personal Liberty" (1952) 30 *Can. B. Rev.* 378 at p. 389. See also Egan, "Bail in Criminal Law" [1959] *Crim. L. Rev.* 705 at p. 706: "Unless the person laying the information has good reason for opposing bail, a warrant should always allow bail so as to keep at a minimum the injury caused to the accused, who, is, of course, at this stage unconvicted of any offence."

[41]See The Summary Convictions Act, R.S.O. 1960, c. 387, s. 15.

the order of the justice, which is to arrest the accused and bring him before a justice of the peace; nevertheless, the power is so eminently practical that it should be given to the police. There is neither historical nor common-sense argument against giving the police this power. The police would not replace the justices but would only supplement their function.

(ii) Releasing an Accused Unconditionally. Whether the police have the right to release an arrested person without taking him before a justice of the peace is at present far from clear. American law does not generally permit the police to release an arrested accused.[42] In Canada, however, the better view is that the police may release an accused person without incurring any liability, civil or criminal.[43] The Toronto police often "reject" an accused person before booking when his innocence seems clear; they will occasionally follow the same practice after the accused is booked, although they may feel somewhat uneasy about whether they are acting properly. Release before booking is a reasonably common practice; release after booking is rare.

On the other hand, this practice is not uniform throughout Canada. Many police officers hold the view that a charge of some kind must be laid when a person has been arrested.[44] Support for this view can

[42]Professor Puttkammer stated, *op. cit. supra* note 33, at p. 67, "Once an arrest has been made, it is no longer lawful for the police to exercise any discretion so far as the retention or release of that individual is concerned." Nevertheless, it is a common practice for the American police to release accused persons without taking them before a justice of the peace. See generally on the question of release without charge: Lafave, *op. cit. supra* note 2, at p. 393 *et seq.*; Warner, "Modern Trends in the American Law of Arrest" *op. cit. supra* note 33, at pp. 212–13; Warner, "The Uniform Arrest Act," *op. cit. supra* note 33, at pp. 336–39; Orfield, *op. cit. supra* note 27, at pp. 35–36.

In some American jurisdictions an action against an officer will fail if there has been an express waiver of a claim for damages or if such a waiver can be inferred from the conduct of the accused. See Bohlen and Shulman, *op. cit. supra* note 27, at p. 853 *et seq.*

[43]See generally Bird, *op. cit. supra* note 15, at p. 75 *et seq.*; Magone, *Police Officers' Manual* (3d ed., 1955) at p. 17; cf. G. A. Martin, "Detention and Arrest," *in* Sowle (ed.), *Police Power and Individual Freedom* (1962) at p. 38.

[44]Bird, *op. cit. supra* note 15, at p. 76. If a court should hold that the power to release does not exist, then there is a strong possibility that the officer would be technically guilty of the offence of "escape." See s. 127(b) of the Code: "Every one who . . . (b) being a peace officer, wilfully permits a person in his lawful custody to escape . . . is guilty of an indictable offence. . . ." It is stated in Archbold, *Criminal Pleading Evidence and Practice* (35th ed., 1962) §3421: " 'Escape' proper is where a person having a prisoner lawfully in his custody voluntarily or negligently suffers him to go at large." See *Rex* v. *Rapp* (1914) 23 C.C.C. 203 at p. 209 (Ont. App. Div.) *per* Riddell J.: "If he leaves the custody of a policeman, he is equally guilty with the policeman who permits it." See also Hawkins, *Pleas*

be gained from the wording of s. 438 of the Criminal Code which provides that "a peace officer . . . who arrests with or without warrant shall . . . take or cause that person to be taken before a justice. . . ." Judicial authority in Canada supports the position that the police may release a person without taking him before a magistrate. In the case of *Mayer* v. *Vaughan* (No. 2), Hall J. stated:[45]

It is plain from the text books upon the duties of constables that it is their duty to take all arrested persons with the least possible delay before a magistrate. But this must be intended to apply to cases in which the charge against the prisoner is persisted in, and clearly should not apply to cases in which the charge for any reason is dropped. Suppose the case of a constable having made a mistake in his instructions and arrested the wrong man. It seems absurd to suppose that the charge may not be dropped and the person released. Such would be the procedure, it appears to me, if the evidence expected to be secured proves to be wanting, as in the case of the supposed pickpocket or counterfeiter, or of the accused letter carrier.[46]

It will be noted that no distinction is made between releasing the accused before or after booking.

There is no clear judicial authority in England on this point. However, the power to release is implicit in the judgment of Scott L. J., in the leading case of *Leachinsky* v. *Christie*, where he stated:[47] "If he arrests on a specific charge, but before he has brought the prisoner before the appropriate judicial authority he changes his mind and decides to keep him on another charge, his power to detain automatically ceases and it becomes his immediate legal duty then to release the prisoner and make a new arrest on the new charge."[48]

It is submitted that the law should be clarified to permit the police to release an accused arrested without a warrant when they believe that the arrest was unfounded.[49] Without clear legislative sanction police

of the Crown (8th ed., 1824) bk. 2, c. 19, s. 5: "It is an escape, in some cases, to suffer a prisoner to have greater liberty than by the law he ought to have. . . ." Cf. *Rex* v. *Leadbetter* (1928) 51 C.C.C. 66 (N.S.S.C.); *Rex* v. *O'Hearon* (No. 2) (1901) 5 C.C.C. 531 (N.S.S.C.).

[45](1902) 6 C.C.C. 68 at p. 71 (Que. C.A.).

[46]See also *Leighton* v. *Lines* (1942) 77 C.C.C. 264 (B.C.S.C.).

[47][1946] 1 K.B. 124 at p. 133 (C.A.) aff'd. on appeal *Christie* v. *Leachinsky* [1947] A.C. 573 (H.L.). See also *Reed* v. *Cowmeadow* (1837) 7 Car. and P. 821, 173 E.R. 358.

[48]The power of the English police to release an accused person is also implicit in the concept of the "delayed charge" (see *supra* note 37) if, in fact, there is such a concept.

[49]The American Law Institute's *Restatement of the Law of Torts* (1934), I, § 134, at p. 312, took the position that failure to release the accused after ascertaining "beyond a reasonable doubt, that the suspicion upon which the

officers will obviously be reluctant to release accused persons. Of course, if the accused wishes to appear in court to clear his reputation officially, he should have the right to do so. In other cases, however, little is gained by completing the drama. When the police do not possess the power of unconditional release, innocent persons are forced to appear in court the following morning, often in custody, simply to have the accusation withdrawn.[50]

Theoretically, the only advantage of the present system is that society, through the magistrates, will have some cognizance of the extent to which the police are exercising their powers of arrest. But the effect of such a theory is to sacrifice the individual for a control over police practice which is in fact non-existent. Magistrates do not concern themselves with cases in which the police wish to withdraw the charge; even if they did, to get a complete picture of police practices in arrests it would be necessary to have all persons arrested and released before booking brought before the court. There are surely better and more expeditious techniques for ensuring that arbitrary arrests and subsequent release do not take place: for example, careful scrutiny of police practices by independent persons and accurate publication of statistics.

(iii) Releasing an Accused in order to Summon Him. An additional means of alleviating the harmful effects of custody would be to give the police the power to release persons from custody in order to summon them. This would be an alternative to police bail and a supplement to summonses issued on the scene by police. Its effectiveness would hinge on the ability of the police, rather than on that of the justice of the peace, to issue summonses.[51]

The present situation constitutes one of the most serious defects in the administration of justice: accused persons (particularly impaired drivers) are being kept in custody overnight because those with the power to bail are not readily available and the police have neither

---

privilege to arrest is based is unfounded," would give rise to a civil action against the police. The burden would appear to be put too high to be at all effective. See also Inbau and Sowle, *op. cit. supra* note 33, at p. 513; Orfield, *op. cit. supra* note 27, at pp. 35–36.

[50]See the A.L.I.'s *Restatement of the Law of Torts, op. cit. supra* note 49; Bohlen and Shulman, *op. cit. supra* note 27, at pp. 843, 853 *et seq.*; *Mayer* v. *Vaughan* (No. 2) *op. cit. supra* note 45.

[51]It was suggested earlier that it would be convenient to permit the police to bail persons arrested with a warrant. It might be considered too insulting to the justices to suggest that the police should have the power to release an accused person arrested with a warrant in order to summon him. Nevertheless, the power is a desirable one.

the power to bail nor clear legal authority to release and then summon.[52] The practice of releasing an accused person in order to summon him has been adopted in some localities. One Crown Attorney in Ontario has pointed out that "in some centres a practice is being established where the drinking driver is either sent home by taxi, or picked up by a relative who has been notified by the police, and summoned at a later date."[53]

An experiment along these lines was recently undertaken by the New York Police Department with the co-operation of the Vera Foundation. A brief description of this project is given by Freed and Wald.

Known as the Manhattan Summons Project, it is designed to test the efficacy of replacing arrest and bail in certain common misdemeanors, such as petit larceny and simple assault, with a station-house summons. Based upon Police Department and Criminal Court regulations which authorize the use of summons for specified offenses, the project utilizes on-the-spot interviews by Vera personnel stationed in the precinct house to determine the community roots of persons brought before the desk officer on the designated charges. If the accused consents, the information he furnishes is immediately verified by phone. No interviews are held when the accused is intoxicated or agitated, or where the police feel that the offense is likely to recur immediately. Recommendations for issuance of a summons are made to the desk officer on a point system similar to that used in the Manhattan Bail Project.

Released defendants are warned that in the event of default, a bench warrant will issue. Where summons recommendations are not made, or when they are rejected by the desk lieutenant, the accused is booked, detained and taken before a magistrate. Wherever the project recommendation is followed, the initial arrest is converted officially into a summons under Section 57 of the New York City Criminal Courts Act. Project personnel assume responsibility for reminding the defendant and, in some cases, a relative, friend or employer, of the scheduled court appearance.

In less than two months of active operation, 101 cases have been interviewed, 58 recommended for summons, and 53 recommendations adopted. All 47 summoned defendants whose arraignment dates have so far arrived, have appeared on time; two had their cases dismissed, one had bail set, and 44 have been released on their own recognizance. In addition to the two dismissals, ten defendants pleaded guilty and received suspended sentences.[54]

It is obvious that this sound practice should be given legislative approval in Canada and that a system to implement it should be set

[52]A striking example was seen in Haggart, *supra* at p. 59.

[53]Affleck, "Notes on Bail" (1963) 6 *Crim. L. Q.* 10 at p. 12.

[54]*Op. cit. supra* note 8, at p. 73. No fingerprinting takes place under this procedure: see Wald's Foreword to "Pretrial Detention and Ultimate Freedom: A Statistical Study" (1964) 39 *N. Y. U. L. Rev.* 631 at 639, note 30.

up. The interviewing could be done by the police, by probation officers, or by an independent body set up for this function.

E. Improved Legal Aid and Advice

A study of the system of legal aid obviously cannot be undertaken in a work such as this.[55] It is proposed here only to outline the direction any legal aid before arraignment should take.

The first step should be to create means of informing accused persons who are brought into custody of the existence of free legal aid for those who require it. For example, the English *Report of the Royal Commission on Police Powers and Procedure* (1929) sets out a notice which is to be posted conspicuously in all police stations informing the accused of, *inter alia*, their right to apply for legal aid.[56] The English *Report on Legal Aid*, 1945, recommended that a printed slip be handed to every accused brought into custody advising him of his right to legal aid.[57] Next, it would be desirable to devise a system to provide free legal advice to accused persons at some point of time prior to their first court appearance, with adequate facilities to be supplied for this purpose. Finally, a proper scheme should ensure that those who desire but cannot afford representation at their first court appearance are represented by counsel. If the case is not disposed of at the first court appearance, counsel can play an important role in relation to bail.

Until such time as adequate legal aid is provided, it would be advisable for magistrates to be reluctant to accept a plea of guilty from an accused, particularly one charged with one of the more serious offences, when he has not had the opportunity of consulting with anyone but the police.

An examination was made of 100 cases involving pre-sentence reports selected at random from the files of the Toronto Probation Office. A significant finding was that at least seven of the persons (all under 21 years of age with an educational level of no higher than grade 9) who pleaded guilty and were remanded for a pre-sentence report subsequently denied their guilt to the officer preparing the report, or described

[55]This subject is presently being explored by the Attorney General's Joint Committee on Legal Aid for the Province of Ontario. Some of the material from this chapter and from chapter 6 was incorporated by the writer in a study prepared for the Joint Committee, dated September 1964: "Legal Aid: Working Papers Prepared for the Joint Committee on Legal Aid for Ontario," Part III.
[56]Cmd. 3297.
[57]The *Report of the Committee on Legal Aid and Legal Advice in England and Wales* (Rushcliffe Report), 1945, Cmd. 6641. See also *Home Office Circular*, No. 79, 1948. See generally, "Legal Aid: Working Papers Prepared for the Joint Committee on Legal Aid for Ontario," *op. cit. supra* note 55: Part I at p. 47, note 87; and at p. 51, note 93; Part III at p. 12.

circumstances which might have constituted a reasonable defence. The offences involved conduct such as possession of stolen goods or writing a bad cheque, offences where the average layman is often not cognizant of the legal requirement of *mens rea*. None of these persons had the benefit of counsel before entering his plea.[58]

The above facts do not necessarily mean that those persons who subsequently denied their guilt were in fact innocent. The cases are of interest because of the number of persons who, having pleaded guilty, did not later acknowledge their guilt in a document which was presented to the court and, more importantly, because the magistrate, presumably having read the report, did not strike out the original plea. There is no record if the magistrate, before passing sentence, questioned the accused concerning his statements to the probation officer, but, unless the accused is represented by counsel or has the plea changed to not guilty, one cannot feel confident that in such circumstances justice is done.[59]

[58]The study was conducted for the writer's course in Criminology in 1962 by Mr. Frank K. Roberts, then a third-year student at Osgoode Hall Law School. See generally the *Report of the Royal Commission on Police Powers and Procedure*, 1929, Cmd. 3297 at pp. 104–5. See also the *Report of the Royal Commission on the Police*, 1962, Cmnd. 1728 at p. 111. The 1929 *Report* refers to the evidence given by the Chief Metropolitan Magistrate (at p. 104) that "unintelligent persons accused of minor offences are surprisingly prone to plead guilty even when they have a good defence in law."

[59]There was a pre-sentence report involved in five of the 42 cases in the present study in which a plea was formally changed from guilty to not guilty; four of these five changes made were by one magistrate.

4. Custody and the First Court Appearance

IN PREVIOUS CHAPTERS the progress of the accused was followed through the initiation of proceedings and the period before the first court appearance. This chapter will examine what happens to the accused at his first court appearance, particularly with respect to those brought into court in custody.

It will be recalled that only 8 per cent of all persons charged with offences against the criminal code initially were summoned, and that 84 per cent of the persons who were arrested for criminal offences remained in police custody until their first court appearance.[1] Most of these accused persons were transferred from the police station lockups (or the Don jail if the arrest took place on the weekend) to the City Hall cells between the hours of 7.00 and 9.00 A.M. and appeared in court between 10.00 and 11.00 A.M.[2]

Table II shows what happened at their first court appearance to those persons who are brought into court in custody.

I. CASES DISPOSED OF AT THE FIRST COURT APPEARANCE

A. By Trial

Very few persons who were brought into court in custody and who pleaded not guilty were tried at the first court appearance, even those charged with relatively minor offences. The data show that only 24 persons who appeared in court in custody (approximately .5 per cent) and pleaded not guilty were tried at the first court appearance. The figure for those who were summoned or bailed before the first court appearance was only slightly higher: 10 out of 1,297 (.75 per cent).

---

[1]The latter figure includes persons charged with driving offences who were released on their own recognizance just prior to their first court appearance.

[2]As noted in chapter 3. I. *A. (iii)*, some accused persons are not brought to the City Hall at this time. The time of appearance in court depends on a number of factors, including the time of arrest, length of investigation, and facilities for transferring the accused to court.

TABLE II

First Court Appearance for those Brought into Court in Custody
(Percentages given in parentheses)

		Summary Offences		Indictable Offences		All Offences	
Case disposed of at first court appearance	Guilty plea	840	(39)	843	(38)	1683	(39)
	Withdrawal	101	(5)	79	(4)	180	(4)
	Not guilty plea and case disposed of	11	($\frac{1}{2}$)	13	($\frac{1}{2}$)	24	($\frac{1}{2}$)
Case not disposed of at first court appearance	Own bail	816	(38)	232	(11)	1048	(24)
	Bail set	352	(16)	824	(38)	1176	(27)
	No mention of bail	21	(1)	83	(4)	104	(2)
	"No bail" or "Hold"	13	($\frac{1}{2}$)	116	(5)	129	(3)
Total		2154	(100)	2190	(100)	4344	(100)

Cases ending in dismissal would not all be actual trials; some would be dismissals in circumstances in which the Crown would normally ask for a withdrawal, or in which, on compassionate grounds, the magistrate would dismiss the charge rather than remand the accused's trial to a later date.

B. Guilty Plea

It was pointed out in chapter 3 that approximately 40 per cent of those who appeared in court in custody pleaded guilty at the first court appearance, while slightly less than 30 per cent of those who were summoned or who were bailed before the first court appearance did so.

C. Withdrawal

Withdrawals at the first court appearance occurred in approximately 4 per cent of the total cases in which the accused appeared in custody. In addition, out of 1,297 persons who were initially summoned or bailed, there were 46 withdrawals at the first court appearance (approximately 3 per cent). When the word "withdrawal" is used here, it refers to a complete withdrawal of all charges relating to the conduct or the transaction in question, not merely to a withdrawal of a greater charge or of one or more of a number of charges.

The withdrawal, exercisable either at the first court appearance or at a later remand, plays a far more significant role in Canadian criminal procedure than is commonly believed and particularly in Toronto. The figures above relate *only* to withdrawals at the first court appearance.

As will be seen, a substantial number of withdrawals takes place at later remands. Table III, giving the conviction rate for *all* cases (in custody and not in custody for the first court appearance and at later remands), shows that more cases were completely disposed of by a withdrawal than by a dismissal or an acquittal.[3] Of course, because of the low number of not guilty pleas concluded, there are more withdrawals than dismissals at the first court appearance. The significant proportion of withdrawals is one of the most interesting findings of the present study, not only because it reveals that there are many persons kept in custody against whom the charge is later withdrawn,

TABLE III

CONVICTION RATE FOR ALL CASES
(Percentages given in parentheses)

	Acquittals	Withdrawals	Convictions	Total
Summary	342 (12)	266 (9)	2,286 (79)	2,894 (100)
Indictable	315 (11)	416 (16)	1,914 (72)	2,645 (100)
Summary and Indictable	657 (12)	682 (12)	4,200 (76)	5,539 (100)

but also because accurate knowledge of its use contributes to a true picture of the workings and efficiency of the administration of justice. The Dominion Bureau of Statistics, for example, completely ignores the withdrawal.[4] As a result, its publications state that the percentage of persons convicted in all of Canada is approximately 90. The figures in this study show the conviction rate for Toronto to be approximately 76 per cent. If the Dominion Bureau of Statistics included withdrawals in its publications, the percentage of convictions for all of Canada would be significantly less than it is at present.

II. CASES NOT DISPOSED OF AT THE FIRST COURT APPEARANCE

Table IV illustrates what happened at the first court appearance to those who came into court in custody and whose cases were not disposed of at that time.

A. Own Bail

"Own bail," or release on one's own recognizance, known in the United States as "r.o.r." (release on recognizance) or "parole," is a

[3]Other dispositions, such as open bench warrants, or cases not yet disposed of at the conclusion of the collection of data, are not included. Their inclusion would have no significant effect on the figures reported.

[4]See generally on this point the review by this writer, "Statistics of Criminal and other Offences, 1960" (1963) 41 *Can. B. Rev.* 475.

TABLE IV

CUSTODY CASES NOT DISPOSED OF AT FIRST COURT APPEARANCE

(Percentages given in parentheses)

	Summary Offences	Indictable Offences	All Offences
Own bail	816 (68)	232 (18)	1,048 (43)
Bail set	352 (29)	824 (66)	1,176 (48)
No mention of bail	21 (2)	83 (7)	104 (4)
"No bail" or "Hold"	13 (1)	116 (9)	129 (5)
Total	1,202 (100)	1,255 (100)	2,457 (100)

procedure whereby the accused is released from custody on signing his own recognizance promising to appear, without having to put up any security in advance. In Canada, the power to be released on one's own bail was originally granted in 1869.[5] This power was apparently not considered clear, however, until the 1953–54 Criminal Code inserted the words "without any deposit" in the sections permitting a court to release an accused on his own recognizance.[6] Table IV shows that "own bail" was granted in 43 per cent of the cases not disposed of at the first court appearance. This is a high percentage but it must be remembered that the procedure is used frequently with respect to certain driving offences. The greatest incidence of "own bail" being granted was found among those charged with impaired driving who are generally released on their own bail from the City Hall cells shortly before their first

[5]32–33 Vict., c. 30, s. 44.

[6]See s. 451 (a) (iii). See *Martin's Criminal Code* (1955) at p. 748. The ability of the accused to act as his own surety was made possible for all offences in England by the Bail Act, 1898. This Act clarified the Indictable Offences Act, 1848, s. 23 of which dealt with bail with respect to felonies and certain misdemeanours, and referred only to "surety or sureties." Section 21 of the 1848 Act, the general section dealing with the powers of the justice when conducting a preliminary inquiry to grant bail, speaks of the accused "entering into a recognizance with or without a surety or sureties." This reference in s. 21 could only contemplate the granting of bail to an accused on his own recognizance, and thus only s. 23 had to be clarified by the 1898 Act. The preamble to the 1898 Act reads as follows: "Whereas accused persons are sometimes kept in prison for a long time on account of their inability to find sureties, although there is no risk of their absconding, or other reason why they should not be bailed, and it is therefore expedient to amend section twenty-three of the Indictable Offences Act, 1848."

Release on recognizance in the American federal system has been defined as "the procedure whereby the accused is granted liberty upon his execution of a personal bond in the bail amount without being required to supply additional assurances of his presence at trial in the form of a surety bond or other acceptable securities." *Report of the Attorney General's Committee on Poverty and the Administration of Federal Criminal Justice* (1963) at p. 74. See also Freed and Wald, *Bail in the United States: 1964* at p. 61 *et seq.*

court appearance. These persons have been included in the category of "own bail at first court appearance." Out of 625 cases of impaired driving in which the accused appeared at the City Hall in custody for the first court appearance, he was released on his own bail in 610 cases; bail was set in only 15 cases. Prostitutes, on the other hand, were very seldom released on their own bail. Out of 171 cases of prostitution (commonly referred to as "Vag. C.," a summary conviction offence) not dealt with at the first court appearance, only one was released on her own bail.

Table V indicates the relative frequency of the use of release on one's own bail at the first court appearance for the various categories of offences.[7]

TABLE V

RELEASE ON OWN BAIL AT FIRST COURT APPEARANCE

Category	Custody Cases Not Dealt with at First Court Appearance	Own Bail	Percentage Use of Own Bail
Driving	744	686	92
Gambling	50	29	58
Assault	233	52	22
Sexual assault against females	52	4	8
Vagrancy	118	24	20
Offences against property	715	152	21
Prostitution	253	4	2
Sexual offences against same sex	12	2	17
Offences against public order	176	97	55
Narcotics	94	0	0
Other offences	7	2	29
Total	2,454	1,052	43

Table VI shows cases not disposed of at the first court appearance, excluding impaired drivers who are normally released just before the court appearance and therefore do not come into court in custody. The exclusion of impaired drivers from the figures significantly reduces the incidence of release on one's own bail from 43 to 25 per cent of all cases in which the accused was remanded. A higher percentage of accused persons may be released on their own bail in Toronto than in most large

[7]This classification of offences was established for the purpose of this study. All offences are included except those that must be tried in the Supreme Court (e.g., murder, manslaughter, and rape). The headings for each category indicate with reasonable certainty the offences contained in the category. It should be pointed out, however, that the offence of robbery has been included in the category, Assault, and that the vagrancy offence known as "Vag. C." (s. 164(1) (c)) has been included in the category, Prostitution. Table XVII in chapter 7 sets out the offences contained in the category Offences against Property.

TABLE VI

CUSTODY CASES NOT DISPOSED OF AT FIRST COURT APPEARANCE EXCLUDING IMPAIRED
DRIVERS

(Percentages given in parentheses)

	Summary Offences	Indictable Offences	All Offences
Own bail	221 (37)	232 (18)	453 (25)
Bail set	337 (57)	824 (66)	1,161 (63)
No mention of bail	21 (4)	83 (7)	104 (6)
"No bail" or "Hold"	13 (2)	116 (9)	129 (7)
Total	592 (100)	1,255 (100)	1,847 (100)

American cities,[8] but release without financial security in advance still does not constitute the principal means of compelling the accused's appearance in court—particularly with respect to indictable offences. For these, release on one's own bail was used in less than 20 per cent of the cases in which the accused who appeared in court in custody had his case remanded to a later date.

All those who have studied the bail system are in agreement on one matter: more use should be made of release on one's own bail.[9] There has been an increasing awareness of the importance of such a practice in the United States.[10] The Manhattan Bail Project, launched in 1961

[8]There are wide variations in the use of r.o.r. in the United States. See Freed and Wald, *op. cit. supra* note 6, at p. 66 *et seq.* In one study conducted by the United States Department of Justice in 1964 it was found that the r.o.r. procedure was used in 17.4 per cent of the cases in the federal system. (Some federal judicial districts had very high percentages of r.o.r., for example, Alaska 72.4, Eastern Michigan 71.7, Connecticut 71.1, and Massachusetts 66.7.) "The New York Bail Study" (1958) 106 *U. Pa. L. Rev.* 685 at p. 721 found r.o.r. to be used in 2.9 per cent of the 3,038 cases studied. In Philadelphia, "bail was required in almost every state case studied," "The Philadelphia Bail Study" (1954) 102 *U. Pa. L. Rev.* 1031 at p. 1074.

[9]See, e.g., "The New York Bail Study," *op. cit. supra* note 8, at p. 730; "The Philadelphia Bail Study," *op. cit. supra* note 8, at p. 1072; Freed and Wald, *op. cit. supra* note 6, at p. 61 *et seq.*; "Bail or Jail" (1964) 19 *The Record* of the Association of the Bar of the City of New York 11 at p. 19 *et seq.*; Sutherland, Cressey, *Principles of Criminology* (6th ed., 1960) at p. 361; Taft, *Criminology* (3d ed., 1956) at p. 422; *Report of the Attorney General's Committee on Poverty and the Administration of Federal Criminal Justice* (1963) at p. 74; "Punishment before Trial" (Review of the National Conference on Bail and Criminal Justice, May 1964) 48 *J. of Am. Jud. Soc.* 6; note, "Bail: An Ancient Practice Re-examined" (1961) 70 *Yale L. J.* 966 at p. 973; Orfield, *Criminal Procedure from Arrest to Appeal* (1947) at p. 132; *Kenny's Outlines of Criminal Law* (17th ed., 1958) at p. 546.

[10]See Freed and Wald, *op. cit. supra* note 6, at p. 61 *et seq.* for a description of the r.o.r. projects being undertaken in various American cities. The number of these projects has grown widely in the last few years. See also the *Report of the Attorney General's Committee on Poverty and the Administration of Federal*

by the Vera Foundation in co-operation with the New York University School of Law and the Institute of Judicial Administration, has focussed attention on the question of bail and encouraged other cities to undertake similar projects. The project is described in *Toward Justice for the Poor: The Manhattan Bail Project* (1964), a report of the activities of the Vera Foundation.

1. When an arresting officer brings an accused person into the detention pens adjoining Manhattan's Criminal Courts, a law student checks the defendant's previous criminal record and the current charge against him.

2. If his record indicates that he is eligible for bail, and if he has not been charged with crimes such as homicide, narcotics offenses, or certain sex crimes—offenses excluded from the experiment because of the special problems they pose—the accused is interviewed to determine whether he is a likely parole risk. The defendant is asked what his job is and how long he has held it, whether he supports his family, has contact with relatives in the city, and is in good health.

3. A point system helps evaluate the answers to the questionnaire, and if the accused appears a good parole risk, the above information is verified by phone—or in the visitors' section of the courtroom. Vera staff members speak only with those persons whom the accused has agreed should be consulted. An interview generally takes 10 minutes and verification about an hour.

4. If the case is still considered a good risk after verification, a summary of the information is sent to the arraignment court, where a recommendation that the defendant be released on his own recognizance is submitted to the judge.

5. When a defendant is so released, Project staff members notify him in writing of the date and location of subsequent court appearances. If the parolee is illiterate, a fact indicated by the questionnaire, he is telephoned as well as notified by letter. If he is literate in a language other than English, he receives a letter in his native tongue. Often a friend or employer agrees to help get the defendant to court. If so, this person is notified as well.

6. During the first year of the Project, a control group was established. Law students checked each questionnaire number against a random number chart to determine whether the case was experimental or control. If the case

Criminal Justice (1963) at p. 74, where the Committee strongly urges the Department of Justice to adopt a policy in federal jurisdictions favouring the release of accused persons before trial. As a result of the recommendation, a directive to this effect was issued on March 11, 1963, to all United States Attorneys. A follow-up survey by the Department of Justice, reported in Freed and Wald, *op. cit. supra* note 6, at p. 68 showed that the rate of r.o.r. releases had tripled in the federal system, from 6.4 per cent in 1960 to 17.4 per cent in 1964. Over 6,000 defendants in federal criminal cases had been released in the year of March 1963 to March 1964, with a default rate of 2.5 per cent. See also the *Second Preliminary Draft of Proposed Amendments to the Federal Rules of Criminal Procedure*, March 31, 1964, Proposed Rule 46.1, and s. 2838 introduced into the United States Senate by Senator Ervin (N.C.) in May 1964 (cited in Freed and Wald, *op. cit. supra* note 6, at p. 60).

fell in the control half, the law student withheld the parole recommendation. If the case fell in the experimental half, the law student handed the recommendation to the judge. (After the first year, the control group was eliminated in order to allow more widespread use of recommendations.)

These experiments have provided statistical evidence favourable to an increased use of release on one's own recognizance. In a recent assessment of these projects, Freed and Wald stated: "To date, these projects have produced remarkable results, with vast numbers of releases, few defaulters and scarcely any commissions of crime by parolees in the interim between release and trial."[11] The failure liberally to use the "own bail" procedure is probably the most serious defect in the present administration of criminal justice.

B. Refusal of Bail

The data show that there were not a great number of cases in which bail was refused outright. The notation "no bail" or "hold" appeared in approximately 5 per cent of the cases disposed of at the first court appearance.[12]

The term "hold" is incapable of precise definition, as its meaning will vary with the user and the context. It may signify that bail has of necessity not been granted because the accused is presently in custody serving a sentence or awaiting trial in another case in which bail had been refused. The term is sometimes used to signify a denial of bail when there are outstanding warrants against the accused for other offences. The *automatic* denial of bail is not justified in these latter cases; a preferable procedure would be to execute the warrant and determine the question of bail on the basis of all charges. To keep the warrant lurking mysteriously in the background is unfair to the accused, for it tends to put him in a less favourable position than if the warrant had actually been executed. If it is not possible to deal with the charge (for example, if the warrant is returnable in another jurisdiction), apart, perhaps from extradition cases,[13] bail should be denied only if

---

[11]*Op. cit. supra* note 6, at p. 62.

[12]No distinction was made between the "no bail" and the "hold" cases in collecting the data. The two notations are often used interchangeably in the court records and thus, without verification from observation in court or possibly from police files, any attempt to divide the cases into meaningful classifications would be misleading. Nevertheless, if the study were to be repeated, such distinctions, even though requiring difficult checking, should be attempted.

[13]See *Re Watts* (1902) 5 C.C.C. 538 at p. 539 (Ont. C.A.) *per* Osler J.A.: "I should be very slow to admit to bail a person who has been arrested or committed for extradition." Cf. note, 5 C.C.C. 539–4. There is no legal obstacle to a Supreme Court in one province releasing an accused on bail for appearance

the magistrate would have exercised his discretion to deny bail had the warrant been executed and returnable before the magistrate.

There is even less justification for refusing bail if there is no outstanding warrant for the accused's arrest, but simply a suspicion that other offences have been committed by him. In such cases the accused should not be deprived of liberty simply because he is charged with a separate offence. It may be that the court is justified in a reasonable delay while the warrant is being sworn, but this is a different situation from that in which bail is refused without any assurance that a warrant will be issued.

The term "no bail" as used in this study signifies an exercise of judicial "discretion" by the magistrate in refusing bail. Bail is presently refused by magistrates in a number of classes of cases: where there is a likelihood that the accused will commit further offences while awaiting trial; where there is a danger that the accused will tamper with witnesses; where the police require further time for investigation; and where there is a likelihood that the accused will abscond. Any attempt to determine the extent to which magistrates refuse bail as an exercise of their discretion is made difficult by a number of factors. The figure of 5 per cent cited above includes "hold" cases, in which in many cases denial of bail is necessarily automatic. On the other hand, it does not include the many cases where bail is effectively and intentionally denied by being set at an excessively high figure by the magistrate. In addition, there will be a number of persons in the category, "no mention of bail," who, had they applied for bail, might have been denied it.

In chapter 10 an analysis of the factors which affect the denial of bail will be made. One proposition merits emphasis at this point, however: custody pending trial should not be imposed through a misuse of the bail system. If it is desirable that certain persons remain in custody pending trial, then bail should be denied openly and directly, using both the proper criteria to determine whether the accused should remain in custody and the necessary safeguards to ensure fair and expeditious treatment, not by setting bail with the expectation that it will not be raised. Using financial security in order to impede release will often result in the release of the very persons who should be kept in custody, and the detention of the very persons who should be released.[14]

---

in another province: see *Rex* v. *Hughes* (1914) 6 W.W.R. 1120 (Alberta S.C.). The same rule should apply if the accused is before a lower court in such a case.
[14]See Freed and Wald, *op. cit. supra* note 6, at pp. 49–55.

5. Custody after the First Court Appearance

IN THIS CHAPTER an examination is made of the length of time spent pending the disposition of the case. A general discussion of time spent awaiting trial will precede an examination of time spent in custody and the conditions in custody awaiting trial. The length of time spent awaiting trial is not a central question in the present study which is concerned principally with time spent *in custody* pending trial. Nevertheless, the length of time spent awaiting trial cannot be ignored because it does contribute to the complete picture and has some bearing on such related matters as the time available to the courts to delve carefully into the question of setting bail, the likelihood that the accused will plead guilty in order to avoid a lengthy period before trial, and the possible consequences to the accused if he is not released from custody. As far as the writer is aware, no figures on this period of time exist in Canada.[1]

Almost invariably remands fall into weeks, the usual remand being for one week. An accused cannot be remanded in custody for more than eight days.[2] For persons not in custody, a remand can be for a longer period, but it is usually set by the magistrate in terms of weeks. There are a number of reasons why the usual remand is for one week. One week is a convenient period of time, and is almost the maximum permitted by the Code if the accused is to be kept in custody. In addition, the daily court calendars can be kept reasonably balanced with a minimum of administration. A remand for one week is certainly understandable,[3] but it is unfortunate that more thought is not given to the proper length of time for each remand; in many cases a very short remand is all that is required.

[1]English figures can be found in the Home Office Study, *Time Spent Awaiting Trial* (London, 1960) (hereinafter referred to as the Home Office Study), which is dealt with and commented upon in the *Report of the Interdepartmental Committee on the Business of the Criminal Courts*, 1961, Cmnd. 1289.

[2]Criminal Code s. 451(b). See also the English Magistrates' Courts Act, 1952, ss. 6, 105(4), and Devlin, *The Criminal Prosecution in England* (1960) at p. 78.

[3]See the Home Office Study at p. 18, para. 45, which states that adjournments "are usually for a week at a time, and cannot be for longer than 8 days if the accused is in custody."

I. Length of Time Spent Awaiting Trial[4]

The data show that few cases are delayed for very lengthy periods, but there is a pattern of consistent delay in the great majority of cases in which the accused pleads not guilty. This in turn causes further delay because the remands tend to reduce the time available for the trial of cases appearing before the court for the first time. (The number of remanded criminal cases on the list each day is usually substantially greater than the number of first appearances in court.) The delays also tend to create confusion in the orderly handling of cases by "cluttering up" court calendars and clerks' dockets, and resultant overcrowding in the courtrooms, corridors, City Hall cells, and vehicles transferring accused persons to court.

No attempt was made in this study to determine the cause of each remand, information not usually noted in any of the court documents. Only by observation in court could one hope to obtain such information and even then it would be difficult to obtain the true facts because of the "bluff" often connected with a request for a remand. Each side wants the other to be responsible for the remand and so, even though neither side is ready to proceed, it may appear from observation in court that only one side wants the case postponed. Thus the fault for delay cannot be categorically assigned.[5] However, even in the absence of statistical

[4]For comparative American figures on the length of time spent awaiting trial, see "The New York Bail Study" (1958) 106 *U. Pa. L. Rev.* 685 at p. 729, and "The Philadelphia Bail Study" (1954) 102 *U. Pa. L. Rev.* 1031 at p. 1050. It should be noted that the time periods spent awaiting trial will tend to be longer than in Toronto because the studies are of the higher courts.

English figures showing a time breakdown for the custody and non-custody cases tried in the higher courts can be found in the Home Office Study, Table 13, which deals with the period between committal and trial. Figures showing the total length of time between the first court appearance in magistrates' courts and trial in the higher courts can be found on p. 21, para. 59. Of cases finally disposed of by magistrates, the study stated at p. 23, para. 66 that "the average time on remand was 2.1 weeks, which differs little from the average time on remand for persons committed for trial." A time breakdown for these cases can be found in Table 21 of the Home Office Study. The mean average is here being used.

[5]It would be interesting to collect data on this. Based on observation of the cases during the course of the study, and excluding the first court appearance where the remand is virtually automatic, the writer would estimate the findings of such a study of not guilty pleas to be as follows: cases where both sides desire a remand, approximately one-third; cases where the Crown desires a remand but the accused appears to oppose it, approximately one-quarter; cases where the accused desires a remand but the Crown appears to oppose it, approximately one-fifth; cases where neither side desires a remand but the case cannot go on owing to overcrowded conditions, approximately one-fifth.

The Home Office Study states at p. 18, para. 45, that in magistrates' courts in England "most adjournments are at the request of the police, who want further information to complete their case, but they may be requested by the defence."

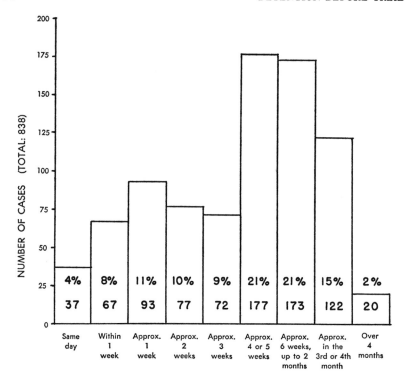

TIME IN WHICH CASE DISPOSED OF IN RELATION TO FIRST
COURT APPEARANCE

FIG. 6. Time spent awaiting trial for not guilty pleas: summary offences.

documentation, routine observation in the magistrates' courts leads one
to the conclusion that the courts are often too free in granting remands
to both sides and that there is an uncomfortable number of cases where
both sides are prepared to proceed but, as a result of heavy calendars
the cases are not reached or cannot be concluded. The Chief Magistrate
of Ontario stated, in December 1964 in a report on magistrates' courts
and court facilities in Toronto, "The courts in the old City Hall have for
some years been so over-loaded that they have been unable to deal with
their cases in the normal course without delay. . . . Moreover, under
present conditions many cases have to be tried piecemeal on various
days and at various intervals because of the lack of courtrooms. . . ."[6]

[6]See the *Survey of Metropolitan Toronto Magistrates' Courts and Court Facilities,* December 11, 1964, by Magistrate A. O. Klein, Chief Magistrate of Ontario
and Senior Magistrate for Metropolitan Toronto at p. 3.

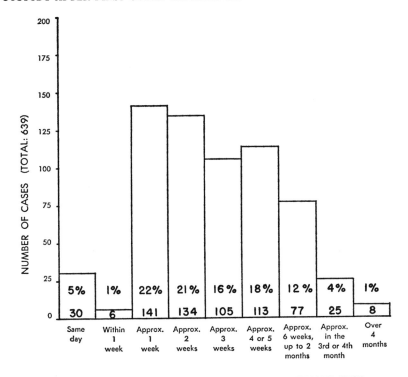

TIME IN WHICH CASE DISPOSED OF IN RELATION TO FIRST
COURT APPEARANCE

FIG. 7. Time spent awaiting trial for not guilty pleas: indictable offences.

The report states that on December 31, 1962, which was within the time period analysed in the present study, there were 1,689 adjourned charges still pending in the City Hall magistrates' courts. There was, according to the report, "an average of 8,504 criminal and liquor (other than drunk) charges per criminal offence court for 1963. . . ."[7]

A. Not Guilty Pleas

Figures 6, 7, and 8 show, in relation to the first court appearance, the length of time spent awaiting trial by persons who pleaded not guilty. In all, the time spent awaiting sentence has been excluded. For the average case (i.e., the median case, having an equal number of cases on either side), the time period spent was approximately as follows: for those charged with summary offences, four to five weeks; for those

[7]Ibid., at p. 4.

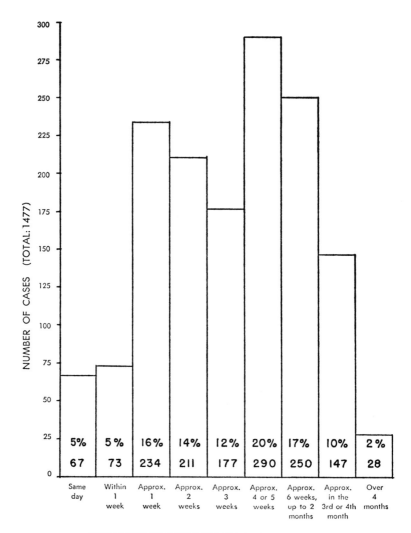

TIME IN WHICH CASE DISPOSED OF IN RELATION TO FIRST
COURT APPEARANCE

FIG. 8. Time spent awaiting trial for not guilty pleas: summary and indictable offences.

charged with indictable offences, three weeks; and for both summary and indictable offences, three weeks. Note that the median *case* is being discussed, not the mean length of time pending trial. The latter would be much greater because the cases which are not concluded until, for example, over four months, would weight the average heavily towards the lengthier periods.

B. Guilty Pleas

Figures 9, 10, and 11 show, in relation to the first court appearance, the length of time pending trial (i.e., the acceptance of the plea by the court) for accused persons who plead guilty. Again, the time spent awaiting sentence has been excluded. The total number of persons who pleaded guilty, whether at their first court appearance or after, is considerable. Of the total number of persons who entered a plea, 69 per cent pleaded guilty (67 per cent of the summary cases and 70 per cent of the indictable cases). There was a greater number of guilty than not guilty pleas for all classifications of offences except assault and sexual assault against a female.[8] Because the majority of guilty pleas are disposed of at the first court appearance, the median figure showing the length of time spent awaiting trial is nil. (This is because well over half of those who plead guilty do so at the first court appearance.) Of particular interest is the number of persons who pleaded guilty after one or more remands. There are many possible reasons for a guilty plea after a number of remands, but one possibility relevant here is that the accused may have desired to have the case disposed of to avoid further remands. The fact that there has already been at least one remand would seem to indicate that some of these persons who later plead guilty originally intended to plead not guilty. The main concern aroused by the possible effect of remands on the plea is that some of the persons who pleaded guilty after remands may have been innocent, a possibility discussed previously.[9] Indeed, it would be regrettable if any person were to enter

[8]The English *Report of the Interdepartmental Committee on the Business of the Criminal Courts*, 1961, Cmnd. 1289 at p. 5, with reference to criminal proceedings in the superior courts (all criminal courts excluding the magistrates' courts), found that "76 per cent pleaded guilty at their trial." See also the Home Office Study *op. cit. supra* note 1, at p. 9. Cf. Rose, *The Struggle for Penal Reform* (1961) at p. 131: "The Select Committee [on the Poor Prisoners' Defence Bill (1903)], to which the Bill was referred, were much impressed by evidence to the effect that 40 per cent of prisoners pleaded guilty. . . ." "The New York Bail Study" *op. cit. supra* note 4, in a survey of all guilty pleas in their study, whether at the first court appearance or later, found that 89.6 per cent of those in jail pleaded guilty compared to 74.6 per cent of those who were on bail.

[9]See *supra* chapter 3.IV.E.

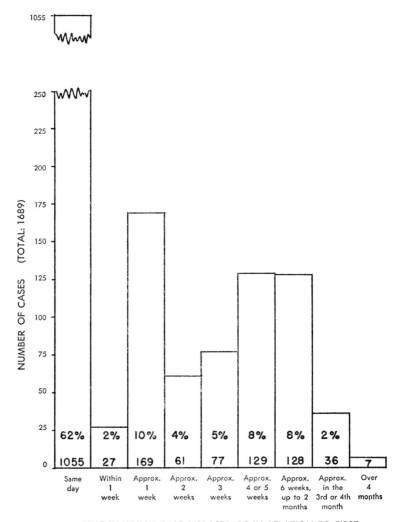

TIME IN WHICH CASE DISPOSED OF IN RELATION TO FIRST
COURT APPEARANCE

FIG. 9. Time spent awaiting trial for guilty pleas: summary offences.

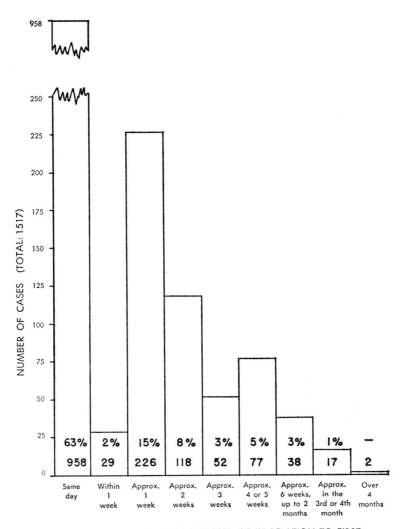

TIME IN WHICH CASE DISPOSED OF IN RELATION TO FIRST
COURT APPEARANCE

FIG. 10. Time spent awaiting trial for guilty pleas: indictable offences.

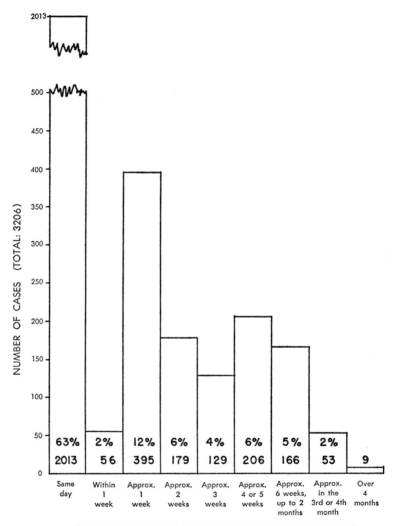

TIME IN WHICH CASE DISPOSED OF IN RELATION TO FIRST
COURT APPEARANCE

FIG. 11. Time spent awaiting trial for guilty pleas: summary and indictable
offences.

a guilty plea simply because he wished to avoid undue delay in waiting for trial. Figures 9, 10, and 11 also show the number of persons who pleaded guilty at the first court appearance.

II. LENGTH OF TIME SPENT IN CUSTODY AWAITING TRIAL[10]

A. *Not Guilty Pleas*

The data show that the majority of those pleading not guilty to a summary offence were not held in custody after their first court appearance but the majority of those pleading not guilty to an indictable offence were held.

The data also show that 62 per cent of all persons charged with summary offences and 71 per cent of all those charged with indictable offences who pleaded not guilty spent at least until the first court appearance in custody; for both summary and indictable offences the figure was 66 per cent.[11] Figures 12, 13, and 14 set out the length of time spent in custody pending trial on a not guilty plea. The percentages represent the percentage of cases, within each time period, of the total number of persons who entered court in custody for their first court appearance.

Only about 22 per cent of persons charged with summary offences who entered the court in custody and who pleaded not guilty spent additional time in custody after the first court appearance; for indictable offences the figure was 66 per cent; for both summary and indictable

---

[10]For comparative American figures on the length of time spent *in custody* awaiting trial see "The New York Bail Study" *op. cit. supra* note 4 and "The Philadelphia Bail Study" *op. cit. supra* note 4.

The English Home Office Study stated the following for all cases finally disposed of by magistrates for both guilty and not guilty pleas (at p. 23, para. 66): "61 per cent were remanded on bail only, for an average period of 2.1 weeks; in addition, 5 per cent were remanded partly in custody and partly on bail, and for these the average total period on remand was 4.6 weeks. 34 per cent were remanded in custody only, for an average period of 1.7 weeks. . . . These periods include time spent on remand both before and after conviction. 215 persons [20 per cent] were remanded for medical, probation or borstal reports, representing about 6,970 persons for the year; these were technically remands after conviction and before sentence, though in some cases they would appear to have occurred during trial." A time breakdown for these cases appears in Table 21 of the Home Office Study.

[11]It will be noted that these figures differ somewhat from those in chapter 3 which did not distinguish between guilty and not guilty pleas. An accused person who is in custody until the first court appearance is more likely to plead guilty than a person who is not in custody; because the analysis is limited to not guilty pleas, the number who remained in custody until the first court appearance is lower than if both guilty and not guilty pleas had been analysed.

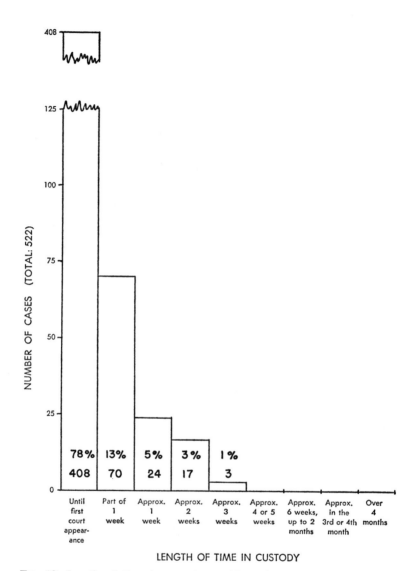

LENGTH OF TIME IN CUSTODY

FIG. 12. Length of time in custody awaiting trial for not guilty pleas: summary offences. In addition to these cases there were 289 (36 per cent of all summary cases in which the accused pleaded not guilty) in which the accused was summoned or bailed before the first court appearance. Including these, the total number of not guilty pleas was 811; excluding them, the number was 522. The percentages were calculated on the basis of the latter figure. On the basis of the former figure, the percentages would read, from left to right: 50, 9, 3, and 2.

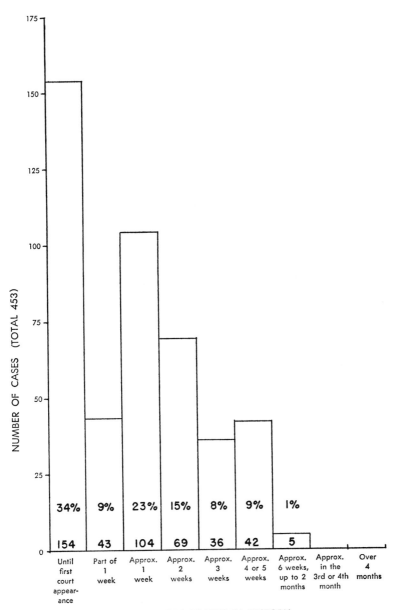

FIG. 13. Length of time in custody awaiting trial for not guilty pleas: indictable offences. In addition to these cases there were 167 (27 per cent of all indictable cases in which the accused pleaded not guilty) in which the accused was summoned or bailed before the first court appearance. Including these, the total number of not guilty pleas was 620; excluding them, the number was 453. The percentages were calculated on the basis of the latter figure. On the basis of the former figure the percentages would read from left to right: 25, 7, 17, 11, 6, 7, and 1.

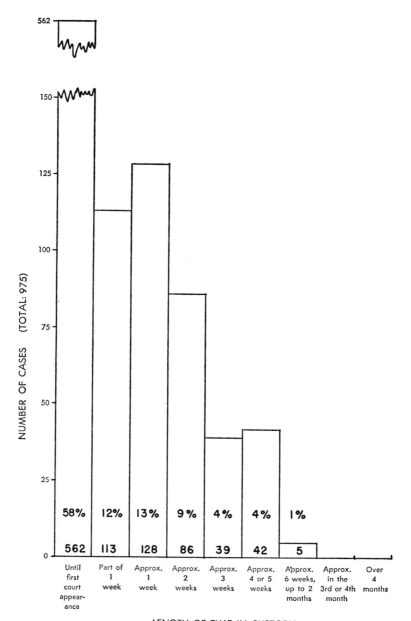

LENGTH OF TIME IN CUSTODY

FIG. 14. Length of time in custody awaiting trial for not guilty pleas: summary and indictable offences. In addition to these cases there were 454 (32 per cent of all summary and indictable cases in which the accused pleaded not guilty) in which the accused was summoned or bailed before the first court appearance. Including these, the total number of not guilty pleas for all offences was 1,431; excluding them, the number was 975. The percentages were calculated on the basis of the latter figure. On the basis of the former figure, the percentages would read, from left to right: 39, 8, 9, 6, 3, and 3.

cases it was 42 per cent. The time spent awaiting sentence has been excluded.

Custody pending trial occurs, therefore, in a significant number of cases where the accused is charged with an indictable offence and pleads not guilty. The periods of time spent in custody *after* the first court appearance for those who were charged with indictable offences, appeared in court in custody for the first court appearance, and pleaded not guilty, were as follows: 66 per cent spent at least part of the first week in custody; 55 per cent spent at least one week in custody; 33 per cent spent at least two weeks in custody; 18 per cent spent at least three weeks in custody; 10 per cent spent at least four to five weeks in custody; and 1 per cent spent at least six to eight weeks in custody. The periods of time spent in custody after the first court appearance for the total number of persons charged with indictable offences who pleaded not guilty (whether appearing in court in custody for the first court appearance or not), are as follows: 49 per cent spent at least part of the first week in custody; 42 per cent spent at least one week in custody; 25 per cent spent at least two weeks in custody; 14 per cent spent at least three weeks in custody; 8 per cent spent at least four to five weeks in custody; and 1 per cent spent at least six to eight weeks in custody.

B. Guilty Pleas

Figures 15, 16, and 17 set out the length of time spent in custody pending trial on a guilty plea. Time spent awaiting sentence has been excluded. The percentages represent the percentage of cases, within each time period, of the total number of persons who entered court in custody for their first court appearance. The data support the possibility that custody pending trial may have a bearing on whether or not the accused pleads guilty.[12]

Data were collected on the number of persons who pleaded guilty at their first court appearance and had the case finally disposed of then, without a further remand in custody for sentence. The data show that, of those who pleaded guilty, 83 per cent of those charged with an indictable offence and over 99 per cent of those charged with a summary offence had the case finally disposed of at the time the plea was accepted by the court without a further remand in custody for sentence. Thus, in

[12]The conclusion in the text is presented with hesitation because the figures show the total time spent in custody without regard to the total time spent awaiting trial. Thus, the guilty plea in any particular case may not have come about while the accused was in custody.

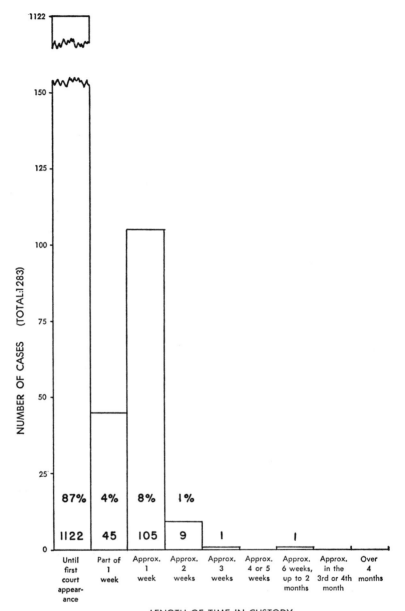

NUMBER OF CASES (TOTAL:1283)

	87%	4%	8%	1%				
	1122	45	105	9	I		I	

| Until first court appear-ance | Part of 1 week | Approx. 1 week | Approx. 2 weeks | Approx. 3 weeks | Approx. 4 or 5 weeks | Approx. 6 weeks, up to 2 months | Approx. in the 3rd or 4th month | Over 4 months |

LENGTH OF TIME IN CUSTODY

Fig. 15. Length of time in custody awaiting trial for guilty pleas: summary offences. In addition to these cases there were 376 (23 per cent of all summary cases in which the accused pleaded guilty) in which the accused was summoned or bailed before the first court appearance. Including these, the total number of guilty pleas was 1,659; excluding them, the number was 1,283. The percentages were calculated on the basis of the latter figure. On the basis of the former figure, the percentages would read, from left to right: 68, 3, 6, and 1.

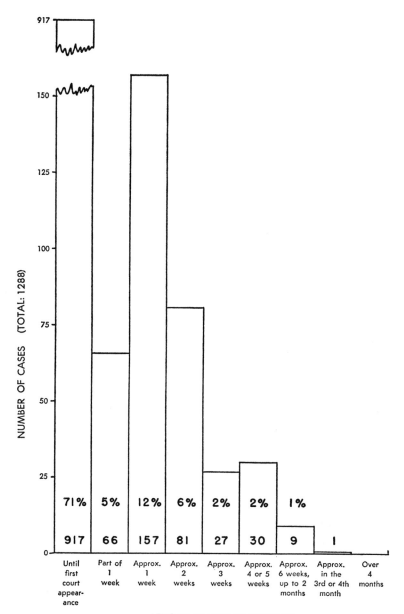

FIG. 16. Length of time in custody awaiting trial for guilty pleas: indictable offences. In addition to these cases there were 209 (14 per cent of all indictable cases in which the accused pleaded guilty) in which the accused was summoned or bailed before the first court appearance. Including these, the total number of guilty pleas was 1,497; excluding them, the number was 1,288. The percentages were calculated on the basis of the latter figure. On the basis of the former figure the percentages would read, from left to right: 61. 4. 10. 5. 2. 2. and 1.

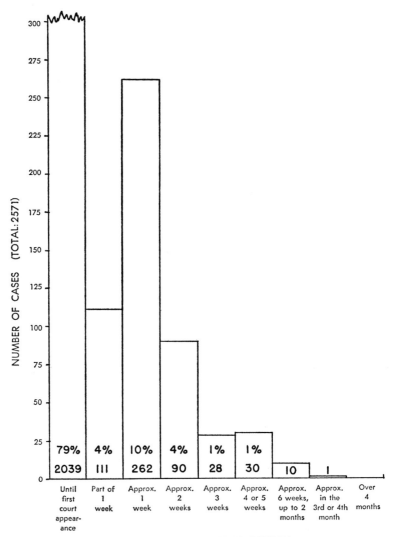

LENGTH OF TIME IN CUSTODY

FIG. 17. Length of time in custody awaiting trial for guilty pleas: summary and indictable offences. In addition to these cases there were 585 (19 per cent of all summary and indictable cases in which the accused pleaded guilty) in which the accused was summoned or bailed before the first court appearance. Including these, the total number of guilty pleas was 3,156; excluding them, the number was 2,571. The percentages were calculated on the basis of the latter figure. On the basis of the former figure the percentages would read, from left to right: 65, 4, 8, 3, 1, and 1.

most cases, a guilty plea usually means a quick disposition of the entire proceeding.

C. Where Charge is Dismissed or Withdrawn

The fact that many persons who spend time in custody are not found guilty does not require statistical demonstration. The point that does require analysis and which will be dealt with in the next chapter is the relationship between custody and the result of the case. Nevertheless, it is of some interest to present the bare figures on the numbers of persons who spent time in custody and were not found guilty (i.e., the charge was either dismissed or withdrawn).

Table VII shows that, out of 1,296 persons studied who were not convicted, 917 or 71 per cent spent *at least* until the first court appearance in custody. Of the 708 persons not convicted for indictable offences, 515 (73 per cent) remained in custody *at least* until the first court appearance and 227 (32 per cent) spent *at least* one week in custody.[13]

III. LENGTH OF TIME SPENT IN CUSTODY AWAITING SENTENCE

After an accused is convicted he may be remanded in custody to a later date for sentencing. This is an additional form of custody possible before a case is finally disposed of. The data show that many of those who are remanded in custody pending sentence are not eventually sentenced to jail.

Table VIII shows the extent to which remands pending sentence were used in the cases studied. It can be seen that such remands were not often employed; the final disposition of the case was usually when the accused pleaded guilty or was found to be guilty. In the majority of cases (77 per cent) in which there was a remand for sentence, it was a remand in custody.[14] Just under half of the remands for sentence (in 159

[13]For comparative American figures on the length of time spent in custody in cases where the charge was dismissed, see "The New York Bail Study" *op. cit. supra* note 4, at pp. 727–28, and "The Philadelphia Bail Study" *op. cit. supra* note 4, at p. 1050.

The Home Office Study at p. 10, para. 27, found that for trials in the English higher courts "only 1.5 per cent of all persons committed for trial were kept in custody and then acquitted. . . ." Though this at first appears to indicate a highly desirable process of selection, one wonders to what extent custody itself was a factor in creating the small percentage of acquittals. The percentage of persons committed for trial who were not kept in custody and were then acquitted was 7.9. See the Home Office Study, Table 6.

[14]The English figures on remanding for sentence in the higher courts are contained in the Home Office Study, Table 10. For all the higher courts, 4.4 per cent of persons who were convicted had the sentencing delayed. In London and

TABLE VII

Length of Time in Custody Pending Trial for Cases where Charge Dismissed or Withdrawn

Length of time in custody	Summary Offences			Indictable Offences			Summary and Indictable Offences		
	Dis-missal	With-drawal	Total	Dis-missal	With-drawal	Total	Dis-missal	With-drawal	Grand Total
Police custody until first court appearance	155	159	314	68	171	239	223	330	553
Part of 1 week	22	25	47	19	30	49	41	55	96
Approximately 1 week	14	14	28	47	69	116	61	83	144
Approximately 2 weeks	9	2	11	29	24	53	38	26	64
Approximately 3 weeks	1	1	2	16	10	26	17	11	28
Approximately 4 or 5 weeks	—	—	—	23	7	30	23	7	30
Approximately 6 weeks to 2 months	—	—	—	—	2	2	—	2	2
Approximately in the 3rd or 4th month	—	—	—	—	—	—	—	—	—
Over 4 months	—	—	—	—	—	—	—	—	—
Total	201	201	402	202	313	515	403	514	917
Summons or bail before first court appearance	125	61	186	103	90	193	228	151	379
Total	326	262	588	305	403	708	631	665	1296

TABLE VIII

TOTAL REMANDS FOR SENTENCE AFTER A CONVICTION

		Remand in Custody	Remand not in Custody	Total	Use of Remand out of Total Number of Cases (per cent)
Summary offences	{ Guilty plea	9	26	35	2
	{ Not guilty plea	2	26	28	3
Indictable offences	{ Guilty plea	252	22	274	18
	{ Not guilty plea	25	12	37	6
Total		288	86	374	8

out of 374 cases: 43 per cent) were to enable probation officers to prepare pre-sentence reports. The majority of the pre-sentence reports (62
per cent) were prepared on persons under the age of 21. Perhaps most
significant was that over 90 per cent of those remanded for the report
were remanded in custody. All but one were in custody for one week or
more.[15] Two-thirds of those remanded in custody pending the pre-
sentence report were not eventually sentenced to jail. Of them, 96 per
cent were given a suspended sentence and the remainder were fined.

It is difficult to assess these figures. They tend to suggest that custody
before sentence is utilized as a means of giving the accused, particularly
the young offender, "a taste of jail."[16] Although the indiscriminate use
of this practice is surely improper, a full examination of it is outside the
scope of this study. An additional cause of concern is that many probation officers feel that they cannot adequately assess the accused in relation to his home environment while he is in custody.

IV. CONDITIONS OF CUSTODY AFTER THE FIRST COURT APPEARANCE

If the accused is remanded in custody, or unable to raise bail at the
first court appearance, he is taken to the Don jail. After the first court

Middlesex Sessions the percentage was 15.3. The Table, however, does not show
whether the remand was in custody or not. Time spent on remand in cases finally
disposed of by magistrates is found on p. 25 et seq. of the Study. Of those magistrates' court cases remanded for reports, 63.7 per cent were kept in custody pending the report (Table 25); of them only 17 per cent were eventually sent to prison
(Table 27).

[15]Approximately 80 per cent were remanded in custody for one week; the other
20 per cent were in custody for more than one week.

[16]The practice has apparently found support among such persons as some court
workers of the Salvation Army. See "Boys Are Helped by Jail—'Sally Ann,'"
Toronto Daily Star, August 25, 1964.

appearance custody is no longer in police lockups under the supervision of the police, but in the Don jail under the custodial care of penal officials.[17]

Persons in custody awaiting trial are virtually indistinguishable from those in custody serving sentences. Apart from the days on which they make their court appearances, those persons awaiting trial follow the same routine, share the same dress and accommodation, and have similar mailing and visiting restrictions as those persons serving sentences. It will be recalled that persons awaiting their first court appearance in a police lockup are, for the most part, treated worse than convicted offenders. Those awaiting trial in the Don jail are at least afforded equality of treatment with those convicted and serving sentences there.

The remanded accused in the Don jail are still in many respects, however, in a less favourable position than most persons serving sentences in other institutions. This anomalous situation would seem to exist throughout North America. Professor Caleb Foote observed with respect to the New York Bail Study that "the most ironic finding in the whole study is the revelation that accused persons, whom our law presumes to be innocent and who are not to be punished, are confined pending trial under conditions which are more oppressive and restrictive than those applied to convicted and sentenced felons."[18] The Don jail, for example, has few of the recreational facilities found in most reformatories and penitentiaries; the daily exercise consists of the brief walk around the inner court yard, and the normal day of an inmate consists mainly of "oppressive inactivity."[19] Very little attempt is made to

[17]In a previous section (C.3.II) describing the conditions in police lockups, brief mention was made of conditions in the Don jail in relation to weekend arrests. It will be recalled that all persons arrested on Saturday or early Sunday morning are transferred to the Don jail and kept in separate facilities there under Metropolitan Toronto Police control.

[18]Foote, "Foreword: Comment on the New York Bail Study" (1958) 106 U. Pa. L. Rev. 685 at p. 689. See also "The Philadelphia Bail Study" op. cit. supra note 4 at p. 1054 et seq. and "The New York Bail Study" op. cit. supra note 4 at pp. 723–24, for descriptions of detention facilities in Philadelphia and New York; Freed and Wald, Bail in the United States: 1964 at p. 9 et seq.; Sutherland, Cressey, Principles of Criminology (6th ed., 1960) at p. 364: "In general, the physical conditions in the county and city detention institutions are decidedly worse than the conditions in the state prisons where criminals are confined after conviction of criminal offences;" and, for a vivid description of conditions in a Philadelphia lockup, see Hallman and Walker, The Rittenhouse Square Meeting (mimeo 1953) cited in "The Philadelphia Bail Study" op. cit. supra note 4, at pp. 1058–59, note 105.

[19]"The New York Bail Study," op. cit. supra note 4 at p. 725. See also the Honourable Alexander Patterson, quoted in Taft, Criminology (3d ed., 1956) at p. 416: "For the most part, they spend the whole day in idleness, reading tattered

separate those awaiting trial from those already sentenced. This inter-mingling of innocent persons or those not eventually sentenced to jail with persons who are serving sentences is undesirable.[20] One feels particular sympathy for the young person awaiting trial who is exposed to confirmed criminals, in some cases for reasonably lengthy periods of time. Some attempt is made at the Don jail to segregate these young persons but they are still subject to the normal jail routine.[21]

It is axiomatic that a person is not kept in custody pending trial as a punishment but primarily to assure that he will appear at his trial.[22]

---

newspapers or playing cards, herded in cages, devoid of proper sanitation, with little chance of exercise or occupation." The conditions in the county jails throughout Ontario are generally no better, and many are worse, than those at the Don. The Department of Reform Institutions is now encouraging the planning of new centres on a regional basis.

[20]Taft, *ibid.*, quoting the Honourable Alexander Patterson: "Young and old, virtuous and depraved, innocent and double-dyed, are thrown into the closest association by night and day."

[21]For a description of the conditions of detention in the United States for *juvenile* offenders (i.e., 18 and under) see Freed and Wald, *op. cit. supra* note 18, at p. 93 *et seq.*

In Canada, the Juvenile Delinquents Act, R.S.C. 1952, c. 160, ss. 13, 14 (applicable in Ontario to persons under 16) provides:

"13. (1) No child, pending a hearing under the provisions of this Act, shall be held in confinement in any county or other gaol or other place in which adults are or may be imprisoned, but shall be detained at a detention home or shelter used exclusively for children or under other charge approved of by the judge or, in his absence, by the sheriff, or, in the absence of both the judge and the sheriff, by the mayor or other chief magistrate of the city, town, county or place. . . .

"(4) This section does not apply to a child apparently over the age of fourteen years who, in the opinion of the judge, or, in his absence, of the sheriff, or, in the absence of both the judge and the sheriff, of the mayor or other chief magistrate of the city, town, county or place, cannot safely be confined in any place other than a gaol or lock-up.

"14. (1) Where a warrant has issued for the arrest of a child, or where a child has been arrested without a warrant in a county or district in which there is no detention home used exclusively for children, no incarceration of the child shall be made or had unless in the opinion of the judge . . . such course is necessary in order to insure the attendance of such child in court."

For young adult offenders in England and summary of work done see the recommendations in *Penal Practice in a Changing Society,* 1959, Cmnd. 645, articles 29, 30, 31. Separate detention facilities for juveniles (under 17) and young adults (17–21) are recommended, and the work begun towards this end is described. See also the English *Report of the Departmental Committee on the Treatment of Young Offenders,* 1927, Cmd. 2831, at p. 40 *et seq.*; *Report of the Interdepartmental Committee on the Business of the Criminal Courts,* 1961, Cmnd. 1289 at p. 7.

[22]Cf. Sutherland *op. cit. supra* note 18, at p. 362: "In the same way that police have sometimes justified punitive methods in making arrests, the suggestion has been made that the hardships of detention should be severe and punitive. . . . [T]here is much evidence to indicate that even when this unofficial policy is not voiced it is the informal principle on which most detention institutions are operated."

There is, therefore, no justification for depriving him of any reasonable facilities. No one should expect luxury; but no one should be forced to accept routine prison treatment.

The best solution to this problem is to have separate detention facilities, preferably in a distinct and separate institution.[23] The stigma attached to spending time in a regular penal institution would be removed and those persons found guilty would be separated from those presumed to be innocent. In addition, persons so segregated would not be looked upon and treated as regular criminals by the prison guards. There is no reason why maximum security is required in all cases; provision for open institutions would not be unreasonable for appropriate cases. There should also be minimal mailing and visiting restrictions for those awaiting trial; in fact, there should be no restrictions on any matter (e.g., food, dress, television etc.) beyond those dictated by administrative necessity. The very fact that these are referred to as "privileges" at the Don jail demonstrates the present attitude to persons awaiting trial. In *The Criminal Prosecution in England*, Lord Devlin makes the following observations on the English treatment of accused persons in custody pending trial:

After that, if he is remanded in custody, he is sent to a local prison, where he comes under the control of the prison service, a distinct body of men from the police, men who have no more interest in the detection and punishment of crime than the ordinary citizen has and whose vocation is the reform of the criminal. Special rules govern the custody of an accused person; he is treated quite differently from those who are convicted and undergoing punishment, and if possible he is not to be put with them. He may, if he can afford it, buy his own food and pay for specially furnished rooms and certain domestic service. He may see his legal advisers in private and his written instructions to them are not subject to censorship. Any infringement of his common-law rights not authorized by the rules would be actionable.[24]

Diagnostic facilities could be provided in a well-conceived remand centre.[25] However, with the exception of remands for psychiatric exami-

[23]Taft, *Criminology, op. cit. supra* note 19, at p. 423 recommends that detention officials provide "secure individual rooms in buildings equipped much like a clean third-class hotel. . . ."

[24]Devlin, *The Criminal Prosecution in England, op. cit. supra* note 2, at pp. 67–68. See also the *Report of the Interdepartmental Committee on the Business of the Criminal Courts*, 1961, Cmnd. 1289 at p. 7: "The prison regime for the unconvicted prisoner is purely custodial: he wears his own clothes, he can have meals sent in, he is not obliged to work. . . ."

[25]See the following articles in the *Canadian Journal of Corrections*, VI, 4 (October, 1964): at p. 467, Diamond, "Some Architectural Considerations for a Modern Remand and Diagnostic Centre;" at p. 474, Turner, "Psychiatric Con-

nations as presently provided to determine fitness to stand trial, care must be taken to prevent remanding persons in custody simply because of the existence of diagnostic facilities. The accused is presumed to be innocent until convicted and is kept in custody pending trial primarily to ensure his appearance in court. The sentencing process must be carefully separated from the determination of guilt or innocence. In general, then, unless the accused consents, these facilities should not come into play until the accused is convicted.

Although the physical and mental discomforts imposed by the present detention facilities are not the most important of the hardships faced by an accused person who is kept in custody pending trial, they are an added reason for developing alternative effective means, short of detention, for ensuring the appearance of the accused at his trial. The changes recommended above are particularly necessary in the case of the young offender between 16 and 21. These youngsters should not be thrown in with acknowledged criminals, left to sit idle all day, guarded by persons who have no real interest in their rehabilitation. The Archambault Report of 1938 stated, after commenting on the importance of not sending youths to prison: "The first consideration of the court should be to see that young offenders are not sent to jail on remand. The machinery of bail and recognizances should be utilized to the fullest extent to keep these youths from contaminating associations they would encounter even while temporarily in jail on remand."[26]

V. Conclusion

This chapter has dealt with the time spent awaiting trial, the time spent in custody awaiting trial, the time spent in custody awaiting sentence, and the conditions of custody during these periods.

Whereas few cases tried in the Toronto Magistrates' Courts were delayed for lengthy periods of time, there was a pattern of consistent delay in the great majority of cases in which the accused pleaded not guilty. When the accused pleaded guilty, the majority of the cases were disposed of completely at the first court appearance, although there was

---

siderations for Remand and Diagnostic Centres;" at p. 477, Boyd, "Our Jails and the Psychiatric Examination and Treatment of the Disturbed Offender;" at p. 483, Mohr, "Potentialities for Research in a Remand and Diagnostic Centre." See also Klare, "The Problem of Remand in Custody for Diagnostic Purposes" in *Studies in Penology Dedicated to the Memory of Sir Lionel Fox* (The Hague, 1964) at p. 113 *et seq.*

[26]*Report of the Royal Commission to Investigate the Penal System of Canada*, 1938, at p. 196.

a substantial number of cases not disposed of until after reasonably lengthy periods of time.

The majority of persons (66 per cent) charged with indictable offences and 22 per cent of persons charged with summary offences who pleaded not guilty spent periods of time in custody after the first court appearance. Many persons who spend time in custody are not eventually convicted. The data showed, for example, that of the 708 persons charged with, but not convicted of indictable offences, 227 (32 per cent) spent one or more weeks in custody. Moreover, large numbers of persons who have spent time in custody are not sentenced to imprisonment if convicted.[27]

Toronto magistrates do not normally remand convicted persons for sentence, but when they do so they usually remand them in custody. Over 90 per cent of persons remanded for a pre-sentence report were remanded in custody, yet two-thirds of these persons so remanded were not eventually sentenced to jail.

The conditions in custody pending trial are almost identical to those for persons already convicted and serving sentences in the Don jail. The conditions for these persons can best be characterized as oppressive inactivity coupled with highly restrictive privileges. If persons must remain in custody pending trial, there is no reason why steps cannot be taken to minimize the punitive aspects of detention by providing special remand centres and not imposing any needless restrictions on activities.

Because time spent in custody before trial necessarily has the effect of acting as a punishment, the time so spent should be taken into account by the magistrate if the accused is convicted. Whether a legislative direction specifying that time spent in custody awaiting trial be taken into account would significantly affect the ultimate sentence is in many cases doubtful. It would appear that magistrates are of the opinion that they presently take time spent in custody into account in their sentences.[28]

[27]At one point elaborate tables were prepared to show that many persons who spent time in custody prior to the trial and were convicted were not returned to jail. These are not presented here because the information can be gathered from the tables in chapter 6 showing the sentence imposed for custody cases. It is difficult to prove statistically that many of these persons would not have been sent to jail even if they had not been in custody pending trial; however, an analysis of the generally lower sentences imposed when the accused was not in custody suggests that this is so.

For English figures on persons who are kept in custody prior to the trial but not returned to jail see the Home Office Study, Table 8.

[28]See the *Report of the Committee on the Detention in Custody of Prisoners Committed for Trial in England and Wales*, 1921, Cmd. 1574 at p. 4: "a Judge, when sentencing a prisoner generally takes into account the time the prisoner has already been detained."

Nevertheless, the provision is desirable for a number of reasons: it would give legislative approval to the practice and would permit the Courts openly to take this factor into account in their sentences; it would encourage those magistrates who presently do not take this time spent into account to do so in the future; and it would counter the opinion, apparently widely held by convicted persons who have spent time in custody awaiting trial, that they were dealt with unfairly.[29] An alternate procedure for taking time spent in custody into account in the sentence, which is perhaps fairer to the accused, is to do so administratively after the magistrate has imposed sentence.

Custody pending trial and custody pending sentence are widely employed in Toronto under punitive conditions. By itself the extensive use of custody should be a matter of grave concern. The following chapter explores the possible prejudicial relationship between custody pending trial and the outcome of the trial.

[29]See the *Report of the Interdepartmental Committee on the Business of the Criminal Courts*, 1961, Cmnd. 1289 at pp. 74–75. The *Report* recommended that "any period spent in custody after committal from a magistrates' court should count towards a sentence of imprisonment, corrective training or preventive detention imposed by a superior court, but that the prisoner should not start to earn remission until he is convicted." The Committee did not recommend that the statutory provision apply to the time spent awaiting trial in the magistrates' courts because "in practice it would be an excessive complication for this period to count as well" and, in any event, "if the waiting period at the magistrates' court stage is abnormally long, the sentencing court can still take it into account." See also Williams, *The Reform of the Law* (1951) at p. 190: "If bail is refused sentence should automatically date from the day when the accused was first received into prison. At present this earlier period of detention is not always taken into account when the time is not long." It is interesting to note that there is an explicit provision to this effect in Soviet Law. See *Law in Eastern Europe. Federal Criminal Law*, No. 3 (1959, Leyden) at p. 63: "S.40. The court will deduct the period spent in custody while awaiting trial from the length of the sentence at the rate of one day for one day when the offender is sentenced to deprivation of liberty or detachment to a disciplinary battalion, and the rate of one day for three days, when he is sentenced to corrective labour, exile or banishment." United States Federal Law provides (1948) 62 Stat. 838, 18 U.S.C. § 3568 (Supp. IV, 1963), that time spent in custody be credited for offences carrying a mandatory minimum sentence. See Wald's Foreword to "Pretrial Detention and Ultimate Freedom: A Statistical Study" (1964) 39 *N. Y. U. L. Rev.* 631 at p. 636, note 21. The new Illinois Criminal Code does not credit time spent awaiting trial if the accused is sentenced to imprisonment, but does so at the rate of five dollars a day if he is fined. See the *Tentative Final Draft of the Proposed Illinois Code of Criminal Procedure*, 1963, § 46–13.

6. Relationship between Custody and the Outcome of the Trial

THE RESULTS OF THIS STUDY indicate a disturbing relationship between custody pending trial[1] and the outcome of the case, with respect to both the determination of guilt or innocence and the sentence imposed. The results do not necessarily prove a causal connection but they do lend statistical support to the common-sense conclusion that such a relationship exists.

Many reasons can be advanced to support the theory that custody pending trial is prejudicial to the accused. If he is in custody, the accused cannot easily contact witnesses or uncover evidence helpful to his case. The difficulty in persuading witnesses to give evidence should not be minimized. It is pointed out in Williams, *The Reform of the Law*:

> The effect of refusing bail is to make the preparation of the defence much more difficult. In a great number of cases it can be the turning point between success and failure. For example, defendants have the greatest difficulty in securing ordinary witnesses to attend the preliminary hearing or trial to give evidence. Although they are merely called to state the truth, they are reluctant to attend because they do not like becoming involved in any form of criminal proceedings. Experience has shown that innocent defendants have to travel considerable distances to persuade witnesses to attend their trial, with a view to giving evidence upon which their acquittal may depend.[2]

Moreover, while in prison the accused cannot earn money to help pay for a lawyer and in some cases appears in court without one or is

[1]Custody, in the following sections, refers to custody immediately prior to the trial. If the accused did not enter the court in custody he is classified as a non-custody case, even though he spent earlier periods of time in custody, and if he entered the court for his trial in custody he is classified as a custody case even though he was not in custody during earlier periods. In most cases however, custody will mean custody from arrest to trial. In any event, custody just prior to the trial is probably more important to this analysis than custody earlier. See Patricia Wald's Foreword to "Pretrial Detention and Ultimate Freedom: A Statistical Study" (1964) 39 *N. Y. U. L. Rev.* 631, at p. 635.

[2]Williams, *The Reform of the Law* (1951) at p. 188.

forced to rely on a legal aid lawyer who is often inexperienced and inadequately prepared. These reasons are applicable both to the question of guilt or innocence and to the question of sentence.

There are other factors which may operate to the accused's disadvantage, relating to the psychological impression made on the magistrate by the accused's appearance in court in custody. The accused enters the court from a stairway leading directly from the cells (if he were not in custody he would use the courtroom door); he sits in a caged-in part rather than in the body of the court until the case is reached; and he remains in close custody while the case is being heard. In addition, the magistrate might suspect that he is in custody as a result of bail being denied or high bail being set owing to a bad record or because the police were convinced of the accused's guilt. The accused who enters court in custody does not have the same opportunity to obtain decent clothes for his trial as the accused person not in custody, and often must appear in the same clothes in which he was arrested. All these factors combine to create an atmosphere of guilt at the trial of an accused who appears in court in custody. He is made to look like a convict and is treated like one. Further, the magistrate may not only be less inclined to find a "reasonable doubt" in the case of a person already in custody, but he may also be less hesitant to send such a person back to jail than to send him there initially. The accused who is not in custody often has a job, has not had his links with the community severed, and is, therefore, able to argue more effectively for a suspended sentence than the person in custody.

The rest of this chapter will be devoted to a statistical analysis of the relationship between custody and the outcome of the case. Whereas the individual figures may not by themselves indicate a significant relationship between the effect of custody and the outcome of the trial, the systematic cumulative effect of all the breakdowns does.[3] The results obtained in studies in other jurisdictions reinforce this finding.[4]

[3] The figures were subjected to statistical analysis (the Chi-square test of significant differences) by Dr. J. W. Mohr, Research Associate, the Forensic Clinic, Toronto.

[4] Recent American studies have recognized the possibility of a relationship between custody and the finding of guilt or innocence, and between custody and sentence. The best analyses of the effect of custody pending trial are by Anne Rankin, "The Effect of Pretrial Detention" (1964) 39 *N. Y. U. L. Rev.* 641 and Patricia Wald's Foreword, *op. cit. supra* note 1. Other studies examined by the writer, though tending to show such a relationship, have not been sufficiently sophisticated in their breakdowns to warrant any firm conclusions. A survey of a number of these studies can be found in Freed and Wald, *Bail in the United States: 1964* at pp. 45–48. The results of some of these studies relating to guilt or innocence are presented here in a cursory fashion. In "The Philadelphia Bail

I. RELATIONSHIP BETWEEN CUSTODY AND THE FINDING OF
GUILT OR INNOCENCE

The relationship between custody and the outcome of the case with respect to guilty pleas was examined in chapter 2, where it was shown that a person in custody tends to plead guilty at the first court appearance more readily than a person not in custody. Because a person who pleads guilty is obviously going to be convicted, there would be little point in examining the effect of custody on the finding of guilt or innocence in such cases. Therefore, only cases involving not guilty pleas will be examined here.

A. Not Guilty Pleas

In Table IX A the finding of guilt or innocence for all not guilty pleas is shown in relation to custody. The table shows that for both the summary and the indictable cases the accused stood a greater chance of being convicted when he came into court in custody than when he was not in custody.

B. When Bail is Set at $500

Although the above figures are consistent with the theory that custody adversely affects the outcome of the trial, many of the factors which have a bearing on whether an accused remains in custody, such as the

---

Study" (1954) 102 *U. Pa. L. Rev.* 1031, a study of 946 cases, it was found that 52 per cent of bailed accused were convicted, as compared with 82 per cent of those jailed pending trial. In New York a number of studies were done. In "The New York Bail Study" (1958) 106 *U. Pa. L. Rev.* 693, an analysis of 3,023 cases, a 20.2 per cent rate of acquittal was found for those in jail pending trial, and a 31.4 per cent rate was found for those bailed prior to trial. A breakdown of the 1960 New York City Records into offences, by the Manhattan Bail Project ("The Manhattan Bail Project: An Interim Report on the Use of Pre-Trial Parole" (1963) 38 *N. Y. U. L. Rev.* 67 at p. 84), showed the rate of conviction for felonies to be as follows for those on bail compared to those in custody: assault (23 per cent—59 per cent); grand larceny (43–72); robbery (51–58); dangerous weapons (43–57); narcotics (52–38); sex crimes (10–14); others (30–78). This project also found (cited in Freed and Wald at p. 63) that, though 60 per cent of those recommended and released on bail were acquitted, only 23 per cent of those who were not recommended (in order to act as a control group) were acquitted. A study of a women's detention house in New York, *House of Detention for Women: A Plan to Reduce the High Census* (1963) at p. 6 (cited in Freed and Wald at p. 47), found a 77 per cent rate of conviction among those detained compared to a 40 per cent rate among those bailed.

The English Home Office Study, *Time Spent Awaiting Trial* (1960) shows (Table 14 and Table 6) that in the higher court cases, a greater percentage (46 per cent) of those persons not in custody who pleaded not guilty were acquitted than of those who were in custody (20 per cent).

TABLE IX
A. Relationship between Custody and Finding of Guilt or Innocence
(Percentages given in parentheses)

	Summary Offences		Indictable Offences		All Offences	
	Con-viction	Acquittal	Con-viction	Acquittal	Con-viction	Acquittal
Custody for trial	67 (65)	36 (35)	141 (57)	106 (43)	208 (59)	142 (41)
Non-custody for trial	389 (57)	288 (43)	162 (45)	196 (55)	551 (53)	484 (47)

B. Relationship when Bail Set at $500
(Percentages given in parentheses)

	Summary Offences		Indictable Offences		All Offences	
	Con-viction	Acquittal	Con-viction	Acquittal	Con-viction	Acquittal
Custody for trial	10 (59)	7 (41)	23 (62)	14 (38)	33 (61)	21 (39)
Non-custody for trial	10 (46)	12 (54)	18 (45)	22 (55)	28 (45)	34 (55)

strength of the Crown's case and the accused's previous criminal record, also have a bearing on the outcome of the trial. In Table IX B an attempt is made to equalize the custody and non-custody cases by confining the analysis to cases in which bail was set initially at exactly $500. The custody cases were those in which the amount was not raised. Again, the results support the theory.

C. Previous Convictions

A further attempt was made to stabilize the two groups by breaking down the cases according to the number of previous convictions.[5] Again, the figures, as shown in Table X A, were, without exception, consistent with the theory.[6]

[5]Previous convictions could not be obtained for those charged with summary offences.

[6]Cf. Freed and Wald, op. cit. supra note 4 at p. 48: "Recent analyses of Manhattan Bail Project data have disclosed, for example, that a defendant's prior record does not account significantly for the difference in case results between free and detained offenders. Among defendants with no criminal record at all, a recent tally showed acquittals of 56 per cent of those on bail but only 25 per cent of those detained."

TABLE X
A. Relationship According to Accused's Record
(Percentages given in parentheses)

	No Previous Convictions		One Previous Conviction		Two Previous Convictions		More than Two Previous Convictions		For All with Previous Convictions	
	Con- vic- tion	Ac- quit- tal	Con- vic- tion	Ac- quit- tal	Con- vic- tion	Ac- quit- tal	Con- vic- tion	Ac- quit- tal	Con- vic- tion	Ac- quit- tal
Custody for trial	45 (51)	44 (49)	6 (30)	14 (70)	9 (50)	9 (50)	78 (70)	34 (30)	93 (62)	57 (38)
Non-custody for trial	119 (49)	123 (51)	9 (25)	26 (75)	10 (42)	14 (58)	18 (51)	17 (49)	37 (39)	57 (61)

B. Relationship When Bail Set at $500
(Percentages given in parentheses)

	No Previous Convictions		One Previous Conviction		Two Previous Convictions		More than Two Previous Convictions		For All with Previous Convictions	
	Con- vic- tion	Ac- quit- tal	Con- vic- tion	Ac- quit- tal	Con- vic- tion	Ac- quit- tal	Con- vic- tion	Ac- quit- tal	Con- vic- tion	Ac- quit- tal
Custody for trial	11 (65)	6 (35)	1 (25)	3 (75)	2 (50)	2 (50)	9 (75)	3 (25)	12 (60)	8 (40)
Non-custody for trial	13 (52)	12 (48)	1 (20)	4 (80)	2 (40)	3 (60)	1 (33)	2 (67)	4 (31)	9 (69)

D. Previous Convictions when Bail Set at $500

The figures from Table X A showing the relationship between custody and result, according to the accused's record, were broken down even further and limited to the cases where bail was set at $500 to equalize further the custody and non-custody cases. At this point the numbers involved become too small to warrant drawing any firm inferences.[7] Nevertheless, the figures, as set out in Table X B, are, without exception, consistent with the theory that custody prejudices the accused.

[7]Assuming that the numbers of cases are large enough to allow one to draw conclusions, a surprising result that can be detected from these figures is that those *with* previous convictions tended to be found guilty after a not guilty plea in a lower percentage of cases than those *without* previous convictions. This was so both for cases where the accused appeared in court in custody for his trial and for cases where he was not in custody.

II. Custody and Counsel

A major reason why custody unfavourably affects the finding of guilt or innocence is the difficulty which presently exists for a person in custody in obtaining legal counsel. In this study it was found that accused persons in custody who pleaded not guilty were not represented by counsel in proportionately as many cases as those persons not in custody. Coupled with this are figures which tend to support the conclusion that an accused who has a lawyer is more likely to be acquitted than a person who has no lawyer.

These two factors may partially explain the finding that custody had an unfavourable effect on the determination of guilt or innocence. It may be argued that it was not custody *per se* which affected the finding of guilt or innocence, but rather the fact that custody lessened the accused's opportunity to obtain adequate legal counsel. The data indicate that, though the inability to obtain adequate legal representation may have been a prime factor in the unfavourable results of the custody cases, a comparison of custody and non-custody cases in which the accused was represented indicates that those in custody were convicted in a higher percentage of cases than those not in custody. Again, the discussion is limited to cases involving not guilty pleas.

A. Relationship between Custody and the Retention of Counsel

(i) Not Guilty Pleas. An accused in custody who cannot raise bail, especially if it has been set at a nominal amount, will often be unable to raise the funds to hire counsel. An accused who is not in custody, unlike his counterpart in custody, can usually earn, borrow, or in some way raise the cash to pay counsel, even if he does not immediately have the cash on hand. Thus, in the absence of an effective system of legal aid, an accused who is not in custody has a much better chance of obtaining a lawyer than one who is in custody. It becomes important, therefore, to consider the role of legal aid in assisting the impecunious offender. The present system does not provide adequate representation for the indigent accused. The figures obtained from the study, as shown in Table XI A, concerning the retention of counsel show that a deplorably high proportion (64 per cent) of those who pleaded not guilty and proceeded to trial while in custody did not have a lawyer. In comparison, only 33 per cent of those not in custody who pleaded not guilty did not have a lawyer.

It is obvious that something is lacking in the system of legal aid. Only rarely does the scheme provide any representation for persons

TABLE XI

A. RELATIONSHIP BETWEEN CUSTODY AND THE RETENTION OF COUNSEL FOR
NOT GUILTY PLEAS
(Percentages given in parentheses)

	Summary Offences		Indictable Offences		All Offences	
	Not repre-sented	Repre-sented	Not repre-sented	Repre-sented	Not repre-sented	Repre-sented
Custody for trial	98 (85)	17 (15)	135 (54)	115 (46)	233 (64)	132 (36)
Non-custody for trial	225 (33)	453 (67)	113 (32)	241 (68)	338 (33)	694 (67)

B. RELATIONSHIP WHEN BAIL SET AT $500
(Percentages given in parentheses)

	Summary Offences		Indictable Offences		All Offences	
	Not repre-sented	Repre-sented	Not repre-sented	Repre-sented	Not repre-sented	Repre-sented
Custody for trial	16 (94)	1 (6)	25 (68)	12 (32)	41 (76)	13 (24)
Non-custody for trial	12 (55)	10 (45)	8 (19)	35 (81)	20 (31)	45 (69)

charged with summary offences and over one-half (54 per cent) of those persons who pleaded not guilty to an indictable charge and were in custody for their trial were not represented. These persons presumably had a full trial. While some of them may have declined the services of counsel, it is inconceivable that, had counsel been readily available, over half would have refused his service.

(ii) Bail Set at $500. When bail was set in the sum of $500 and was not raised the chances of obtaining a lawyer while in custody, as shown in Table XI B, were even lower: 76 per cent of those who pleaded not guilty and did not raise the $500 bail did not have a lawyer at the trial. In comparison, 31 per cent of those who pleaded not guilty and raised the $500 bail did not have a lawyer at the trial.

B. Relationship between Custody, the Retention of Counsel, and the Result of the Case

(i) Not Guilty Pleas. The lack of counsel would appear to be pre-judicial to the accused who pleads not guilty at his trial. A major role of statistics is simply to document the obvious. Such is the pursuit now

undertaken: to show that an accused was better off with, than without, a lawyer. This fact is not obvious to all; one occasionally hears the comment that an accused without a lawyer is often in a more favourable position because the court acts as his counsel. It is only in the summary cases when the accused is in custody for trial that the figures, as set out in Table XII A, are not consistent with the theory that an accused without counsel is at a disadvantage.[8]

(ii) Bail Set at $500. This same conclusion was indicated, as shown in Table XII B, when only the cases in which bail was set at $500 were taken: accused persons with lawyers tended to be acquitted more frequently than accused persons without lawyers.

C. Comparison of Custody and Non-Custody Cases when Counsel is Not a Factor

It would appear that counsel does play a significant role in the outcome of the case, and that an accused who is not in custody has a better chance of retaining counsel than an accused who is in custody. However, even if counsel is eliminated as a variable, it can be seen that custody may still have been a factor in the finding of guilt or innocence. An examination of the previous figures indicates that, when both were legally represented, an accused who was in custody was convicted in a somewhat higher percentage of cases than an accused who was not in custody. When neither was represented, however, the figures did not consistently support the hypothesis concerning the relationship between custody and the determination of guilt or innocence.[9]

III. RELATIONSHIP BETWEEN CUSTODY AND SENTENCE[10]

A pronounced cumulative statistical relationship between custody pending trial and the sentence imposed tends to support the hypothesis that custody is prejudicial to an accused. Although in some cases it can be argued that custody pending trial may help the accused by enabling counsel to argue for a suspended sentence or a lesser jail term, because

---

[8]It will be noted, however, that relatively few persons (17) in this group were represented and so the figures are less reliable than if the group involved had been larger.

[9]There were only 6 cases in the non-custody, non-represented category for indictable offences when bail was set at $500 and so the conviction rate of 83 per cent is less reliable than if the group involved had been larger.

[10]Comparative American figures on the relationship between custody and sentence are available. See, in particular, Rankin, *op. cit. supra* note 4 and Wald, *op. cit. supra* note 1. "The Philadelphia Bail Study" *op. cit. supra* note 4 found

TABLE XII

A. RELATIONSHIP BETWEEN CUSTODY, RETENTION OF COUNSEL, AND RESULT OF CASE
(Percentages given in parentheses)

| | Summary Offences | | | | Indictable Offences | | | | All Offences | | | |
| | Not represented | | Represented | | Not represented | | Represented | | Not represented | | Represented | |
	Convic-tion	Acquit-tal	Convic-tion	Acquit-tal	Convic-tion	Acquit-tal	Convic-tion	Acquit-tal	Convic-tion	Acquit-tal	Convic-tion	Acquit-tal
Custody for trial	54 (64)	31 (36)	13 (76)	4 (24)	84 (66)	43 (34)	57 (50)	56 (50)	138 (65)	74 (35)	70 (54)	60 (46)
Non-custody for trial	143 (65)	76 (35)	247 (56)	195 (44)	58 (55)	48 (45)	104 (45)	129 (55)	201 (62)	124 (38)	351 (52)	324 (48)

B. RELATIONSHIP WHEN BAIL SET AT $500
(Percentages given in parentheses)

| | Summary Offences | | | | Indictable Offences | | | | All Offences | | | |
| | Not represented | | Represented | | Not represented | | Represented | | Not represented | | Represented | |
	Convic-tion	Acquit-tal	Convic-tion	Acquit-tal	Convic-tion	Acquit-tal	Convic-tion	Acquit-tal	Convic-tion	Acquit-tal	Convic-tion	Acquit-tal
Custody for trial	9 (56)	7 (44)	1 (*)	— (*)	17 (68)	8 (32)	6 (50)	6 (50)	26 (63)	15 (37)	7 (54)	6 (46)
Non-custody for trial	6 (50)	6 (50)	4 (40)	6 (60)	5 (83)	1 (17)	12 (38)	20 (62)	11 (61)	7 (39)	16 (38)	26 (62)

*Figures too small to be meaningful.

the accused has already spent time in jail, the general effectiveness of such an argument can easily be exaggerated.

A. For all Offences

For all the convictions, whether arising out of guilty or not guilty pleas, the data, as set out in Table XIII A, show that 41 per cent of those in custody for their trial were sent to jail (i.e., imprisonment in any form) as opposed to only 13 per cent of those not in custody.[11]

A breakdown of the jail sentences, as set out in Table XIII B, shows that when an accused was sent to jail he was usually sent there for a longer period when he had appeared for his trial in custody than when he had not. Whereas 79 per cent of those in custody who were sent to jail received sentences of one month or more, only 36 per cent of the non-custody cases received comparable sentences.

The figures in Table XIII include both guilty and not guilty pleas. It was shown previously that there was a higher proportion of guilty pleas for the custody than for the non-custody cases, and it may be that those pleading guilty tend to receive longer sentences than those pleading

---

that 22 per cent of those on bail who were convicted were sent to prison, while 59 per cent of those in jail pending trial who were convicted were sent to prison. "The New York Bail Study" op. cit. supra note 4 found that 83.9 per cent of convicted persons kept in jail before trial were sentenced to penal institutions, as compared to 45 per cent of those bailed. "The Manhattan Bail Project" op. cit. supra note 4, at p. 85, found the following contrast in prison sentences for felony convictions in New York in 1960 for those on bail compared to those in custody: assault (58 per cent—94 per cent); larceny (48–93); robbery (78–97); dangerous weapons (70–91); narcotics (59–100); all other offences (56–88). For misdemeanours, prison terms were given in 87 per cent of the jail cases, and in only 32 per cent of the bail cases. A District of Columbia study (Preliminary Study by the D.C. Bar Association's Junior Bar Section, referred to in Freed and Wald, op. cit. supra note 4, at p. 16) found that 25 per cent of those on bail received suspended sentence, but only 6 per cent of those in jail received probation. The Report of the Attorney General's Committee on Poverty and the Administration of Federal Criminal Justice (1963) at pp. 142–44 states that prison sentences received by bailed accused compared with those who remained in custody were, respectively, 33 per cent and 57 per cent in the Sacramento Division of the Northern District of California, 49 per cent and 82 per cent in the San Francisco Division of the Northern District of California, and 20 per cent and 52 per cent in the District of Connecticut. The English figures found in the Home Office Study, Table 28, are consistent with the theory that custody adversely affects the sentence.

[11]See the Report of the Interdepartmental Committee on the Business of the Criminal Courts, 1961, Cmnd. 1289 at pp. 6–7: "In some of these [cases not involving detention] the period spent in custody awaiting trial may have been an important factor making it possible for the court not to pass a sentence of imprisonment. But there must be a considerable number of cases where imprisonment would not have been imposed in any event."

TABLE XIII

A. RELATIONSHIP BETWEEN CUSTODY AND SENTENCE
(Percentages given in parentheses)

	Summary Offences				Indictable Offences				All Offences			
	Fine	Suspended sentence	Jail	Total dispositions	Fine	Suspended sentence	Jail	Total dispositions	Fine	Suspended sentence	Jail	Total dispositions
Custody for trial	735 (70)	158 (15)	162 (15)	1055	209 (16)	292 (22)	797 (61)	1298	944 (40)	450 (19)	959 (41)	2353
Non-custody for trial	1009 (86)	35 (3)	134 (11)	1178	312 (54)	181 (31)	88 (15)	581	1321 (75)	216 (12)	222 (13)	1759

B. DISPOSITION OF JAIL CASES
(Percentages given in parentheses)

	Summary Offences						Indictable Offences						All Offences					
	Under 1 month	1–6 mths.	6 mths. to 2 yrs.	2–5 yrs.	5 yrs. and over	Total dispositions	Under 1 month	1–6 mths.	6 mths. to 2 yrs.	2–5 yrs.	5 yrs. and over	Total dispositions	Under 1 month	1–6 mths.	6 mths. to 2 yrs.	2–5 yrs.	5 yrs. and over	Total dispositions
Custody for trial	105 (65)	54 (33)	3 (2)	—	—	162	97 (12)	202 (26)	366 (46)	107 (14)	19 (2)	791	202 (21)	256 (27)	369 (39)	107 (11)	19 (2)	953
Non-custody for trial	110 (83)	22 (17)	—	1 (1)	—	133	30 (34)	19 (22)	33 (38)	4 (5)	1 (1)	87	140 (64)	41 (19)	33 (15)	5 (2)	1	220

not guilty. Custody would thus have affected the sentence indirectly, by inducing more guilty pleas.[12]

B. Not Guilty Pleas[13]

In the following tables the guilty pleas are excluded from the figures. Only convictions after a not guilty plea are examined. Again, as shown by Table XIV A, the theory that custody adversely affects the sentence is supported. Even when broken down into categories of offence, the general pattern is clearly evident.

When the jail sentences are broken down according to duration it can be seen that those who were tried in custody tended to receive longer sentences than those who were not in custody, as can be seen from Table XIV B. Whereas 84 per cent of the persons in custody who were convicted and sent to jail after a not guilty plea received sentences of one month or more, only 30 per cent of their counterparts not in custody received comparable sentences.

C. Not Guilty Pleas where Bail Set at $500

One possible weakness in the interpretation of the figures is that there is no guarantee that the custody cases for all offences or for any particular classification of offence do not generally involve more serious cases than the non-custody ones. An attempt was made to equalize the custody and non-custody cases by taking only those where bail was initially set at $500.[14] The resulting figures, as set out in Table XV A, are consistent with the general theory that custody is prejudicial to the accused. Whereas 40 per cent of the custody cases resulted in jail

[12]Tables were prepared, but are not set out in this study, showing the relationship between the plea and the sentence imposed. The data did not, however, show very great variations between the sentences imposed after guilty and not guilty pleas. The guilty plea may be a point in the accused's favour because the court either consciously or unconsciously appreciates the fact that the accused saved the state the expense of proving the case and the court the time required to try it. (See the *Report of the Royal Commission on Police Powers and Procedure*, 1929, Cmd. 3297, at p. 104.) On the other hand, the not guilty plea which results in a conviction is obviously not as clearly a case of guilt in the eyes of the magistrate as the guilty plea: a conviction does not represent the magistrate's absolute certainty that the accused is guilty. His uncertainty may be reflected in the sentence imposed.

[13]It would have been of interest to break down the not guilty pleas according to whether the accused was represented by counsel. This was not done, however.

[14]Again, such an operation results in the problem of numbers too small for reliable inferences; in seeking greater accuracy, there is a greater possibility of statistical error. It might have been helpful, for example, to have stabilized the custody and non-custody cases further, according to previous convictions *and* counsel, but clearly the numbers would have been too small to be meaningful.

TABLE XIV

A. RELATIONSHIP BETWEEN CUSTODY AND SENTENCE FOR NOT GUILTY PLEAS
(Percentages given in parentheses)

Offence Classification	Custody for Trial				Non-custody for Trial			
	Fine	Suspended sentence	Jail	Total dispositions	Fine	Suspended sentence	Jail	Total dispositions
Driving	7 (47)		8 (53)	15	255 (82)	2 (1)	54 (17)	311
Gambling	5 (56)		4 (44)	9	14 (93)	1 (7)		15
Assault	9 (21)	4 (10)	29 (69)	42	38 (59)	12 (19)	14 (22)	64
Sexual offences against females		1 (8)	12 (92)	13	6 (40)	4 (27)	5 (33)	15
Vagrancy	10 (32)	11 (35)	10 (32)	31	8 (89)	1 (11)		9
Offences against property without violence	5 (6)	9 (11)	67 (83)	81	32 (48)	26 (39)	9 (13)	67
Prostitution	11 (73)		4 (27)	15	6 (35)	2 (18)	3 (27)	11
Sexual offences against same sex		1 (33)	2 (67)	3		1 (100)		1
Public order	6 (50)	5 (42)	1 (8)	12	39 (75)	10 (19)	3 (6)	52
Narcotics			10 (100)	10			2 (100)	2
Other							2 (100)	2
All offences	53 (23)	31 (13)	147 (64)	231	398 (72)	59 (11)	92 (17)	549

B. DISPOSITION OF JAIL CASES
(Percentages given in parentheses)

Offence Classification	Custody for Trial						Non-custody for Trial					
	Under 1 month	1-6 mths.	6 mths. to 2 yrs.	2-5 yrs.	5 yrs. and over	Total dispositions	Under 1 month	1-6 mths.	6 mths. to 2 yrs.	2-5 yrs.	5 yrs. and over	Total dispositions
Driving	4 (50)	2 (25)	2 (25)			8	47 (87)	7 (13)				54
Gambling		2 (50)	2 (50)			4						
Assault	5 (17)	3 (10)	16 (55)	4 (14)	1 (3)	29	8 (57)	4 (29)	2 (14)			14
Sexual offences against females	5 (42)	1 (8)	4 (33)	1 (8)	1 (8)	12	4 (80)		1 (20)			5
Vagrancy	4 (40)	3 (30)	3 (30)			10						
Offences against property without violence	15 (22)		42 (63)	10 (15)		67	2 (22)	2 (22)	5 (56)			9
Prostitution	2 (50)	2 (50)				4	1 (33)	2 (67)				3
Sexual offences against same sex			2 (100)			2						
Public order			1 (100)			1	2 (67)	1 (33)				3
Narcotics	2 (20)		5 (50)	2 (20)	1 (10)	10			2 (100)			2
Other									2 (100)			2

(Percentages given in parentheses)

Offence Classification	Custody for Trial				Non-custody for Trial			
	Fine	Suspended sentence	Jail	Total dispositions	Fine	Suspended sentence	Jail	Total dispositions
Driving	1 (33)		2 (67)	3	3 (60)		2 (20)	5
Gambling					4 (100)			4
Assault	4 (36)	2 (18)	5 (45)	11	2 (25)	3 (38)	3 (38)	8
Sexual offences against females		2 (40)	3 (60)	5		2 (50)	2 (50)	4
Vagrancy								
Offences against property without violence	2 (7)	8 (29)	18 (64)	28	7 (29)	14 (58)	3 (13)	24
Prostitution	68 (59)	9 (8)	38 (33)	115	39 (78)	3 (6)	8 (16)	50
Sexual offences against same sex	1 (100)			1	1 (50)	1 (50)		2
Public order	2 (50)	1 (25)	1 (25)	4	1 (100)			1
Narcotics								
Other			1 (100)	1		1 (100)		1
All offences	78 (46)	22 (13)	68 (40)	168	57 (58)	24 (24)	18 (18)	99

B. DISPOSITION OF JAIL CASES
(Percentages given in parentheses)

Offence Classification	Custody for Trial						Non-custody for Trial					
	Under 1 month	1-6 mths.	6 mths. to 2 yrs.	2-5 yrs.	5 yrs. and over	Total dispositions	Under 1 month	1-6 mths.	6 mths. to 2 yrs.	2-5 yrs.	5 yrs. and over	Total dispositions
Driving	2 (100)					2		2 (100)				2
Gambling												
Assault	2 (40)	1 (20)	2 (40)			5	3 (100)					3
Sexual offences against females	2 (67)		1 (33)			3	2 (100)					2
Vagrancy												
Offences against property without violence	2 (11)	5 (28)	10 (56)	1 (6)		18	2 (67)		1 (33)			3
Prostitution	17 (45)	21 (55)				38	3 (38)	5 (62)				8
Sexual offences against same sex												
Public order			1 (100)			1						
Narcotics												
Other												
All offences	25 (37)	28 (41)	14 (21)	1 (1)		68	10 (56)	7 (39)	1 (6)			18

sentences, only 18 per cent of the non-custody cases were sentenced to jail. A breakdown of the figures, as shown in Table XV B, discloses that the custody cases received more severe jail sentences.

IV. CONCLUSION

The statistical evidence presented in this chapter offers cogent support to the theory that custody is prejudicial to the outcome of the case. The figures presented have shown the relationship between custody and the ability to retain counsel, between the retention of counsel and the outcome of the case, between custody and the outcome of the trial, and, finally, between custody and the sentence imposed. All of these point to the conclusion that custody, directly or indirectly, affects the accused's ability to engage counsel, hinders his attempt to present a proper defence, and increases the likelihood that he will be sentenced to imprisonment if convicted. Data presented in chapter 3 have already documented the effect on the plea of the accused of custody before the first court appearance. The lack of counsel for those in custody is probably the dominant reason why the outcome of the trial tends to be less favourable for them. A scheme of legal aid, properly conceived and providing adequate representation for all indigent persons, is imperative. A further step which should be taken which would tend to lessen the prejudicial effect of custody is to construct and arrange court facilities in such a manner that the magistrate would not know automatically whether the accused was in custody pending trial.

In addition to the possible effects of custody on the outcome of the trial, it has been pointed out that custody infringes upon the personal life and dignity of the accused; it creates an unnecessary financial burden upon the state; and it lowers the status of the administration of justice in the eyes of the public. The cost of custody includes the building and maintaining of police lockups and the supervision of accused persons until they are brought to court. If the accused is not released from custody at his first court appearance, the accused must be housed, fed, clothed, and guarded at the Don jail and transported to and from court.[15]

[15]A rough estimation of the cost of detention before trial in the Don jail can be made by multiplying the average daily population awaiting trial in the jail by the average daily cost for all prisoners held at the jail. The daily average number of persons awaiting trial during one week in October 1963 was approximately 170 and the daily cost per prisoner during 1963 was approximately five dollars, according to the *Annual Report of the Department of Reform Institutions,* 1963, Part I at p. 82. This works out to a yearly cost of approximately $300,000. Because this figure includes certain fixed costs (which would remain constant

Further costs may result when the state is forced to finance a defence for the accused or to finance his family when his incarceration makes him unable to do so.

It is obvious, therefore, that custody pending trial should be confined to those cases where it is clearly necessary. One means of accomplishing this, discussed in chapter 2, is by increased use of the summons procedure. Theoretically, the bail system should provide a further means of limiting the use of custody before trial. Regrettably, the theoretical advantages of the bail system are offset by its practical shortcomings, which are presented in the following chapters.

---

unless there was a sizable decrease in the prison population) the variable cost of maintaining prisoners awaiting trial would, of course, be less than this. For comparative American figures see Freed and Wald, *op. cit. supra* note 4, at p. 39 *et seq.*

7. The Setting and Raising of Bail

I. The Setting of Bail

IT HAS BEEN SEEN that bail was set at the first court appearance in approximately half (48 per cent) of the cases which were not disposed of then. In this chapter a detailed examination of the practices of setting bail and the ability of the accused to raise the bail set will be made.

The practice in Metropolitan Toronto is for the magistrates to set bail in court at a fixed amount without specifying whether one or more sureties are required or, in most cases, whether the bail should be raised in the form of cash or real property.[1] The justices of the peace who are delegated to accept the bail[2] are not concerned with whether the cash is put up by the accused or a surety or whether the surety puts up cash or real property: the option is with the accused.[3]

A. Judicial Discretion in Setting Bail

Because the main purpose of bail is to ensure that the accused will show up for his trial, and because the accused's roots in the community differ from case to case, one might expect that magistrates exercise a judicial discretion in setting the amount of bail required to keep the accused from absconding.[4] Not surprisingly, however, the amounts

[1]Magistrates will occasionally set property bail at a higher amount than cash bail.

[2]This is considered to be a ministerial act and so can be delegated by the magistrate to a justice of the peace. See *Johnston* v. *Attorney-General* (1910) 16 C.C.C. 296 (N.S.S.C.).

[3]See Galligan, "Advising an Arrested Client," *Law Society of Upper Canada Special Lectures 1963* 35 at p. 44: "Generally speaking, bail can either be posted in cash or property can be put up as the security."

[4]See, e.g., Archbold, *Criminal Pleading Evidence and Practice* (35th ed., 1962) § 202: "the duty of a magistrate as to admitting a prisoner to bail is judicial. . . ." See also *Johnston* v. *Attorney-General op. cit. supra* note 2, at p. 304 (N.S.S.C.) *per* Meagher J.: "The allowance of bail is a judicial act, and cannot, I take it, be delegated. . . ;" *Re Rex* v. *Lepicki* (1925) 44 C.C.C. 263 at p. 265 (Man.K.B.); see also Puttkammer, *Administration of Criminal Law* (1953) at p. 103: "Setting the amount of bail is a judicial task and can be performed

set by magistrates in Toronto tend to be standardized according to the offence. To a certain extent standardization is the result of crowded dockets, harried magistrates, and the fact that little assistance as to the amount of bail to be set is gained from the accused, who is usually not represented at this point.[5] To an even greater extent standardization is the result of an unspoken realization by magistrates of the virtual impossibility of choosing a proper figure. A sound system would presumably have amounts of bail high enough reasonably to ensure the appearance of the accused and yet low enough to afford him a reasonable chance of raising it. The fact that these two limits seldom, if ever, overlap makes it difficult, if not impossible, for the magistrate to exercise a proper discretion in most cases. The result is often a compromise figure, usually too low to act as a serious deterrent against absconding, yet too high to be raised easily by the accused.

The extent to which the setting of bail has become standardized can be seen from an investigation of one of the categories used for this study: cases in which bail was set between $301 and $500 inclusive. There were 406 cases within this category, yet in 393 of them (96.8 per cent) bail was set at the convenient figure of exactly $500.

Standardization is virtually absolute for the offence of prostitution. Of 169 cases of prostitution in which bail was set, it was set at exactly $500 in all but one. (In this solitary exception bail was set at $200.) It should be noted that standardized amounts will vary from time to time, however. For example, the standard amount for prostitution has risen in the past ten years from $50 to $200 to the present $500. The standard amount for bootlegging, on the other hand, has dropped from $500 to $250.

B. Amounts at which Bail Set

In a recent article dealing with some of the practical aspects of bail, a Crown Attorney in Ontario supplied the following list of offences

---

only by a member of the judiciary. . . ;" *People* v. *McDonnell* (1947) 296 N.Y. 109; 71 N.E. 2d 423 (N.Y.C.A.); *Federal Rules of Criminal Procedure*, Rule 46: "If the defendant is admitted to bail, the amount thereof shall be such as in the judgment of the commissioner or court or judge or justice will insure the presence of the defendant. . . ."

[5]The extent of standardization in the United States is documented by Freed and Wald, *Bail in the United States: 1964* at p. 9 *et seq.* In the studies of bail in New York and Philadelphia, cited by Freed and Wald, it was found that there were lists of standard amounts of bail based on the category of offence. In fact, at p. 21, Freed and Wald point out that a municipal judge in Baltimore recently announced a revision of the court's bail schedule to meet "inflation."

coupled with the amounts of bail which "over a period of years . . . have been relatively standard in many countries:"[6]

Drunk or impaired driving	$500
Breaking and entering; theft over $50	$1,000
Theft under $50	$500
Assault	$100
Rape	$5,000
Armed robbery	$10,000[7]

The reader will appreciate that the existence of such a list negates the concept of a judicial discretion exercised mainly on the likelihood of the individual appearing for his trial.

(i) For Categories of Offences. The above amounts are more or less in line with those found in the present study. The figures for impaired driving and theft under $50 are somewhat higher than those found in Toronto, whereas that for assault is somewhat lower. Table XVI shows the amounts at which bail was set by the Toronto magistrates for certain categories of offences.

A more complete understanding of these figures can be gained from Table XVII which gives the median amount of bail set for various categories of offences. As pointed out previously, almost all cases within the category of $301–$500 had bail set at exactly $500. Therefore, the median amount of bail was $500.

(ii) Offences against Property (without Violence). A breakdown for particular offences within the category of offences against property (without violence) is set out in Table XVIII.

The median amount of bail set was as given in Table XIX.

C. Cash or Property

Magistrates will occasionally set property bail at a higher amount than cash bail, almost invariably at double the cash figure. Some magistrates never draw a distinction between the amount necessary for cash or property bail, and among those who do make the distinction there is a wide variance as to the frequency of the practice. In the present study it was found that one magistrate alone accounted for approximately one-quarter of all the cases in which cash and property bail were set at different amounts. This lack of uniformity in practice is an indication of a general lack of awareness by the magistrates of the purpose of bail.

[6]Affleck, "Notes on Bail" (1963) 6 *Crim. L. Q.* 10 at p. 15.

[7]See also Galligan, *op. cit. supra* note 3, at p. 43: "In most jurisdictions there is a pretty standard quantum of bail for certain types of offences, for example, offences such as impaired driving, shoplifting, petty theft, minor assaults and the like."

TABLE XVI

The Setting and Raising of Bail According to Offence Classification

(The figures in parentheses show the number of cases in which the bail set was raised)

Offence Classification	Total Number of Cases in which Bail Set	Number of Cases in which Bail Was Set at Various Amounts (in dollars)									
		25 and under	26–50	51–100	101–200	201–300	301–500	501–1,000	1,001–2,000	2,001–5,000	Over 5,000
Driving	56 (37)	1 (1)	3 (2)	16 (13)	14 (11)	5 (3)	10 (3)	6 (3)		1 (1)	
Gambling	20 (16)			1 (1)	2 (1)	3 (3)	9 (9)	5 (2)			
Assault	152 (61)		7 (6)	13 (7)	22 (12)	7 (5)	40 (19)	21 (3)	14 (4)	27 (5)	1 (0)
Sexual offences against females	42 (19)		1 (1)		7 (4)		18 (10)	7 (2)	4 (1)	5 (1)	
Vagrancy	67 (10)	35 (6)	24 (3)	3 (0)	2 (0)		2 (1)	1 (0)			
Offences against property (without violence)	416 (156)	5 (3)	14 (10)	30 (20)	49 (25)	23 (9)	92 (38)	75 (20)	46 (13)	77 (15)	5 (3)
Prostitution	242 (82)		2 (2)	1 (0)	1 (0)	1 (1)	213 (72)	7 (5)	5 (0)	12 (2)	
Sexual offences against the same sex	9 (4)			1 (1)			5 (3)	3 (0)			
Public order	65 (36)	3 (1)	10 (9)	7 (4)	19 (13)	1 (1)	11 (3)	9 (3)	3 (1)	2 (1)	
Narcotics	86 (9)					2 (2)			2 (2)	82 (6)	2 (1)
Other	15 (11)	1 (1)	1 (1)	2 (2)	2 (1)		4 (2)	1 (1)		2 (1)	
Total	1170 (441)	45 (12)	62 (34)	74 (48)	118 (67)	42 (24)	404 (160)	135 (39)	74 (21)	208 (32)	8 (4)

TABLE XVII

MEDIAN AMOUNT OF BAIL SET

Offence	Amount (in dollars)
Driving	101– 200
Gambling	301– 500
Assault	301– 500
Sexual offences against females	301– 500
Vagrancy	25 and under
Offences against property (without violence)	301– 500
Prostitution	301– 500
Sexual offences against the same sex	301– 500
Public order	101– 200
Narcotics	2,001–5,000
Other	201– 300
All offences	$301– $500

In 7 per cent of the cases in which bail was set at the first court appearance (76 out of 1,177) property bail was set at a higher amount than cash bail. Table XX shows the relationship between cash and property bail for each amount classification.

II. THE RAISING OF BAIL

A. Ability to Raise Bail

The most important question in the whole area of the administration of bail concerns the number of persons kept in custody through inability to raise bail.

(i) For all Offences. The figures that emerged from the study show that a significant proportion of all persons for whom bail was set were unable to raise it. Out of a total of 1,170 cases in which bail was set, only 441 were able to raise the bail, i.e., 62 per cent of all persons for whom bail was set at the first court appearance were unable to raise it. These persons remained in custody until their trial or until bail was lowered. The percentages for summary and indictable offences were approximately the same: bail was not raised in 61 per cent of the summary conviction cases and 63 per cent of the indictable cases. The inability to raise bail is shown graphically in Figure 18.

(ii) Categories of Offences. Table XXI shows bail raised when all cases are broken down into general categories of offences.

(iii) Offences against Property (without Violence). One of the largest categories of offences is that of offences against property. The percentage

TABLE XVIII

The Setting and Raising of Bail for Offences Against Property (without Violence)

(The figures in parentheses show the number of cases in which the bail set was raised)

Offence	Total Number of Cases in which Bail Was Set	Number of Cases in which Bail Was Set at Various Amounts (in dollars)									
		25 and under	26–50	51–100	101–200	201–300	301–500	501–1,000	1,001–2,000	2,001–5,000	Over 5,000
Theft over $50	76 (26)		1 (1)	4 (1)	7 (2)	4 (1)	30 (8)	16 (7)	5 (2)	8 (3)	1 (1)
Theft under $50	83 (48)	3 (3)	12 (8)	16 (12)	21 (10)	11 (3)	11 (8)	3 (1)	2 (1)	4 (2)	
Auto theft and joyriding	36 (6)				4 (3)		16 (0)	8 (1)	4 (1)	4 (1)	
Breaking and entering	70 (13)	2 (0)		2 (2)		6 (2)	21 (6)	1 (0)	35 (2)	3 (1)	
False pretences and fraud	61 (29)		1 (1)	4 (2)	7 (4)	7 (4)	11 (6)	10 (2)	11 (4)	8 (4)	2 (2)
Possession of stolen property	54 (24)			3 (2)	6 (4)	1 (1)	14 (11)	9 (2)	8 (3)	13 (1)	
Forgery and uttering	17 (7)			1 (1)	3 (1)	3 (2)	5 (2)	3 (0)	2 (1)		
Possession of burglar's tools	7 (3)				1 (1)		1 (1)	3 (0)	2 (1)		
Total	404 (156)	5 (3)	14 (10)	30 (20)	49 (25)	32 (13)	109 (42)	53 (13)	69 (15)	40 (12)	3 (3)

TABLE XIX

MEDIAN AMOUNT OF BAIL SET

Offence	Amount (in dollars)
Theft over $50	301– 500
Theft under $50	101– 200
Auto theft and joyriding	301– 500
Breaking and entering	1,001–2,000
False pretences and fraud	501–1,000
Possession of stolen property	501–1,000
Forgery and uttering	301– 500
Possession of burglar's tools	501–1,000
All offences against property (without violence)	301– 500

TABLE XX

COMPARISON OF CASH AND PROPERTY BAIL

Amount (in dollars)	Cash and Property Bail Set at same Amount	Property Bail Set Higher than the Cash Figure	Percentage of Cases where Cash and Property Bail Differed
25 and under	43	2	4
26– 50	60	3	5
51– 100	70	4	5
101– 200	115	5	4
201– 300	33	9	21
301– 500	378	28	7
501–1,000	120	15	11
1,001–2,000	71	6	8
2,001–5,000	205	3	1
Over 5,000	6	1	14
Total	1101	76	7

of persons in this category who were able to raise the bail set was approximately the same (38) as the percentage of persons who were able to raise bail for all offences, although within the category there were variations, as given in Table XXI A.

The figure for the cases of auto theft appears to be somewhat out of line. The explanation would seem to be that often young persons are involved in these offences and have greater difficulty than older persons in raising bail. The low number who were able to raise bail for the offence of breaking and entering is probably because high bail is often set for this offence.

When the above offences taken collectively are broken down into the various amounts in which bail was set, in general, the pattern is that

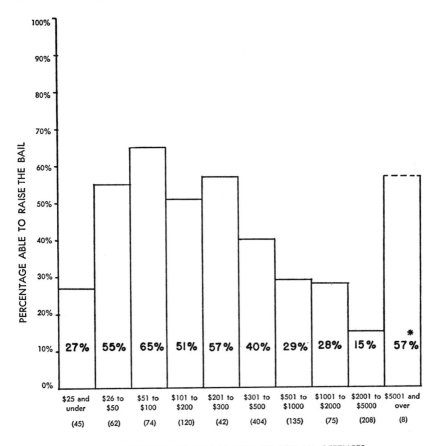

AMOUNT IN WHICH BAIL WAS SET FOR ALL OFFENCES

*As there were only eight cases in this group the percentage shown may be misleading.

FIG. 18. Percentage who were able to raise bail when set at various amounts for all offences. (The number of cases in which bail was set within each category is shown at the bottom of each column.)

as the amount of bail required increases, the probability of raising it decreases.

The main difference between Figure 19, involving offences against property without violence, and Figure 18, involving all categories of offences, is that the likelihood or raising bail set at very low amounts is greater for offences against property without violence. Although magistrates tend to set bail for the true vagrancy-type offences at very low amounts, vagrants can seldom raise even a modest sum. Because

TABLE XXI

A. The Ability to Raise Bail for all Categories of Offence

Offence Category	Number of Cases in which Bail Was Set	Number of Persons able to Raise the Bail	Percentage of Persons Able to Raise the Bail
Driving	56	37	66
Gambling	20	16	80
Assault	152	61	40
(robbery—included in above figures)	(40)	(7)	(18)
Sexual offences against females	42	19	45
Vagrancy	67	10	15
Offences against property (without violence)	416	156	38
Prostitution	242	82	34
Sexual offences against the same sex	9	4	44
Public order	65	36	55
Narcotics	86	9	10
Other	15	11	69
Total	1,170	441	38

B. The Ability to Raise Bail for Offences against Property (without Violence)

Offence	Number of Cases in which Bail Was Set	Number of Persons Able to Raise the Bail	Percentage of Persons Able to Raise the Bail
Theft over $50	76	26	34
Theft under $50	83	48	58
Auto theft and joyriding	36	6	17
Breaking and entering	70	13	19
False pretences and fraud	61	29	48
Possession of stolen property	54	24	44
Forgery and uttering	17	7	41
Possession of burglar's tools	7	3	43
Total	404	156	39

vagrancy offences constitute a large percentage of the cases in which bail was set at low amounts, the figures for all offences therefore show a general inability to raise bail when set at low amounts. Prostitution, commonly referred to as "Vag. C." has not been included in the

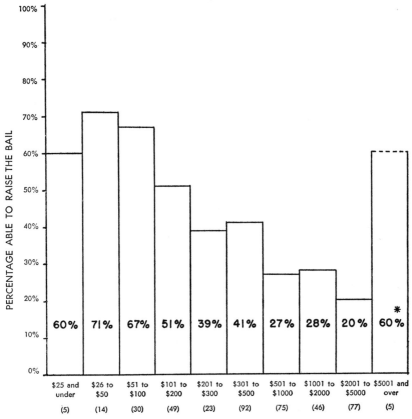

AMOUNT IN WHICH BAIL WAS SET FOR ALL OFFENCES

*As there were only five cases in this group the percentage may be misleading.
FIG. 19. Percentage who were able to raise bail when set at various amounts for offences against property (without violence). (The number of cases where bail was set within each category is shown at the bottom of each column.)

vagrancy category.[8] Out of a total of 45 cases in which bail was set at $25 or under, there were 35 cases involving vagrancy, and out of 63 cases in which bail was set between $26 and $50, 24 cases involved vagrancy. It was no surprise to discover that, out of the 35 vagrancy

[8]Section 164(1)(c). Only s. 164(1)(a) and (b) are included.
"S. 164(1) Every one commits vagrancy who
         (a) not having any apparent means of support is found wandering abroad or trespassing and does not, when required, justify his presence in the place where he is found;
         (b) begs from door to door or in a public place. . . ."

cases in which bail was set at $25 or under, only 6 persons (17 per cent) were able to raise it or that, out of the 24 cases where bail was set between $26 and $50, only 3 persons (13 per cent) were able to raise it.[9]

(iv) Comparison with American Figures. It will be recalled that a fairly large proportion (approximately 400 cases) of accused persons had bail set in the sum of $500, of whom 240 persons (60 per cent) were unable to raise it. In the study conducted in New York City by the University of Pennsylvania Law School it was found that only 28 per cent of those who had bail set at $500 were unable to raise it.[10] An earlier study in Philadelphia showed that when bail was set at $500 in the Philadelphia state courts 15 per cent were unable to raise it and in the Philadelphia federal courts 32 per cent were unable to do so.[11]

When bail was set at $1,000 the same pattern emerged. In the New York, Philadelphia state, and Philadelphia federal courts, 38 per cent, 22 per cent, and 50 per cent respectively were unable to raise the $1,000 bail. In Toronto slightly over 70 per cent were unable to raise it.[12] The divergence between the Toronto and the American figures was equally striking when bail was set at $2,000: in New York 35 per cent were unable to raise that amount; in Toronto 72 per cent were unable to raise it. Any comparison with American figures on bail over $5,000 might be somewhat misleading because of the small number of cases in this study in which bail was set at over $5,000.[13]

[9]There were only eight vagrancy cases in which bail was set at a sum over $50 and bail was raised in only one (a case in which bail was set and raised in the sum of $500 though an essential ingredient of the charge was "not having any apparent means of support").

[10]The "New York Bail Study" (1958) 106 *U. Pa. L. Rev.* 685 at p. 707. There were variations between the localities studied. Bail was furnished when set at $500 by 78 per cent in the Bronx, 62 per cent in New York, and 85 per cent in Queens. Broken down into categories of offences (at p. 711) the percentages of persons able to raise bail were as follows (the number of cases is shown in parentheses): robbery—26 per cent (298); burglary—37 (307); narcotics—45 (402); assault—57 (318); dangerous weapon—63 (67); grand larceny—64 (451); rape—67 (109); forgery—68 (98).

[11]The "Philadelphia Bail Study" (1954) 102 *U. Pa. L. Rev.* 1031 at pp. 1032–33.

[12]The comparison is even more striking in view of the fact that our study includes cases where bail was set between $500 and $1,000, the latter figure being the maximum in our category.

[13]Other American figures on the ability to raise bail can be found cited in Freed and Wald, *op. cit. supra* note 5, at p. 9 *et seq.* A preliminary study of bail in the District of Columbia by the D.C. Bar Association's Junior Bar Section showed that two-thirds of the persons eligible for bail were unable to raise it (188 out of 285): at $500, 17 per cent could not raise bail; at $1,000, 40 per cent could not raise it; at $2,500, 78 per cent failed to raise it. In the *Report of the Attorney*

These figures cannot be compared with precision;[14] however, they do demonstrate that proportionately more persons remain in custody, through inability to raise bail, in Toronto than in New York or Philadelphia. Though the periods of time spent in custody were less in the present study than those found in the American studies, the latter concentrated on cases in the higher courts, whereas this study deals exclusively with cases tried in the lower courts.

(v) Comparison with English Figures. It is important to recognize the one major difference between English and Canadian bail practices: the English bail system does not require any security in advance. Dr. R. M. Jackson states that "bail in our courts rests on recognizances, which are really promises; there are no deposits of money or the pledging of property or bondsmen."[15] The surety in England does not "put up" anything; he simply undertakes to pay a designated sum if the accused does not show up for his trial. Thus an accused who has bail set will not be kept in custody because he is indigent or cannot arrange to have anyone put up money in advance; if he is unable to obtain his release it is normally because he knows no one who considers him a sufficiently good risk to take the chance of forfeiting money in the future. It would therefore be expected that the number of persons unable to raise the bail in England would be very much lower than in Canada. The Home Office Study bears out this expectation. A study was made of 1,934 magistrates' court cases, comprised of 781 persons committed

---

General's Committee on Poverty and the Administration of Federal Criminal Justice (1963) p. 67 and Tables III and IV, it was found in a survey of four districts that 23 per cent of accused persons could not raise bail in the District of Connecticut, 43 per cent in the Northern District of Illinois, 58 per cent in the San Francisco Division of the Northern District of California, and 83 per cent in the Sacramento Division of the Northern District of California.

[14]For example, cases where the bail was not raised and was subsequently lowered have been included as inability to raise bail in the figures for Toronto. In the New York study these cases were excluded. If the figures were included in the New York study the percentage of those who were unable to raise the bail initially set would be slightly higher (but not much; bail was reduced only in about 6 per cent of the cases—see "The New York Bail Study" *op. cit. supra* note 10, at p. 716). A further difficulty in comparing the figures stems from the fact that in Toronto some accused persons were released on bail prior to the first court appearance and they are not included in these figures. If they were, the Toronto percentage with respect to those unable to raise bail would be somewhat lower. All the persons who raised bail before the first court appearance would not have to be taken into account but only those who did not plead guilty or have the charge withdrawn and were remanded to a later date. There was not a sufficient number within this category to affect the general picture. In any event, we are not taking into account persons who were unable to raise bail before the first court appearance and were not remanded for trial.

[15]*The Machinery of Justice in England* (4th ed., 1964) at p. 133.

for trial and 1,153 persons tried summarily and remanded either before or after conviction (including 75 committed to quarter sessions for sentence). It was found that:

26 persons were stated to have been remanded or committed in custody solely because of inability to find sureties. Three of these were committed for trial in custody; two were remanded for probation reports only; 21 were ordinary remand cases. In seven of the cases the police opposed bail, so that lack of sureties may not have been the only reason for custody, although it was the reason stated. . . . The amount of surety required is shown in Table 36, from which it is apparent that the sureties demanded, although in the upper part of the range, were not abnormally high. Of the 23 persons tried summarily, only six were sentenced to imprisonment; seven were put on probation (including the two remanded for reports), four were fined, three were discharged and three were acquitted.[16]

Table 36 of the Home Office Study is here reproduced as Table XXII.

TABLE XXII

INABILITY TO RAISE BAIL IN ENGLAND

Amount of Bail (in pounds)	Persons Granted Bail Proportion Finding Sureties of Different Amounts		Number of Persons Unable to Find Sureties of Different Amounts	
	Committed for trial (per cent)	Tried summarily (per cent)	Committed for trial	Tried summarily
Under 5	—	3.7	—	—
5– 10	1.9	27.9	—	2
10– 15	20.5	40.9	—	2
15– 25	35.2	12.2	—	8
25– 50	23.0	9.7	2	3
50–100	12.4	4.2	1	1
100–200	5.1	1.0	—	—
200 and over	1.9	0.4	—	2
Amount not stated	—	—	—	5
Total	100	100	3	23

Thus, for all the cases in the English sample only 1 per cent (26 out of 1,934) were in custody owing to inability to raise bail. This was 4 per cent (26 out of 751) of the cases in which the accused was remanded or committed in custody only, and at the same time comprised 2 per cent (26 out of 1,209) of the cases in which the accused had bail set. Data taken from the Home Office Study have been compiled in Table XXIII to show inability to raise bail for the various categories studied.

[16]Home Office Study, *Time Spent Awaiting Trial* (1960) at p. 34 para. 89.

TABLE XXIII

THE RAISING OF BAIL IN ENGLAND: TABLE ADAPTED FROM
HOME OFFICE STUDY
(The figures in parentheses show the percentage of persons unable to raise bail)

Those Unable to Raise the Bail Set	Procedure	Total Number of Cases Studied	Those Remanded in Custody Only	Those Who Had Bail Set
3	Committed for trial	781 (1/2)	328 (1)	456 (1/2)
23	Tried summarily and remanded	1078 (2)	363 (7)	738 (3)
0	Tried summarily and committed for sentence	75 (0)	60 (0)	15 (0)
26	Total	1934 (1)	751 (4)	1209 (2)

B. Previous Convictions and the Ability to Raise Bail

We have seen that 62 per cent of all persons who had bail set were unable to raise it. In the following pages an analysis is made of the relationship between the ability of the accused to raise bail and his previous record. Only cases of indictable offences where bail was set were studied, 827 cases in all. Because the police do not keep any data on previous convictions for summary conviction offences, the analysis is limited further to previous convictions for indictable offences.

One might expect that raising the bail set would be easier for a person without a previous record than for one with a previous record. The over-all figures tend to support this but a fuller analysis suggests that a person with a record possibly has a better chance of raising bail than a person without a record.

(i) For all Indictable Offences. Table XXIV gives the figures for previous convictions in relation to the ability to raise bail for all indictable offences. Perhaps the most striking fact demonstrated by these figures is that, of all persons charged with an indictable offence without a previous record for indictable offences, 57 per cent were unable to raise the bail that was set. This fact alone is sufficient to demonstrate the ineffectiveness of the bail system.

(ii) Indictable Offences where Bail Set at $500. A somewhat more sophisticated analysis was made, examining only the indictable offences where bail was set in the sum of $500 in order to extract cases which, perhaps in a crude way, were comparable. It may well be that, taking all indictable offences, the accused's chance of raising the bail decreased as his record became longer because bail was set at higher amounts for

TABLE XXIV

PREVIOUS CONVICTIONS AND THE ABILITY TO RAISE BAIL
FOR ALL INDICTABLE OFFENCES

Previous Convictions	Number of Cases	Number who Raised the Bail	Percentage who Raised the Bail
No previous convictions	361	156	43
One previous conviction	79	28	35
Two previous convictions	69	21	30
More than two previous convictions	262	66	25
Total for all indictable cases in which bail was set	771	271	35

TABLE XXV

PREVIOUS CONVICTIONS AND THE ABILITY TO RAISE BAIL
SET AT $500

Previous Convictions	Number of Cases	Number who Raised the Bail	Percentage who Raised the Bail
No previous convictions	124	57	46
One previous conviction	20	11	55
Two previous convictions	15	7	47
More than two previous convictions	42	16	38
Total for all indictable offences in which bail was set at $500	201	91	45

persons with records. When only the cases in which bail was set at $500 are taken, however, the figures show that a person's chance of raising $500 bail does not decrease in relation to the length of his record. Table XXV shows that large numbers of persons without previous recorded convictions are unable to raise bail. Moreover, though it cannot be stated with certainty, it may well be that a person without previous convictions does not stand as good a chance of raising bail as a person with previous convictions. The existence of the professional bondsman makes this understandable. The professional bondsman or money-lender will probably offer his services more readily to a person who is known in the criminal world or has proven to have been a reliable risk on a previous occasion. In addition, the person with previous convictions is more likely to know of the existence of bondsmen. The figures indicate, then, that the ultimate result of the bail process for a person without a record is no more favourable than that for a person with a record.

C. Delay in Raising Bail

Even if an accused is able to raise the bail that is set, there is often a considerable delay before it can be furnished by him or on his behalf, particularly when bail is set in the higher amounts and property bail is used. The following advice was recently given to the practising bar of Ontario:

For a number of very good reasons there has been a very considerable amount of tightening-up with regard to the accepting of property bail. At the present time the release of your client is not likely to be speedy if property is to be put up as bail. Generally speaking the Crown attorney will have to be satisfied that the bondsman has good title. Sometimes the Crown attorney will wish to search the title or have it searched or have a solicitor's abstract and certificate of title together with a Registrar's abstract. He will also require proof that the property has sufficient value so that the bondsman's equity in the property is equal to the amount of the bail. Usually the property will have to be appraised by a real estate appraiser and a certificate as to the value of the property will have to be filed. Also, a sheriff's certificate as to executions will have to be obtained. For obvious reasons therefore the process of having property bail posted is not a speedy one. It would be my suggestion that if at all possible cash bail should always be used as it is much simpler to post and effects a much more speedy release of your client.[17]

(i) For all Offences. The study shows that approximately one-half (47 per cent) of the persons who were able to raise the bail set at the first court appearance were not released from custody on the day bail was set. Some 16 per cent were not released until they had spent at least one week in custody.

It is understandable that there must necessarily be some delay in arranging bail. There is often difficulty in contacting persons who might put up bail for the accused, and in making arrangements to raise the bail, whether it be cash or property. The difficulty is compounded by the fact that bail magistrates are available only at certain times in the afternoon at the Don jail, from where most accused persons are released on bail. Though the accused can be released from the City Hall cells between the first court appearance and removal to the Don jail, it is often too difficult for him to arrange bail in such a short period of time.

Delay in raising bail is set out in Table XXVI which shows the day on which bail was raised and the accused was released, in relation to the day on which bail was set.

[17]Galligan, op. cit. supra note 3, at pp. 44–45.

TABLE XXVI

DELAY IN RAISING BAIL FOR ALL OFFENCES

Date Bail Raised	Per cent who Raised Bail at that Time (Number who raised bail in parentheses)	
Same day	53	(206)
1 day after 1st court appearance	9	(36)
2 days after	8	(30)
3 days after	7	(26)
4 days after	5	(19)
5 days after	7	(26)
6 days after	4	(17)
One week or more after	8	(29)
Total	100	(389)

(ii) For Prostitutes. One fact tends to make the figures in Table XXVI slightly misleading: prostitutes are not released from custody until they have had a medical examination, which normally takes a number of days to complete.[18] Only 7 per cent of the prostitutes arrested were released on the date of the first court appearance or during the following two days and approximately one-third were released on exactly the fifth day after the first court appearance. Table XXVII shows the delay in raising bail for prostitutes.

TABLE XXVII

DELAY IN RAISING BAIL FOR PROSTITUTES

Date Bail Raised	Per cent who Raised Bail at that Time (Number who raised bail in parentheses)	
Same day	6	(4)
1 day after 1st court appearance	0	(0)
2 days after	1	(1)
3 days after	16	(11)
4 days after	13	(9)
5 days after	33	(22)
6 days after	16	(11)
One week or more after	13	(9)
Total	100	(67)

(iii) For all Offences Except Prostitution. If the prostitution cases are removed from Table XXVI the percentage of those unable to raise bail on the day it was set decreases from 47 to 38, a figure still high enough to cause concern, however. Table XXVIII shows the delay in raising bail for all offences except prostitution.

[18]The Venereal Diseases Prevention Act, R.S.O. 1960, c. 415, ss. 8, 9, authorizes the inspection and treatment in custody of those who are under arrest or in custody when the medical officer of health believes the person may be infected.

TABLE XXVIII

DELAY IN RAISING BAIL FOR ALL OFFENCES EXCEPT PROSTITUTION

Date Bail Raised	Per cent who Raised Bail at that Time (Number who raised bail in parentheses)	
Same day	62	(202)
1 day after 1st court appearance	11	(36)
2 days after	9	(29)
3 days after	8	(25)
4 days after	3	(10)
5 days after	1	(4)
6 days after	2	(6)
One week or more after	5	(16)
Total	100	(328)

It is obvious from the foregoing that, under the existing bail system, a system which requires full security in advance, some delay is inevitable. Changing the system would, of course, eliminate much of the delay in release. If the present system is continued, however, to decrease the delay presently found there should be someone at the Don jail at all times to accept bail that has already been set. Accepting bail previously set by a magistrate in court is, in almost all cases, a routine administrative act, particularly when full security in advance is employed. The federal government should pass legislation permitting persons in charge of a jail or police station to accept such bail. The English have wisely permitted such a practice.[19] If federal legislation is not passed, no harm could result in appointing certain jail officials as justices of the peace for the sole purpose of accepting bail when the regular justice is not available.

D. The Form of the Security: An Additional Obstacle to Release

Assuming that security in advance is a necessary part of our bail system, certain rules preventing the posting of particular types of security require re-examination. The following particular rules will be discussed here: the refusal by the justices to accept cheques; the lack of provisions permitting the accused to post real property as security; and the refusal by the justices to accept property bail from a surety when the accused owns the property jointly with the surety.

In many cases accused persons are unable to obtain their release prior to the first court appearance because they and their friends and relatives are unable to obtain at night the cash required by the justice

[19]See s. 95 of the English Magistrates' Courts Act, 1952 and Rule 68(1) of the English Magistrates' Courts Rules, 1952. Rule 68(1) is set out in chapter 3.

of the peace. The extent of custody before the first court appearance has been discussed. It would be decreased if the justices followed the practice of accepting, from a surety or the accused, a cheque which could be cashed when the banks opened. Little harm could possibly result from such a practice. There is, of course, a slight possibility that there might not be adequate funds to cover the cheque when presented. It is doubtful, however, if there would be many such cases; few persons would blatantly undertake such a course of action which not only constitutes the criminal offence of false pretences[20] but is also certain to be discovered. In any event, because the cheque would in most instances be presented the following morning, if it were not honoured, the accused could be re-arrested soon after his release.[21]

Although provision is made in the Criminal Code for cash bail by the accused, no reference is made to the posting of real property by him. Again, assuming that security in advance is desirable, there can be no justification for such a distinction. Real property bail can be as secure as cash bail. The present anomalous situation is surely a good indication that there is a basic misunderstanding of the function of the bail system.

Furthermore, in Toronto a wife cannot use the family home to bail her husband if it is jointly owned by the husband and wife. A reasonably large proportion of married couples take title to property in their joint names. A couple that wish to use their property as bail, when one of the spouses is arrested, is no doubt surprised when their lawyer explains that what may be desirable for estate planning will not satisfy the bail magistrate. The origin and reason for this rule is somewhat uncertain and difficult to justify. The surety's interest in property held jointly can be sold if the accused absconds.[22] It is only remotely possible that the

[20]S. 304 of the Criminal Code.

[21]Archbold, *op. cit. supra* note 4, § 203 stating that "if the sureties become afterwards insufficient, the defendant may be ordered by any magistrate to find sufficient sureties, and in default may be committed to prison."

[22]The rule preventing one joint tenant from putting up his undivided interest in land as security, unless all the joint tenants interested in the land enter into the recognizance, may have been based on the anomalous and repudiated rule followed by Barlow J. in *Re Tully and Tully and Klotz* [1953] O.W.N. 661 in which it was held that the filing of a writ of execution against the interest of one joint tenant in mortgaged land did not bind the land and therefore the joint tenants together could convey the land to a third person who would take free of any claim by the execution creditor. Such a rule would permit joint tenants to sell their land, in spite of the Crown's execution, during the waiting period before the land could be sold.

The reasoning is not applicable, however, for a number of reasons: the *Tully* case was probably not consistent with earlier authorities (*Re Craig* (1928) 63 O.L.R. 192 (App. Div.); *Re Kates and Kates* v. *Morrison* [1951] O.W.N. 701

surety may die and the property pass to the accused spouse.[23] In such a case the accused can be required to obtain further sureties. In any event, should the surety die and the accused abscond, the accused will have assets available to pay for the estreated recognizance which he also signed. The justification given by the bail magistrates for the rule appears to be based upon the reasoning that all owners of property held jointly must sign the recognizance and, if required, the affidavit of justification; the accused cannot sign the affidavit of justification because one of the items stated in it is, "That I am not awaiting trial for any criminal offence;" thus, a wife cannot use the property held jointly to bail her husband. The premises used are faulty, however; not only should it not be necessary for all owners of property held jointly to join in the recognizance, but also the affidavit of justification presently being used should not be treated as if it were a statute. The affidavit has no legislative backing; it simply evolved to aid magistrates in deciding on the sufficiency of the surety.[24]

III. Varying the Bail Set

An accused who has bail set or denied by a magistrate may have his bail application reviewed in two ways: a magistrate at a later remand date may re-assess the previous bail decision, or the accused may apply for a review by a High Court judge.

(High Ct.)); has been doubted in later cases (see Re Klagsbrun v. Stankiewicz [1953] O.W.N. 910 (High Ct.)); would seem to have been effectively overruled by the 1957 amendment to The Execution Act, Stat. Ont. 1957, c. 31, s. 4; and, finally, can be avoided by the Crown by the creation of a lien under the 1957 Bail Act (now R.S.O. 1960, c. 28).

I am grateful to my colleague, Dennis Hefferon, for his assistance on this point.

[23]*Quaere* whether this would in fact happen. It is arguable that the posting of one joint tenant's interest in a property held jointly converts joint tenancy into a tenancy-in-common and suspends the right of survivorship until the lien is discharged. (See *In re Penn Application* (1951) 4 W.W.R. (N.S.) 452 (B.C.S.C.); but cf. *Re Brooklands Lumber & Hardware Ltd. & Simcoe* (1956) 3 D.L.R. (2d) 762 (Man. Q.B.)). Perhaps legislation should make it clear that a complete severance, which would probably surprise the husband and wife, does not take place.

[24]The present form attempts to follow slavishly the example of an affidavit of justification set out in an annotation, Armour, "Bail in Criminal Cases" (1926) 47 C.C.C. 1, 12–13. The inadvertent omission in s. 9 in the present form of the word "or" makes the provision, swearing there has been no indemnification, incomprehensible. Yet the last section of the form (s. 12) states: "That this affidavit and the recognizance have both been read over to me and explained and I fully understand the same."

A. In the Lower Courts

The practice of a magistrate varying, in favour of the accused, the bail that was initially set is quite prevalent.[25] Bail was lowered, or set where it had previously been denied, in approximately one-third of all the cases in which the opportunity for variance existed.[26] Of cases where bail was set and not raised, later variation by a magistrate took place in approximately half.

Table XXIX contains a breakdown of the cases in which there was a later variation of bail. The fact that bail is subsequently varied does not necessarily mean the accused will be released. As Table XXIX shows, in 33 per cent (45 out of 136) of the cases in which the bail was varied, the accused was still unable to procure his release.[27]

Although a variation in the bail may seem desirable as an attempt to accommodate an accused who is in custody, the extent of its use indicates certain deficiencies of the present system. If the amount subsequently set is proper, then it is arguable that the amount originally set was excessive. This appears to indicate that bail was initially set without sufficient investigation of the accused's resources, his roots in the community, and the role of these factors in ensuring his appearance for trial. It is all too easy for a busy magistrate, knowing that he has the power to vary bail, to take the position that he will consider the matter with more care at a later time if the accused is still in custody.

While collecting the data, the writer was struck by the fact that

[25]See s. 401 of the Criminal Code. Bail was increased after it was initially set in only ten out of those cases where the accused was not kept in custody and did not have his case disposed of at the first court appearance. This may serve as some indication that there were few cases in which the accused was re-arrested for further offences committed while awaiting trial; if a further offence is committed the prosecutor would probably recommend that bail be raised or cancelled. This conclusion is presented with some hesitation, however, because the figure of ten may be unduly low owing to the difficulty encountered in extracting from the data the cases where bail was altered to the prejudice of the accused. In "The New York Bail Study" *op. cit. supra* note 10, at p. 718 it was found that bail was increased in 33 out of 2,501 cases in which bail was initially set (1.3 per cent). Of these, only 5 (15 per cent) were able to raise the increased amount.

[26]This figure of one-third was arrived at by comparing the number of cases in which bail was varied in the accused's favour with the total number of cases in which the accused remained in custody for over one week and did not have his case disposed of at the end of the first week. Those cases disposed of at the end of a week were not included as it was felt that there would be no true opportunity for a magistrate to vary bail in them because the accused would not usually appear on remand before the end of one week.

[27]In "The New York Bail Study" *op. cit. supra* note 10, at pp. 716–17 it was found that of 2,501 cases in which bail was set, 158 persons (6.3 per cent) successfully had the amount lowered. Of these 158, 56 (35 per cent) were unable to furnish the reduced amount.

TABLE XXIX

VARIATION OF BAIL IN THE LOWER COURTS ACCORDING
TO THE RESULT OF THE CASE

Type of Variation		Result of Case				
		Conviction	Acquittal	Withdrawn	Other result	Total
Bail initially set	Bail initially set was lowered and the accused raised it	7	4	6	3	20
	Bail initially set was lowered but the accused did not raise it	2	11	4	1	18
	Accused subsequently released on his own recognizance after bail initially set was not raised	6	20	15	3	44
"No bail" initially set	Bail subsequently set and raised after "no bail" at first court appearance	11	2	1	5	19
	Bail subsequently set and not raised after "no bail" at first court appearance	21	2	4	*	27
	Accused subsequently released on his own recognizance after "no bail" at the first court appearance.*	2	2	3	1	8
Total		49	41	33	13	136

*These include cases where bail was subsequently set and not raised.

many of the individual cases followed a familiar pattern: an accused would be charged with, say, breaking and entering; high bail or no bail would be set, effectively keeping him in custody; later, bail would be set or lowered, but it would still be too high for him to raise; after spending a number of weeks in custody he would be released on his own recognizance; and, finally, the charge would be dismissed or withdrawn. Over 80 per cent of the persons who were eventually released on their own recognizance as the result of a variance by the magistrate had the case disposed of in their favour by a withdrawal or a dismissal. Over one-half of this group who had the charge withdrawn or dismissed had been charged with offences against property; one-quarter of the group had bail initially set at more than $2,000. In almost all of these cases the period of time spent in custody was greater than one week.

The fact that so many persons eventually released on their own recognizance were kept reasonably long in custody because of inability to raise bail, only to have their cases eventually dismissed or withdrawn, demonstrates another unfortunate aspect of the existing bail system. It also may indicate the existence of a highly questionable practice on the part of the police of arresting a person without sufficient proof of guilt and suggesting high bail to the court to keep him in custody; if the accused fails to plead guilty or if evidence of guilt cannot be found, the charge is withdrawn or dismissed.

B. *By Review in the Higher Courts*

An accused in custody who is denied bail or is unable to raise bail has the theoretical right to have a High Court judge review his bail application.[28] It would appear, however, that this right is rarely used. In 1961 there was only one case for all of Ontario in which an application to vary bail as set or denied in magistrates' court was heard in the High Court. In this one case, bail had been set at $4,000 for stealing a traveller's cheque valued at $200, and bail was reduced by the High Court judge to $500. One other application to the High Court to vary bail as set in magistrates' court was struck off the court list without being heard because no one appeared at the hearing.

This study is concerned principally with cases commenced and concluded in the magistrates' courts. In examining the High Court records it was apparent that the number of applications to the High Court with respect to setting bail generally was very small. In 1961 there were only seven applications to set or vary bail for all cases in all courts: two were discussed above; two were murder cases in which bail can only be set by a High Court judge;[29] and the remaining three (which were unsuccessful) were applications after a committal for trial. There is no reason to believe that these figures are not typical of those for other years. Many reasons can be suggested for the dearth of applications to the High Court for bail variance: the procedure is not expeditious at a time when speed is of the essence;[30] it requires money for legal fees when lack of funds is often the very reason for the application; and the chance of success is probably slight owing to the deference accorded to the discretion of the judicial officer initially setting bail.

In contrast to Ontario, applications to the High Court to vary bail in England are becoming increasingly more common.[31] Lord Devlin has pointed out that "before 1939 there were less than 100 of these applica-

[28]See the Criminal Code ss. 463, 465.

[29]Criminal Code s. 464.

[30]See Williams, *The Reform of the Law* (1951) at p. 189: "there is no reason why this application should not be made within the matter of a few hours."

[31]For the situation in the United States, see Freed and Wald, *op. cit. supra* note 5, at p. 87: "Since the amount of bail is within the discretion of the lower court, appellate courts rarely set it aside as 'excessive'. Quick appeal, if available, would likely meet with quick affirmance, unless the accused could show that the trial court relied on improper criteria, or refused to consider the facts."

tions annually to the judge; in 1956 the total was 1,665. . . . Out of the 1,665 applications in 1956, 7 per cent. were granted, and that is quite a normal proportion. . . ."[32] There are a number of possible reasons for the discrepancy in practice between England and Ontario. Many of the substantial number of accused persons in Ontario who do not have the aid of counsel are often unaware of their legal rights. Even if they were aware of their right to apply to a High Court judge for review of the bail set, lack of counsel could nullify it. Apparently at one time a printed application form for bail variance was available in Ontario, but when they ran out some years ago no additional ones were printed. Handwritten applications by the prisoner encounter procedural difficulties in the courts; therefore the accused is forced to obtain the services of a lawyer. Because there appears to be no adequate provision for providing legal assistance on such applications for impecunious offenders, many accused persons are not able to avail themselves of their right to apply to the High Court. In England, on the other hand, the prisoner is made aware of his rights by a notice posted in the police cells, and "the most common form of application for bail is by the prisoner himself in writing and it is presented through the Official Solicitor."[33] The recent increase in applications for bail variance in England has been attributed by Lord Devlin to the notice posted in the police cells.[34]

IV. CONCLUSION

The obvious conclusion is that the existing bail system is not functioning properly. It has been shown that magistrates generally set bail at standardized amounts according to the offence charged rather than according to the likelihood that the accused will appear for his trial. The

[32]Devlin, *The Criminal Prosecution in England* (1960), at p. 72. The Home Office Study at p. 20, para. 53, states: "Anyone refused bail by the magistrates' court may apply to the High Court, the application being heard by a judge in chambers. From figures obtained from the Prison Commission, it appears that between one and two per cent of persons committed for trial in custody are released on bail in this way."

[33]Devlin, *op. cit. supra* note 32, at p. 72. Rule 9 of the English Magistrates' Courts Rules, 1952, states that where a magistrates' court committing a person for trial of an offence other than treason or murder does not release him on bail, it shall inform him of his right to apply for bail to a judge of the High Court. See Archbold, *op. cit. supra* note 4, § 206.

[34]Devlin, *op. cit. supra* note 32, at p. 72. Prisoners in England have occasionally proceeded by *habeas corpus* on the ground that the amount fixed by the justices is so excessive as to amount to a grant of no bail and thus contravenes the *Bill of Rights*, 1688–9: see *Ex parte Thomas* [1956] *Crim. L. Rev.* 119 (Div. Ct.); cf. *Ex parte Speculand* [1946] K.B. 48 (K.B.).

main question explored was the ability of accused persons to raise the bail that was set. Perhaps the most important, as well as the most disturbing fact in the entire study is that the data showed that well over half of all accused persons did not raise the bail that was set at the first court appearance. A comparison with the results of certain American studies showed that fewer persons were able to raise the bail initially set in Toronto than in the American cities studied. A study of the English data showed that in England the number of persons who were unable to raise the bail set was very low. In England, security in advance is not the practice; thus, few persons are kept in custody because of inability to raise bail once it has been set. A number of additional undesirable features of the present system were examined. It was found that even in the cases where the accused was able to raise the bail there was often a period of delay before he was released from custody. Moreover, there were very few applications to the higher courts to vary the bail that was set. An examination was also made into such anomalous rules as the inability of the accused to use his own house as security or his wife to use property held jointly with the accused. The next two chapters explore additional defects in present bail practices.

8. The Professional Bondsman

PROFESSIONAL BONDSMEN exist to meet the needs of the vast numbers of persons unable to raise the requisite amount of bail themselves. For a fee they supply the security which enables an accused to obtain his release from jail. The operations, legality, and desirability of these professional bondsmen will be examined in this chapter.

I. How the Bondsmen Operate

There are basically two types of professional bondsmen operating in Toronto: the professional surety and the professional "money-lender." Their operations are well known to many court officials and lawyers. In essence both accomplish the same end.

The professional surety will, for a fee (usually 15 per cent of the face value of the bond), put up the requisite amount of security for the accused in either real property or cash. He may either have this real property or cash himself, or be in contact with persons who can supply it. Cash is rarely provided in this manner in Toronto, however, because the cash surety can operate with some semblance of legality as a money-lender.

The money-lender does not consider himself to be a professional bondsman, but an examination of his activities discloses that, in point of fact, he is. He operates in a manner different from that of the professional surety; for a fee, or "interest" (also usually 15 per cent of the face value of the bond), he lends money to accused persons or to their sureties to use for posting bail. This 15 per cent fee for both the money-lender and the surety is not per annum, but for the length of time the accused is out on bail pending trial. Assuming, for example, that bail is set at $500, the professional will give this sum to the accused or his surety on payment of interest of $75. The borrower then goes to the bail magistrate, who takes the money and issues a receipt acknowledging the deposit. The back of this receipt is signed by the borrower and turned over to the money-lender, who in turn writes over the signature assigning the bail money to himself. In some cases the procedure is expedited by not having the borrower handle the money. The professional and the borrower attend together before the bail magistrate; the professional hands $500 directly to the magistrate, receives $75 from the borrower, and has the borrower sign the back of the receipt as soon as it is issued. In either case, if the accused shows up for his trial, the professional will present the bail receipt at the cash wicket at the City Hall and be given $500. He signs a register acknowledging receipt of this sum from the bail cashier.

II. EXTENT OF THEIR OPERATIONS

The following exchange is reported to have taken place recently in a Toronto Magistrate's Court:

> When Trew asked for two weeks to pay the $100 fine, Magistrate Bolsby suggested he pay it from his $500 bail. Trew replied he had obtained the $500 from a professional bondsman.
> "But that's illegal," said Magistrate Bolsby. Mr. Humphrey assured him it was happening all the time and the rate was about 15 per cent. . . .[1]

The money-lending procedure seems to be used more frequently in Toronto than the surety. No systematic attempt was made to assess the extent of the professional surety's operations by analysing, for example, the number of times a surety's name appeared on a cash bond. However, in the course of the routine collection of statistical data it became apparent that the same surety's name sometimes recurred in circumstances from which the only reasonable inference was that the surety was a professional. One individual, for example, owned a house, in which he had an $8,000 equity (according to his sworn affidavit), which was used for three individuals who had been charged at different times with breaking and entering, and had been granted bail at $3,000 each, and at one point of time all three of these persons were out on bail by virtue of this property. The property was thus used to provide bail for three persons at one time in a sum that was greater than the surety's equity, in spite of the fact that the owner of the property swore an affidavit at the time of entering into each of these bonds that he was "not bail or surety for any other person." A quick check of other property recognizances showed that, in addition to these three, the same property was used to bail three other persons during the same calendar year.

It was much easier to obtain an indication of the extent of the opera-

[1]*Toronto Daily Star*, July 22, 1964.

tions of the professional money-lender who must sign a register on presenting the bail receipt to reclaim the bail money. An analysis made of the register, to determine the extent to which the same names recurred, determined that a reasonably large proportion of the amount of cash bail handled by the courts is put up by professionals. One particular individual is apparently very active. An examination of the records revealed that over a period of five months he was involved in just over one-eighth of the total cash bail posted by or on behalf of all accused persons tried in Magistrates' Courts in Toronto. Table XXX shows the extent of his involvement.[2]

TABLE XXX

CASH BAIL DISTRIBUTED TO ONE PARTICULAR INDIVIDUAL

| Month | Bail Picked Up by One Particular Individual | | Total Disbursements from the City Hall (in dollars) | Percentage of Total Amount |
	Amount (in dollars)	Number of cases		
Sept. 1961	9,250	24	76,535	12
Oct. 1961	6,525	13	83,890	7
Nov. 1961	10,275	26	62,427	16
Dec. 1961	10,220	27	63,966	16
Jan. 1962	6,565	26	55,570	12

III. THE LEGALITY OF THEIR OPERATIONS

It is clear that the professional surety is operating illegally. Section 119(2)(e) of the Criminal Code provides that a person is "deemed wilfully to attempt to obstruct, pervert or defeat the course of justice who . . . being a bondsman, accepts or agrees to accept indemnity, in whole or in part, from a person who is released or is to be released from custody under a recognizance." The professional bondsman, because of the fee that he charges, "accepts . . . indemnity, in whole or in part."[3]

There is less certainty about the criminal illegality of the professional money-lender. He cannot be caught by the specific provision mentioned above because that applies only to a person who is a bondsman. The Code provides, however, that the specific provisions should not restrict

[2]The extent of this individual's involvement with respect to the offences included within the study may be even greater than indicated here because the figures shown include provincial offences with which this individual was seldom involved.

[3]Even if, on a narrow construction of the section, the fee charged is not considered indemnification, the general provision under s. 119(1) would cover the case.

the generality of s. 119(1). The better opinion would appear to be that the conduct is illegal under the general words of s. 119(1) which provides: "Every one who wilfully attempts in any manner to obstruct, pervert or defeat the course of justice is guilty of an indictable offence and is liable to imprisonment for two years." It is also arguable that the conduct constitutes an offence under s. 408(2)(a)—a conspiracy to effect an unlawful purpose.[4] If the prosecution fails because the conduct is straight money lending, the conduct would in any event constitute an offence under the Dominion Small Loans Act.[5]

If the professional is acting illegally, so is the accused. Similarly, the accused's lawyer who "counsels, procures or incites" the accused to commit this offence is himself guilty of an indictable offence under s. 407(a) of the Code. Most lawyers would welcome a system whereby they could avoid the hypocrisy in the present system of advising a client about a professional money-lender without seeming to profess any knowledge of his existence.

IV. OBJECTIONS TO THE BONDSMAN

In spite of the probable illegality of the activities of the professional money-lenders, there have been no prosecutions recorded against them and no serious attempts to eliminate them. Moreover, there appears to be no strong feeling that bail magistrates should refuse to accept bail from a person who has received the security from a bondsman. Most magistrates know that the practice is prevalent; some of the money-lenders operate openly in front of them.[6] Their open existence can be attributed in part to a lack of awareness of the harm caused by the system and in part to a clear awareness that the professional makes a potentially intolerable situation somewhat bearable. It is readily apparent that without the professional money-lender our jails would be even more crowded than they are at present. What is needed, of course, is some system which does not depend on the professional bondsman or money-lender in order to be workable, one in which release is not dependent on monetary sanctions which require security in advance.

[4]See *R. v. Porter* [1910] 1 K.B. 369 (C.C.A.) overruling the earlier cases of *R. v. Broome* (1851) 18 L.T. (O.S.) 19 and *R. v. Stockwell* (1902) 66 J.P. 376.
[5]1952, R.S.C., c. 251, s. 3.
[6]The writer was informed that in the past in the case of prostitutes who could not be released until after their medical was completed, it was sometimes the practice for the money-lender to leave the money for the prostitute with one of the sergeants at the Don jail, who would turn it over to the accused to give to the bail magistrate. This is no longer followed.

The arguments against any form of professional bondsman are overwhelming. It appears reasonably clear that the acceptance by bail magistrates of money obtained from them constitutes a complete rejection of the theoretical and historical basis of any sound concept of bail. Further, it is degrading to the administration of justice to have a system of questionable legality operating in a reasonably open fashion.

Among the more serious objections to the professional bondsman are that the system does little to ensure the appearance of the accused in court; the bondsman reaps large profits; the accused often needs the money he pays to the bondsman; some accused, in order to raise money, commit further offences while awaiting trial; the accused is often represented by lawyers involved in the operation; the system results in the bondsmen, not the courts, controlling who is released; the system tends to favour the professional criminal; and, finally, the existence of the bondsman tends to increase the amount of bail required for all accused persons.

A. Appearance in Court

The services of both the professional money-lender and the professional surety offer little incentive for the accused to appear at trial. When money is "loaned" to the accused or security is "put up" on his behalf, the accused has no *financial* interest in showing up for his trial. The fee of 15 per cent has already been paid to the professional. If the accused shows up for trial he will get nothing back; if he does not show up he will not be required to pay anything in addition. Further, the accused will in no way be influenced in his actions by the fact that an impersonal professional, as opposed to a surety who may be a friend or relative, may lose money if he does not show up for trial.

When the transaction is handled by "lending" money to a friend of the accused who will act as the accused's surety, similar financial considerations apply. The accused and his surety gain nothing financially if the accused shows up for his trial, and lose nothing if he does not show up.

Thus, the financial burden falls on the "professional" if the accused does not appear.[7] This individual has neither the facilities nor the inclination to keep an eye on the accused and ensure that he appears in court. If he does not appear, in most cases the professional treats the estreating of bail as a normal business loss. Of course, he attempts, usually successfully, to have only a portion of the bail estreated. In some

---

[7]The professional would not be able to sue the surety or the accused, as the case may be, on an implied contract of indemnification. See the cases cited in *R. v. Porter, supra*, note 4.

cases, though, particularly if there is a fair amount of money at stake, the professional will take steps to find the accused. However, it would surely be preferable to have police officers undertake the task of tracking down accused persons who have not shown up for their trial. The detection of crime and the apprehension of criminals has become primarily a police function. There is no reason, other than historical, why the private citizens' role should remain so dominant in this area. The extent of this phase of the professional bondsman's activities in the United States is often exaggerated. As the drafters of the new Illinois Code of Criminal Procedure stated: "As to the value of bondsmen being responsible for the appearance of accused and tracking him down and returning him at the bondsman's expense—the facts do not support this as an important factor. While such is accomplished occasionally without expense to the country, the great majority of bail jumpers are apprehended by the police of this and other states."[8]

B. Profits of the Bondsman

It is impossible to estimate the amount of money made by bondsmen. However, some indication of the profit involved can be gained by examining the dealings of the individual mentioned above (and see Table XXX). It will be recalled that the rate of remuneration is 15 per cent of the face value of the bond no matter how long the accused awaits trial.[9] Assuming that the average length of time pending trial in the magistrates' courts is one month, and that 5 per cent of the total amount of money put up for bail is eventually estreated (a figure much higher than the true amount), the total net profit of the individual mentioned previously would be slightly over $10,000 for the year from the magistrates' court cases alone.[10] The rate of return on the capital invested is thus over 100 per cent per annum.

C. Position of the Accused

It is obvious that the accused will often require this money to assist himself in preparing for his trial and paying for legal assistance. Apart from this, the money is needed in most cases for the accused's own

[8]See the Comments of the Committee in the *Tentative Final Draft of the Proposed Illinois Code of Criminal Procedure*, 1963, at p. 113.

[9]In general, American bondsmen charge less, the standard premium rate appearing to be 10 per cent. See generally, Freed and Wald, *Bail in the United States: 1964* at p. 23. In addition to the lower premium rates, the length of time during which the bond operates is, in general, longer in the United States. The American bondsmen, however, do not have to hand over to the court the total amount of the bond as Canadian money-lenders are indirectly obliged to do.

[10]The exact figure in the hypothetical case works out to $10,280.

expenses and those of his family while he is awaiting trial. The sum involved is not merely nominal; to raise $1,000 bail the accused must pay $150 in advance, and the very fact that the accused is forced to resort to a professional is in itself some indication that he is in need of the money.

D. Raising Money by Committing Further Offences

It would seem reasonable that payment to the professional bondsman or money-lender increases the possibility of further offences being committed during the period before trial.[11] In fact, the accused who does indulge in further criminal acts may feel justified in recouping the price which society has permitted the bondsman to force him to pay for his liberty.

E. Lawyers and Bondsmen

The accused stands a good chance of being represented by a lawyer involved in the operation because some lawyers are themselves in the business of money-lending or providing surety for bail or have concluded an arrangement with a bondsman.[12] In either event, it is somewhat uncertain whether these lawyers are providing the quality of representation expected from the legal profession (especially in those cases where the bondsman represents the accused on their applications for bail).

F. Power of the Bondsman

As we have seen, the majority of accused persons are unable to raise the bail that is initially set. The professional bondsman or money-lender often has effective control over whether the accused is released or kept in custody and thus, as an American judge has pointed out, the "professional bondsmen hold the keys to the jail in their pockets."[13] It is the bondsman who, without adequate investigation, assesses the risk of whether the accused will turn up for his trial and, in so doing, judges whether the accused should be released.[14] This is obviously undesirable,

[11]See Freed and Wald, *op. cit. supra* note 9, at p. 25: "Reports from some cities indicate that some defendants who owe bondsmen money commit further crimes, especially burglaries, to pay bond premiums."

[12]For a discussion of this situation in the United States, see the "New York City Bar Report" (1964) 19 *The Record* 11, at p. 16; Freed and Wald, *op. cit. supra* note 9, at p. 35.

[13]*Per* Circuit Judge J. Skelly Wright in *Pannell* v. *United States* (1963) 320 F. 2d 698, at p. 699 (D.C. Cir.); see also Freed and Wald, *op. cit. supra* note 9, at p. 32.

[14]See *People* v. *Smith* (1949) 91 N.Y.S. 2d 490 at p. 494, 196 Misc. 304 at p. 307 (*per* Sobel J.).

for control over the accused's liberty is shifted to a person who is operating on the dark fringes of the legal order.

There are no controls over the operations of the bondsman: he may act on caprice or whim, he may be prejudiced against certain offences or offenders, and he may act on mere rumour. It may well be that the bondsman in Canada is more reluctant to perform his service than his counterpart in the United States: the American bondsman generally will protect himself by seeking collateral security in cases he considers high risks.[15] In Toronto, on the other hand, collateral does not play a significant role in the operations of the bondsman: in doubtful cases the Toronto bondsmen will simply refuse to take the risk of the accused absconding. Another bondsman might assess the risks differently but it appears that the forces of competition do not usually operate in this area.

G. The Professional Criminal

A professional criminal has a much greater chance of making contact with a professional bondsman and being released on bail than an accused who has not previously been in contact with the law. There are a number of reasons for this: the first offender will often not readily be aware of the existence of the professional bondsman; contacting the bondsman is more difficult for him than it is for the accused person who "knows the ropes;"[16] the bondsman will probably prefer to deal with persons who have proven to be good risks by showing up for trial and not causing him any trouble with the authorities; acting for the professional criminal who may have a high bail set offers greater financial rewards to the bondsman; and, finally, there is probably a greater chance that the first offender will be more reluctant knowingly to enter an illegal transaction with a surety than would a seasoned offender. This last point merits attention: if it is illegal for the surety or money-lender to take remuneration under s. 119(2)(d) of the Code, it is equally illegal for the accused to give compensation; the two activities are reciprocal.

H. Increasing the Amount of Bail

One of the most harmful consequences of the existence of the professional bondsmen is that magistrates, knowing of the existence of these

[15]For discussion of the use of collateral, see the "New York City Bar Report" *op. cit. supra* note 12, at pp. 12–13, and Freed and Wald, *op. cit. supra* note 9, at p. 27. Freed and Wald report that in cities which strictly enforce forfeitures the bondsmen attempt to obtain full collateral. Collateral is sometimes taken in Toronto, but is not the general practice.

[16]This also occurs in the United States where professional bondsmen are legally recognized. See Freed and Wald, *op. cit. supra* note 9, at pp. 22–23, 35; "New York City Bar Report" *op. cit. supra* note 12, at p. 17; *People* v. *Smith, op. cit. supra* note 14.

persons, and perhaps wishing to impose a certain burden on the accused, tend to set bail at higher levels than if there were no professional bondsmen. The present system therefore becomes circular and self-defeating: because of the existence of the bondsmen, the system is forced to rely on their services. An interesting example of the amount of bail demanded can be seen in relation to the offences of prostitution.[17] Ten years ago the standard amount of bail required for this offence was $50. Because professional money-lenders have been widely available for these offenders, the standard amount of bail gradually has risen, first to $200, and then to $500 where it stands today. Probably one of the reasons for the increase is that magistrates know that a prostitute readily can obtain the services of a professional bondsman. The present fee for obtaining $500 bail is approximately the same as the total amount of bail required a decade ago. This sum is difficult to raise without resorting to a professional bondsman. Thus an accused prostitute who either does not know of the professional bondsman, or will not become involved with him, or is refused by him, is obviously in a much worse position than she would have been ten years ago.

V. The Bonding Company

Professional bondsmen play a significant role in the United States, where they are legal. Bonding companies would seem to have grown up in the United States to help alleviate the difficulty faced by the accused in providing security in advance of release and to provide a *quid pro quo* if the accused absconded. Freed and Wald state: "A study conducted by the United Nations recently disclosed that the United States and the Philippines are the only countries to allot a significant role to professional bail bondsmen in their systems of criminal justice."[18] Allowing professional bonding companies to write bail bonds is a solution only superficially attractive, however—a form of painkiller which does nothing to root out the disease. Many of the objections raised previously to the professional bondsman apply with equal force to the professional bonding company, along with a number which are of particular application to the bonding company. For example, once the bondsmen become legally recognized, there is pressure to have their activities regulated, thereby creating problems of supervision and control.[19] One consequence of regulation is that the remuneration of the bondsman is

---

[17]S. 164(1)(C).

[18]Freed and Wald, *op. cit. supra* note 9, at p. 22.

[19]See generally, for a discussion of the regulation of bondsmen in the United States, Freed and Wald, *op. cit. supra* note 9, at p. 36 *et seq.*

limited. As a result, the bonding company often insists on collateral being posted in addition to the premium and this, of course, makes it more difficult for the accused to be released. An unfortunate additional side effect of the system is that: "The professional bail bond business is plagued by charges of corruption and collusion between bondsmen and court officials, police, lawyers, and organized crime. Regular payoffs by bondsmen to police have sometimes been described as essential to survival in the bonding business."[20]

It would be senseless to introduce the American system at the very time when the Americans are discovering its shortcomings and attempting to diminish the scope of its operation.[21] One such attempt to decrease the importance of the professional bondsman can be found in the recommendations outlined in the *Proposed Illinois Code of Criminal Procedure*, 1963, which would permit the accused to execute a bail bond and deposit 10 per cent of its face value with the court. If the accused turns up for his trial 90 per cent of his deposit will be returned to him: 10 per cent (i.e., 1 per cent of the face value of the bond) is kept as compensation for running the system. The object of such a scheme is to drive persons away from the professional bondsman because no addi-

---

[20]Freed and Wald, *op. cit. supra* note 9, at p. 34.

[21]The desired goal in the "New York City Bar Report" *op. cit. supra* note 12, was "the final abolition of the professional bondsman." One could sense at the National Conference on Bail and Criminal Justice in Washington in May 1964, which the writer attended, that the bondsmen were aware that their importance was declining and would decline further in the future. One of the principal arguments used against their elimination by one of their spokesmen was "creeping socialism."

A good description of the operations of the bonding companies in New York County can be found in the "New York City Bar Report" at pp. 12–13. The companies simply provide a sure means of obtaining the bail money if the accused absconds and if it is not obtained elsewhere. However, the companies do not play a significant role in the administration of the business of bail bonds and do not in practice run any risk of loss. The "Report" states (at p. 12):

"Once written, the bonds are those of a particular company licensed by the State Department of Insurance. In New York County 43 per cent of the bonds were written by one company and 99 per cent were written by five companies. In all of these companies the writing of bail bonds is a relatively minor part of their entire business. The financial stability of the Companies is carefully reviewed by the Insurance Department and a questionnaire must be completed by them which is quite comprehensive. There is little doubt as to the financial responsibility of these approved companies. Yet such a company lends merely its name to the administration of bail, for although it is on the bond, it runs no risk. Indeed, it has been stated that the insurance companies have never suffered a financial loss through the writing of bonds, or hardly ever."

The result is that the insurance companies are collecting fees and in return fulfil the dubious role of giving a certain measure of respectability to an otherwise shady operation.

tional collateral is required and 90 per cent of the deposit is returned to the accused, whereas, if the deposit had been paid as a fee to the bondsman, it would not, of course, be returned. This proposal was accepted by the United States Attorney General's Committee on Poverty and the Administration of Federal Criminal Justice,[22] and, though it is obviously a desirable step in eliminating the professional bondsman, he will probably still be active as a money-lender to enable accused persons to raise the 10 per cent deposit. The provision is merely a temporary half-way house to the eventual removal of all financial conditions requiring security in advance. The final step to eliminate even this minimal deposit will probably be taken when the practice, under the proposed scheme, demonstrates its possible defects: professional money-lenders will play an active role in providing the funds for the deposits and therefore the accused's risk of loss is very slight; many accused persons will not be able to raise even the modest deposit; this deposit, even though returnable at a later date (and only partially negotiable at an earlier stage) will deprive the accused of cash needed to prepare for his trial and to care for his family; there are far better "inducements" against absconding; finally, bail will tend to be set at higher levels because of the new provisions.[23]

Professional bondsmen or bonding companies cannot be the solution to the problems connected with detention before trial.

[22]*Report of the Attorney General's Committee on Poverty and the Administration of Federal Criminal Justice* (1963) at pp. 81–82. See also the "New York City Bar Report" *op. cit. supra* note 12 at pp. 20–21 (increased use of cash bail). The practice has been in use in New York for some time and legislation was introduced in the United States Senate on May 14, 1964 (s. 2840) to authorize the system in the federal courts. See Freed and Wald, *op. cit. supra* note 9, at p. 79. See also the *Second Preliminary Draft of Proposed Amendments to the Rules of Criminal Procedure before the United States District Courts,* Rule 46(d).

[23]See the *Chicago Sun Times,* Feb. 28, 1964 (cited in Freed and Wald, *op. cit. supra* note 9, at p. 79) where it is reported that the Chief Justice of Cook County's Circuit Court suggested raising the statutory bail schedule tenfold for defendants with police records to meet the proposed procedures for Illinois.

9. Consequences of Absconding

THREE POSSIBLE DETERRENTS to absconding are discussed in this chapter: a prosecution for "skipping" bail, the estreat of the bail, and recapture of the accused. Although no bail system can operate effectively without imposing and enforcing consequences for absconding, it will be seen that in Toronto the present practices of release before trial are not accompanied by any serious or consistent attempt to enforce the consequences for absconding.

I. CRIMINAL PENALTY FOR "SKIPPING" BAIL

Many informed Americans have, over the years, recognized the need for vigorous enforcement of a provision against jumping bail in addition to, or as a substitute for, purely financial sanctions.[1] Legislatures in the United States are becoming increasingly receptive to the adoption of the criminal penalty to ensure the appearance of the accused in court.[2]

The Canadian Criminal Code as early as 1925 provided a penalty for skipping bail.[3] The present s. 125(c) states that everyone who "having been charged with a criminal offence and being at large on recognizance fails, without lawful excuse, the proof of which lies on him, to appear in accordance with the recognizance at the proper time and place for his preliminary inquiry, to stand his trial, to receive

[1]See, e.g., Freed and Wald, *Bail in the United States: 1964* at p. 81; *Report of the Attorney General's Committee on Poverty and the Administration of Federal Criminal Justice* (1963) at p. 78; "Bail: An Ancient Practice Reexamined" (1961) *Yale L. J.* 966 at p. 973; Orfield, *Criminal Procedure from Arrest to Appeal* (1947) at p. 127.

[2]See Freed and Wald, *op. cit. supra* note 1, at p. 81, note 20, for a list of American jurisdictions having bail-skipping statutes. It includes seven states and the federal jurisdiction. The federal statute, 18 U.S.C. § 3146 provides for up to five years imprisonment and a $5,000 fine for skipping bail on a felony charge, and up to $1,000 and one year for a misdemeanor. It is interesting to note that the federal statute does not cover release on one's own recognizance, while the California section covers only release on one's own recognizance.

[3]Stat. Can. 1925, c. 38, s. 3, amending R.S.C. 1906, c. 146, s. 189.

sentence or for the hearing of an appeal, as the case may be, is guilty of an indictable offence and is liable to imprisonment for two years." Regrettably, this provision, although potentially a most effective one for ensuring the appearance of the accused in court, is seldom invoked by prosecuting attorneys. In addition, imprecise legislative drafting and strict interpretations by the courts have detracted from the utility of the section.[4] There were only two prosecutions recorded for jumping bail in the present study: one person pleaded guilty and was convicted; the other pleaded not guilty (was again released, on bail set at $5,000) and was convicted. These two prosecutions represent but a small proportion of the total number of cases in which a prosecution could have been brought.

Information was obtained through the co-operation of the Dominion Bureau of Statistics on all the prosecutions throughout Canada for the offence of jumping bail for the years 1959 and 1960. For the whole of 1959 there were only two prosecutions at the Toronto City Hall Magistrates' Courts; in 1960, there were but three. In York County there were five prosecutions in 1959 and seven in 1960. The data for the rest of the country show a similar reluctance to prosecute for this offence: throughout all of Canada there was a total of 40 cases for 1959 and 41 for 1961.[5]

[4]Just prior to the 1953–54 revision of the Code the section read as follows: "S. 189. Every one is guilty of an indictable offence and liable to two years' imprisonment who . . .

"(c) having been charged with a criminal offence and being on bail does not, without lawful excuse, the proof whereof shall lie on him, present himself at the proper time and place for his preliminary inquiry or to stand his trial or to receive his sentence or for the hearing of an appeal, as the case may be."

R. v. *Singer* (1939) 73 C.C.C. 399 (Que. Ct. of Sess.) held that failure to appear at an adjourned preliminary inquiry did not come within the section as it then read. In *R.* v. *Bowers* (1945) 85 C.C.C. 58 the Ontario Court of Appeal held that the section, then reading "being on bail prior or subsequent to his conviction" required proof that the accused was actually convicted of the principal offence. Roach J. A. stated at p. 65: "The words 'prior or subsequent to his conviction' cannot be ignored. If Parliament had intended the section to have the broader meaning of being on bail pending trial, regardless of the result of the trial, then there was no necessity for using the words quoted. Having used them, effect must be given to their plain and ordinary meaning." A legislative amendment in 1947 covered these situations. It should be noted that an amendment in 1943 added the words "or subsequent to" which presumably allowed a prosecution if the accused absconded after conviction but pending sentence. Also, prior to the 1953–54 Code, the section spoke of "being on bail" rather than "on recognizance" and so may not have been applicable to cases where the accused was released on his own recognizance.

[5]It is interesting to note the disproportionate number of prosecutions for this offence in certain areas. In 1959, one-fifth of the total prosecutions in Canada occurred in Edmonton. (For 1960, Edmonton had one-tenth of the total

The provincial and territorial breakdown for 1959 and 1960 is as given in Table XXXI.

TABLE XXXI

PROSECUTIONS FOR SKIPPING BAIL

Province	1959	1960
Alberta	8	4
British Columbia	5	11
Manitoba	1	1
New Brunswick	0	0
Newfoundland	3	0
Nova Scotia	1	0
Ontario	17	21
Prince Edward Island	0	0
Quebec	2	1
Saskatchewan	2	2
Yukon	1	1
Total	40	41

A perusal of the jail sentences imposed leads one to the conclusion that, even in the cases where a prosecution is brought, the offence is not usually treated with the seriousness it warrants. Because there are generally so few prosecutions, it might be suspected that s. 125 was invoked only in instances of the most blatant disregard for court orders. Yet in many of the cases recorded only a nominal fine was imposed; in others the sentence was made concurrent with that imposed for the principal charge; and in still others the penalty was only a very short prison sentence. For example, in the three prosecutions in the Toronto Magistrates' Courts in 1960, two resulted in a $100 fine and the third in a concurrent sentence. In the two prosecutions in 1959, one resulted in an acquittal and the other in a concurrent sentence.

There is little question that increased enforcement of the penalty for skipping bail would be desirable.[6] The court releasing an accused should inform him clearly of the criminal consequences of failure to appear, and the warning should in addition appear on the recognizance that the accused signs.[7] This would necessitate an amendment to the

prosecutions.) Though this may be due to a large number of persons jumping bail, it is more likely due to an appreciation of the importance of vigorous prosecution under the section. In New Brunswick, on the other hand, there were no prosecutions reported in 1959 or 1960.

[6]See references cited in note 1, particularly the *Report of the Attorney General's Committee on Poverty and the Administration of Federal Criminal Justice* at p. 78.

[7]See the *Report of the Attorney General's Committee, ibid.* at p. 78: "Great care should be taken at the bail hearing that the accused understand the nature of the obligation to appear for trial and that this understanding be reinforced by the sending of letters to persons at liberty restating the accused's obligation to present himself for trial."

existing recognizance form, Form 28, which at present does not mention the criminal penalty for absconding. Such a warning, combined with vigilant police activity to recapture persons who do not appear and increased readiness on the part of prosecuting attorneys to invoke s. 125, would constitute a workable substitute for the present financial sanction in advance. Although in most areas the police initiate criminal proceedings, it appears that for the offence of jumping bail initiation of proceedings is left to the Crown attorney who may, in turn, be leaving it to the police. The result is that bail jumpers are in most cases not prosecuted for this offence. It is most vital, therefore, that both the police and the Crown attorneys recognize the importance of the provision and of their joint responsibility for seeing that it is enforced.

To make s. 125 more effective as a deterrent against absconding it would be desirable to include skipping bail as an extraditable offence in international extradition treaties. The affront to the administration of justice warrants the return of the accused even if the principal offence does not.

II. Estreats

As a means of ensuring the appearance of the accused in court, prosecutions for skipping bail have been found ineffective as presently employed. The same holds true with respect to what is commonly considered to be the fundamental consequence of absconding: the estreating of bail. It might be expected that, under a system relying heavily on the threat of financial sanction as a deterrent against absconding, appropriate steps would be taken to ensure that the threat was carried out where possible. Yet it will be seen that the estreating of bail in the Toronto Magistrates' Courts is not pursued in earnest, with the result that the financial sanction (at best an unsound system) becomes not only ineffective but farcical. It will be seen that the degree to which bail is estreated and the manner in which it is done are both indicative of a general confusion regarding the bail system in the minds of those who administer it.

A. Estreat Procedure

A brief outline of the estreat procedure as envisaged by the Code will provide the background for an examination of the existing practice in Toronto. If an accused person does not appear according to the terms of his recognizance, a bench warrant for his arrest should be issued by the magistrate. Section 676 (1) of the Criminal Code provides that whenever a person who is bound by recognizance does not comply with a condition of the recognizance the magistrate shall endorse on the back of the recognizance a certificate setting out the nature of and the reason for the default, the names and addresses of the principal sureties, and whether the ends of justice have been defeated or delayed by reason of the default. This recognizance shall then be sent to the clerk of the court (s. 676(2)). Thus far the bail has not been estreated: it has only been noted for estreat. In the County of York, applications for estreat are heard four times a year (September, December, March, and May) before the Senior County Court Judge. Before the hearing, notice will have been sent to the principal and surety named in the recognizance (s. 677(1)). At the hearing, the Judge "may, after giving the parties an opportunity to be heard, in his discretion grant or refuse the application and make any order with respect to the forfeiture of the recognizance that he considers proper" (s. 677(2)).

The Criminal Code thus envisages a system whereby the discretion not to estreat or to reduce the amount to be estreated is given solely to the County Court Judge. It is the *duty* of the magistrate to note the recognizance for estreat and then give it to the Clerk of the Court. Beyond that, the magistrate has no power. In spite of this, however, it was found that in many cases in Toronto the magistrate did not note the recognizance for estreat or, where he did, he later cancelled the notation. These practices vary among magistrates, but it would appear that some, out of a feeling of sympathy for the accused or his surety, feel that the ends of justice have been met if the accused appears, either voluntarily or pursuant to the bench warrant, at a later date. The fact that a noted recognizance was already sent to the Clerk of the Court or, indeed, was already on the County Court Judge's list of bail applications, did not prevent magistrates in some cases from cancelling their notation. Although there is no provision made in the Criminal Code for the cancellation by the magistrate of his endorsement of default, most magistrates feel they have this power. More effective and uniform enforcement of the estreat provisions undoubtedly would be ensured if discretionary concessions were to be granted by the County Court Judge, as is presently required, and not by magistrates, as is presently done.[8]

[8]Petersdorff, *Law of Bail* (1824) describes early English estreat procedures as follows (at p. 536): "The various causes which operate as a discharge of the recognizance, have been already considered. If any of the conditions of that instrument be not complied with, it becomes liable to be estreated (that is, taken out from among the other records, and sent up to the Exchequer), which renders the party an absolute debtor to the crown for the sum or penalty therein mentioned. But as a forfeiture of that security is frequently incurred through mere inattention and ignorance, the statute of 4 Geo. 3. c. 10. empowers the barons of the Exchequer to relieve, on petition, any person whom they may deem a proper object for indulgence."

B. Number of Estreats

In the present study, there were approximately 145 cases in which a bench warrant was issued because the accused did not appear. In only 21 did an application for estreat eventually come before the County Court Judge. Of these 21, there were eight cases in which no forfeiture at all was ordered by the County Court Judge. In the remaining 13, the total amount that was noted for estreat was $15,250; of this, only $4,490 was estreated. It is interesting to note that out of this sum, $3,070 (over two-thirds) was accounted for by four accused persons from the United States who failed to appear for their trials. The nature of the charges against three of these persons would tend to indicate that, if guilty, they were professional criminals: two were charged with keeping a gaming house and one was charged with living off the avails of prostitution. In these three cases the accused persons put up and lost $1,000, $1,000, and $950, respectively. It was probably anticipated (indeed, hoped) that the Americans would return home, not appear for trial, lose their bail money, and relieve Canada of the burden of trying and executing the sentence against them. Obviously, it is undesirable to allow a probable professional who will not show up for trial to purchase his freedom simply by posting money in this manner. These cases are somewhat atypical and, if they are excluded from consideration, the extent to which the estreat procedure is normally employed is even further decreased.

There are a variety of reasons for the fact that 124 bench warrant cases did not reach the County Court Judge. In some, the accused had been released on his own recognizance and the practice is not to make application for estreat in these cases; some were due to a failure by the magistrate to note the recognizance for estreat; and still others were due to the cancellation of the estreat notation by magistrates.

A precise assessment of the percentage of bail estreated was not possible on the basis of the figures on hand. However, even a conservative estimate must be that less than 10 per cent of the bail that could have been estreated was eventually forfeited.[9]

C. Consequences of Non-Enforcement

When steps are not taken regularly to forfeit bail bonds, the bondsmen, and in particular professional bondsmen, will flourish at the expense of the bail system. They will "put up" bail for accused persons without

[9]American writers have observed a similar lack of enforcement in the United States. See, e.g., Moreland, *Criminal Procedure* (1959) pp. 190–92; Freed and Wald, *op. cit. supra* note 1, at pp. 28–30; at p. 30 it is stated: "Collection of forfeited bonds has often been found lax or tinged with scandal."

much concern over the degree of risk involved; they will have even less incentive to supervise the movements and activities of the accused; and they will have little reason to take any active steps to trace an accused in the event that he absconds. A surety who will not regulate the activities of the accused is valueless as a deterrent against the accused absconding.[10]

One of the cases in the study provides a good example of the malfunctioning of present estreat practices. An accused who had a long record was charged with two counts of breaking and entering and one count of possession of burglar's tools. At the time that bail was set for these offences, the accused was already on bail while awaiting trial for other offences. His mother arranged with "acquaintances," a husband and wife who owned property but who did not know the son at all, to use their property as security for his $8,000 bail. The accused did not show up at the next remand date and some time later it was discovered that he was serving a sentence in Nevada. An application was brought by the Crown to have the bail estreated. It was acknowledged by counsel for the bondsman at the hearing of the estreat application that the sureties were informed by the Justice of the Peace of the consequences of default. The argument before the County Court Judge was that the sureties did not know that the accused had a bad record or that he was likely to skip bail. In substance, their plea was that they did not know the accused at all; they had only a passing acquaintance with his mother. The order of the County Court Judge was that if the sureties paid $200, the notation of estreat would be cancelled. Although one may be inclined to feel that it would be unduly harsh to deprive the sureties of $8,000 under the circumstances, in the long run the consequences of non-enforcement are more severe.

If we are going to keep the present system, we must ensure that it is effective by enforcing it[11] not only for cases where security is posted in advance but also for cases where the accused is released on his own recognizance without sureties.[12] If we do not have the heart to enforce

---

[10]See Tappan, *Crime, Justice and Correction* (1960) at p. 336: "Beyond this, where the bondsman is responsible and the bail collectible, courts frequently have failed to levy against the property. Naturally where forfeitures are not exacted, bail comes to have little value for assuring the appearance of defendants or material witnesses. Thus 'jumping of bail' becomes common."

[11]See *Re R. v. Scosky* (1955) 17 W.W.R. 94 (B.C.C.C.); *R. v. Bronson* (1956) 19 W.W.R. 527 (B.C.C.C.); *R. v. Lauder* [1963] 2 C.C.C. 142 (Alta. Dist. Ct.), *Re Ingebrigtson* (1961) 37 C.R. 21 (Man. Q.B.). See also Devlin, *The Criminal Prosecution in England* (1960) at p. 73.

[12]Release on one's own recognizance is apparently taken more seriously in England. See, e.g., Sybille Bedford, *The Faces of Justice* (New York, 1961) at p. 41.

the recognizance, we must find some alternate approach. Surely there are better techniques for ensuring that the accused will turn up for trial than the threat that if he does not show up an often impersonal third party may lose a negligible percentage of the bail noted for estreat. It is certainly arguable that the accused in the above example should not have been released on bail at all, considering the nature of the offences, his long record, and the fact that the offences charged were allegedly committed while he was already on bail. If he was to be released, the deterrent to prevent him from skipping trial should have been awareness of the vigilance of search, the certainty of capture, and the criminal penalty for not showing up at trial.

III. Recapture

Certainty of recapture, when coupled with a penalty for skipping bail, is the most effective deterrent against an accused absconding. In the absence of a serious policy of recapture, bail tends to be a means of purchasing freedom rather than of ensuring appearance.

At the present time there appears to be no consistent policy in Metropolitan Toronto with respect to recapturing accused persons who have absconded. When an accused absconds from Toronto to another area, even within the province, the Toronto police usually make no serious effort to recapture him. Even when it is known that another police force is holding such an accused, there is often reluctance to take active steps to bring him back unless a private complainant is willing to pay the expenses. The Toronto police will leave it to the other municipality, if it so desires, to expend the time and money necessary to return him. Certainly, there is little likelihood that the police will set out to bring back an absconded accused where the offence is minor and the distance great. The probability of recapture varies in direct proportion to the seriousness of the offence and the proximity of the accused to Toronto. The cases involving the allegedly professional American criminals, discussed above, are good examples. It will be recalled that in these cases the court accepted both the bail money and the fact that the accused had left the jurisdiction as a proper *quid pro quo* for his absconding.

Some Crown attorneys can see nothing wrong with the above approach. It is true that the immediate advantages to the police district involved are readily apparent; however, the serious consequences in the long run easily outweigh any immediate advantages. Failure to recapture accused persons who abscond serves as an invitation to professional criminals when they know that if they are caught they may be able to buy their freedom. In addition, it does nothing to counteract crime on a national basis. Lack of a firm policy of recapture plays havoc with the bail system by forcing magistrates to place undue emphasis on the only possible deterrent that remains—money. As a result bail is often set at amounts too high to be raised by the non-professional, yet low enough to be raised by the professional criminal. The tendency therefore is that the professional is not deterred and the non-professional is not released.

Many of the cases publicized in which the police have gone out of the city to obtain an accused's return have resulted from the insistence and financial backing of large organizations such as banks, which recognize the importance of recapture in safeguarding their future operations. It would be well if the police recognized the importance of recapture too. In England, the practice of the police apparently is to ensure that very few persons escape trial by absconding. In 1960, for example, out of 174,659 persons proceeded against for indictable offences in England, only 249 cases were not disposed of by the justices by reason of the persons absconding and being still at large at that time.[18]

At present, ss. 421 and 421A of the Criminal Code give jurisdiction to a court in the same or in another province to try an accused charged with an offence over which the court would normally not have jurisdiction. These sections, however, apply only where the accused has pleaded guilty and so do not remove the need for recapture. If the accused knows that there is little likelihood of his being returned to the place where the offence was committed, he is not likely to plead guilty. Extending these sections to cases where the accused pleads not guilty would not provide an effective solution because the expense of sending witnesses might be greater than the expense of returning the accused. These sections would be more useful in cases where the accused is prepared to plead guilty if there were a serious and consistent policy of seeking the return of an absconded accused. Indeed, the sections are wide enough to cover the offence of jumping bail as well as the principal offence.

The fact that police forces do not actively pursue accused persons who abscond is due only in part to the short-sighted view of the necessity for such steps; it is mainly a result of a shortage of police manpower and finances. Even if an accused is in the custody of another police force, and no detection is necessary, two men must be taken off their regular duties and sent to pick him up. When detection is necessary,

[18]*Criminal Statistics England and Wales,* 1960, at p. 24. At pp. 28–29 it is shown that out of 912,535 persons proceeded against for non-indictable offences, only 1,739 were not disposed of because the accused absconded.

the time and expense involved are immeasurably greater, but the problems involved in recapture go beyond time and finances. It would be unreasonable to rely on a local police force to carry out a policy necessitating provincial, national, and, indeed, international activity. The ideal solution would be for the federal government to implement a policy of recapture on a national basis. A precedent may be found in other areas of conduct which require a broad base of enforcement; for example, control of narcotics has been placed in the hands of the Royal Canadian Mounted Police.

Failing the establishment of a federal scheme, the next best solution would be a provincial plan for Ontario. To a certain extent, the province now lends some financial support to recapturing accused persons, but this is not enough.[14] The province simply provides a fund for the payment of certain out-of-pocket expenses, if the Attorney General so directs, when a police force seeks the return of an accused who has been charged with an indictable offence. It neither provides nor organizes the manpower for this task, nor does it pay the salaries of those from local forces engaged in it.

[14]The fund was established by statute in 1959 (see 1959 Stat. Ont., c. 1, s. 1), now The Administration of Justice Expenses Act R.S.O. 1960, c. 5, s. 12. The fund also applies to accused persons who have not yet been arrested.
"S. 12. Where the Attorney General is of the opinion that it is advisable to bring a person charged with an indictable offence from a place out of or in Ontario to the place of trial in Ontario, he may direct that such be done and in every such case the expenses incurred in carrying out the direction shall be paid out of the moneys appropriated by the Legislature for the administration of justice."

10. An Assessment of Release Practices before Trial

THE FACTUAL MATERIAL set out in the previous chapters is sufficient to demonstrate that the release practices before trial which exist for cases tried in the Toronto Magistrates' Courts operate in an ineffective, inequitable, and inconsistent manner. A complete re-thinking of these release procedures is clearly required.

The period before trial is too important to be left to guess-work and caprice. At stake in the process is the value of individual liberty.[1] Custody during the period before trial not only affects the mental, social, and physical life of the accused and his family, but also may have a substantial impact on the result of the trial itself. The law should abhor any unnecessary deprivation of liberty and positive steps should be taken to ensure that detention before trial is kept to a minimum.[2]

It is not strictly necessary to rely on the "presumption of innocence" to form the conclusion that indiscriminate detention before trial is unsound. One is not forced to rely on a notional presumption when one knows that there is, in fact, a reasonable likelihood that the accused may be innocent. It will be recalled that in the present study 24 per cent of those brought to court were not convicted. Nevertheless, the "presumption" is important as a statement of a basic policy in our law and it adds force to the arguments in favour of a liberal use of release before trial; for example, the United States Supreme Court stated in *Stack* v. *Boyle*: "Unless this right to bail before trial is preserved, the presumption of innocence, secured only after centuries of struggle, would lose its meaning."[3] The "presumption of innocence" has not been relied on in the argument against unnecessary detention before

[1] *Report of the Attorney General's Committee on Poverty and the Administration of Federal Criminal Justice* (1963) at p. 58.

[2] See Rule 46 (c) of the *Second Preliminary Draft of Proposed Amendments to the Rules of Criminal Procedure before the United States District Courts*, which includes as one of the considerations to be used by the court in setting the terms on which the accused can be released: "the policy against unnecessary detention of defendants pending trial."

[3] (1951) 342 U.S. 1 at p. 4 *per* Vinson C.J.

trial in order to avoid entering into the controversy about the extent to which the principle applies to the period before trial.[4]

Apart from the present study there are no Canadian statistics available on the extent of detention before trial. This is unfortunate. It is only when the facts are known, and particularly when they can be compared with those found in other areas, that an intelligent appraisal can be made of existing practices. This is an area in the administration of criminal justice which merits the collection and presentation of data by the Dominion Bureau of Statistics.[5] It should not be forgotten that detention before trial occurs in more cases than detention after trial.

The following summary of the major points in the previous chapters should serve to highlight some of the inadequacies in the present system. Most of the changes recommended, set out here and in the previous chapters, would require implementation by federal legislation; other changes could be brought about only by provincial legislation; still others would depend upon changes in the structure and procedures of the local courts and police forces.

I. Summary of the Major Findings and Recommendations in the Previous Chapters

The arrest procedure was used by the police in over 90 per cent of the cases studied and in over 90 per cent the arrest was made without a warrant. Even under the present Canadian law it is obvious that greater use could and should be made of the summons procedure. Comparative English figures on the use of the summons, set out in chapter 2, show its liberal use in that jurisdiction. Adoption of the numerous recommendations for legislative changes set out in that chapter would facilitate the use of the summons to a greater degree and would tend to ensure that the arrest procedure is not employed where not strictly necessary. Among the changes recommended are such matters

[4]It can be argued with some validity that the presumption is mainly an evidentiary rule applicable to the trial itself. See, for example, the discussion on the presumption of innocence in Thayer, *A Preliminary Treatise on Evidence at the Common Law*, Appendix B at p. 551 *et seq.*, particularly at pp. 561–62; Smith, "Bail before Trial: Reflections of a Scottish Lawyer" (1960) 108 *U. Pa. L. Rev.* 305 at p. 309. It can apply only with difficulty to the arrest itself although even in the area of arrest it can be useful as a statement of principle. See, e.g., *R. v. Wentworth Magistrate's Court, Ex parte Reeves* [1964] 2 O.R. 316 at pp. 318–19 *per* McRuer, C.J.H.C.; *Dumbell* v. *Roberts* [1944] 1 All E.R. 326 at p. 329, *per* Scott L.J.; *R.* v. *McDonald* (1932) 59 C.C.C. 56 at p. 63 (Alberta C.A.) *per* Harvey C.J.A.

[5]See Mostyn, "Bail and the Presumption of Innocence" (1964) 61 *The Law Society's Gazette* 799.

as: authorizing summonses issued by the police; imposing civil and criminal liability for unreasonable use of the arrest procedure; providing for the publication of statistics showing the use of the summons; imposing criminal liability on the accused for failure to obey a summons or for giving a false name or address with intent to escape liability after he has been notified that he will be charged with an offence; and permitting the police to obtain the accused's fingerprints when a summons is used.

Of those arrested by the police (i.e., over 90 per cent of those charged), approximately 85 per cent are kept in police custody until their first court appearance, many for substantial periods of time. Most persons arrested during the day are not brought into court that day, even though the court is sitting. In chapter 3 the study revealed, for example, that in one division station over 80 per cent of all those booked between 7.00 A.M. and midnight were kept in police custody for over 10 hours before their first court appearance. For all of Metropolitan Toronto, 84 per cent of all persons arrested for criminal offences were kept in custody until their first court appearance. Approximately 40 per cent of those who appeared in court in custody for their first court appearance, 95 per cent of whom did not have a lawyer, pleaded guilty at that time. A thorough revision of the procedural aspects of release before the first court appearance is clearly necessary. A number of recommendations are set out in chapter 3 including: increasing the number and effectiveness of the justices of the peace; granting the police the power to set bail and, in any event, to accept bail that has been set by a justice of the peace; authorizing the police to release accused persons from police custody either absolutely or in order to summon them; improving the conditions in the police lockups; ensuring an early appearance in court for the accused by establishing special remand courts which would sit during the day and at night; and improving the system of legal aid by providing assistance before the first court appearance or, at least, adequate notice to the accused of the availability of counsel.

Many persons whose cases are not disposed of at the first court appearance spend substantial periods of time in custody pending the disposition of their cases. Statistics on custody after the first court appearance are presented in chapter 5. Not only were a considerable number of these persons who spent time in custody before trial not eventually convicted or, if convicted, not returned to jail, but also the conditions under which persons awaiting trial are kept in custody are often more restrictive and onerous than those that exist for persons already convicted and serving their sentences. As one writer has observed: "We first administer the major part of the punishment and then enquire whether he is guilty."[6] Recommendations with respect to physical conditions for those in custody awaiting trial at the Don jail can be found in the same chapter where it is argued that there is no logical justification for the conditions which exist and for the type of measures presently taken in these cases. An accused awaiting trial should not be deprived of any reasonable facilities. If possible, there should be separate detention facilities for him. A further step that should be taken is to provide specifically by legislation that the time spent in custody awaiting trial should automatically be taken into account in the sentence imposed.

The fact that time is often spent needlessly in custody is not of itself the only matter for concern; an additional consideration is the clear and alarming relationship that appears to exist between custody pending trial and the trial itself. Thus the seriousness of the problem extends beyond the question of unnecessary deprivation of liberty. In chapter 3 it is shown that custody before the first court appearance is a possible factor in inducing guilty pleas at the first court appearance. As was mentioned previously, approximately 40 per cent of those who appeared in court in custody pleaded guilty at their first court appearance. In chapter 6, which explores in detail the relationship between custody and the outcome of the trial, it is shown that those who were not in custody for their trial were more likely to be acquitted than those who were in custody and, if convicted, were more likely to receive lighter sentences. Apart from taking steps to decrease the use of custody before trial, the prejudicial effects of custody would partially be eliminated if there were a scheme of legal aid, properly conceived and providing adequate representation for all indigent persons, and if court facilities were so constructed that magistrates would not know automatically whether the accused was in custody pending trial.

The prejudicial effects on the accused of custody pending trial demand that the system which determines whether or not he will be released pending trial be a well-considered one. Unfortunately, the bail system as it operates in the Toronto Magistrates' Courts falls far short of any reasonable standard. Little, if any thought is given to the purposes to be accomplished by the granting or denying of bail. The present system is unfortunately often subverted into a form of punishment before trial. Occasionally this use of detention before trial is openly admitted. For example, a Deputy Chief of the Metropolitan Toronto Police force has

---

[6]Puttkammer, *Administration of Criminal Law* (1953) at p. 69.

recently stated publicly, in relation to the apparent rise in the rate of juvenile delinquency and the fact that juveniles are now normally remanded before trial to the custody of their parents: "Years ago we used to remand them in custody for a week after they were picked up. That gave them something to think about and often put them back on the right path."[7]

In the setting of bail there is an undue preoccupation with its monetary aspects. Security in advance is generally required in our courts: release on one's own recognizance was used in less than 20 per cent of the indictable offence cases where bail was set. In addition, standard amounts of bail for various offences were found to exist; bail was evidently set more with an eye on the offence than the offender. Because the primary purpose of bail is to ensure that the accused will show up for his trial one might expect that the fact that offenders obviously vary would be reflected in the amounts of bail set.

The tragedy of this preoccupation with money is that a large percentage of persons are unable to raise the bail that is set. In chapter 7 it is shown that 62 per cent of all persons for whom bail was set at their first court appearance were unable to raise it and, in particular, when bail was set at $500, 60 per cent were unable to raise it. Thus, the ability of the accused to marshall funds or property in advance determines whether he will be released, and as a consequence may have an effect on the outcome of the case. A system which requires security in advance often produces an insoluble dilemma. In most cases it is impossible to pick a figure which is high enough to ensure the accused's appearance in court and yet low enough for him to raise: the two seldom, if ever, overlap. The result is that magistrates tend to throw up their hands and set amounts of bail arbitrarily between the two extremes, at sums which ensure neither the release of accused persons nor their appearance if released. The ability to raise the bail set is simply a barrier to release which the accused may or may not be in a position to surmount. Further, bail is sometimes set punitively with the clear expectation that it will not be raised. By employing the technique of security in advance the police and the courts can more easily use bail as a deliberate means of keeping the accused in custody. For example, in one case examined, bail was set for a waitress implicated in a bad cheque ring at $100,000.

The reliance on security in advance has brought into existence the professional bondsman and money-lender. Although it would appear

[7]See the Toronto *Globe and Mail*, October 12 (news story) and October 14 (editorial), 1963.

that these persons are acting illegally, they have been operating more or less openly; their operations have been tolerated because they meet the pressing need created by the existing bail system. In chapter 8 the following overwhelming objections to their practices were discussed: the system does little to ensure the appearance of the accused in court; the bondsmen and money-lenders reap large profits; the accused often need this money; some accused in order to raise this money commit further offences while awaiting trial; the accused is often represented in court by lawyers involved in the operation; the bondsmen and money-lenders, not the courts, effectively control who is released; the system tends to favour the professional criminal who is more likely to know of and be trusted by the bondsmen; and the existence of the bondsmen tends to increase the amount of bail required for all accused persons.

In spite of this rigid reliance on security in advance as a deterrent against absconding, if the accused does not show up for his trial, only half-hearted steps are taken to estreat the bail. In fact, few if any active steps at all are taken against most accused who abscond. Even if the accused is in custody in another city in Ontario the Toronto police will often make no serious effort to bring him back; in addition, a prosecution for skipping bail is rarely brought. This general lack of enforcement of the system, discussed in chapter 9, is a further illustration that the ability to raise the amount of bail is considered simply a ticket to freedom. In chapter 9 it is recommended that vigorous steps be taken against an accused who wilfully absconds. Not only should the recognizances be forfeited, but special funds and officers should be available, preferably on a national basis, to seek the accused, bring him back for trial, and prosecute him for the offence of absconding as well as for the principal offence. If convicted of absconding, more than a nominal sentence should be imposed. At the time of his release the accused should be made plainly aware of the consequences of failure to appear.

II. A Proposal for a Basic Reform in Present Bail Practices: The Elimination of Security in Advance

A proper system of bail should require the magistrate to make a determination whether the accused should or should not be released pending trial. If he determines that the accused need not remain in custody pending trial, the accused should not be deprived of his liberty merely because of his inability to raise bail. Conversely, if the accused is not deemed to be a good enough risk for release before trial, he should remain in custody, whether or not he has the ability to raise bail. In other words, the magistrate should be forced in all cases to meet and deal directly with the issue concerning the release of the accused from custody. At present, magistrates are meeting and dealing with many of the obviously good risks by release on the accused's own recognizance and with many of the obviously bad risks by denying bail or by setting prohibitive bail. However, it is the persons in the middle group—which constitutes by far the largest group of cases—who are not dealt with directly. Release in these cases is left to be determined by the ability of the accused to raise a set amount of money, usually fixed according to the offence he is alleged to have committed.

Security in advance appears to be the standard practice throughout Ontario. In a recent lecture to Ontario practitioners it was stated: "Usually the justice of the peace will fix bail in the usual amount and you will then arrange for the bondsman to meet the justice of the peace at a particular time and enter into the recognizance, deposit the cash and have the accused released. . . . Generally speaking, bail can either be posted in cash or property can be put up as the security."[8]

The major solution to the defects in bail-setting practices is to eliminate the practice of requiring security in advance, a practice which, inter alia, has the effect of keeping many persons in custody unnecessarily while not acting as a substantial deterrent against absconding for those released. There are better deterrents against absconding: knowledge by the accused of virtual certainty of recapture followed by a prosecution for skipping bail would certainly be more effective and would by itself be sufficient.

It is the requirement of security in advance rather than the creation of a subsequent debt which creates the present problems. No consequences prejudicial to the accused can result in most cases from creating a debt in a reasonable amount due from the accused, or, if easily obtainable, his sureties, to the Crown in the event that the accused fails to appear.

The concept of bail which is advocated here is not a new one: it is the one envisaged by the Canadian Criminal Code and the one presently in operation in England. The practice in Toronto of requiring security in advance is simply an undesirable and unjustifiable gloss on the traditional concept of bail.

The Canadian Criminal Code, like the English practice, envisages a bail system which derives its effectiveness from supervision of the accused by sureties who acknowledge in a recognizance that if the

[8]Galligan, "Advising an Arrested Client," *Law Society of Upper Canada Special Lectures 1963* at pp. 43–44.

accused fails to appear for his trial they will owe a designated debt to the Crown. An examination of the provisions for bail in the Code makes this clear. Section 451(a)(i) of the Code provides for the admitting of the accused to bail by a justice "upon the accused entering into a recognizance in Form 28 before him or any other justice, with sufficient sureties in such amount as he or that justice directs." No mention is made in the Criminal Code of any *deposit* by the surety. Signing a recognizance simply creates a debtor–creditor relationship. A definition of a "recognizance" which has been cited with approval by the courts is "the acknowledgment of a debt due to the King, defeasible upon the happening of a certain event, *viz.*, the appearance of the party in Court, pursuant to the terms of the condition."[9] The cases reported tacitly bear out the fact that security in advance is not envisioned by the Code.[10] In other subsections the justice is permitted to bail the accused without sureties either on the accused's own recognizance or after deposit of security by the accused.[11] These approaches facilitate the accused's release in cases where he would have difficulty in finding sufficient sureties. No provision is made in the Criminal Code for the posting of real property by the accused. If the drafters of the Code were simply looking to the security *per se*, they would surely have permitted the accused to use real property.[12] Form 28, referred to above, which is the bail recognizance form set out in the Code, clearly contemplates the creation of a debt by the surety in the event of default rather than a deposit of security by the surety in advance of release. Form 28 reads as follows: "Be it remembered that on this day the persons named in the following schedule personally came before me and severally acknowledged themselves to owe to Her Majesty the Queen the several amounts set opposite their respective names, namely. . . . to be made and levied of their several goods and chattels, lands and tenements, respectively, to the use of Her Majesty the Queen, if the said A.B. fails in the condition hereunder written."[13]

One can perhaps understand the comfortable certainty in the mind of the justice of the peace in requiring security in advance: if the justice

[9]See *R.* v. *McDonald* [1958] O.R. 373 at p. 378 (Ont. C.A.) and cases cited therein.
[10]See, e.g., *R.* v. *Greig* (1914) 23 C.C.C. 352 (Sask. Dist. Ct.); *Johnston* v. *Attorney General* (1910) 16 C.C.C. 296 (N.S.S.C.); *R.* v. *Lepicki* (1925) 44 C.C.C. 263 (Man. K.B.).
[11]See also Petersdorff, *Law of Bail* (1824) at p. 506. Cf. note, "Bail: An Ancient Practice Reexamined" (1961) 70 *Yale L. J.* 966 at p. 971, note 34; Perkins, *Cases on Criminal Law and Procedure* (1959) at p. 914.
[12]See *supra*, chapter 7.II.D.
[13]For summary conviction cases, see s. 710(2) which also refers to Form 28.

requires it, no one can later claim that the surety which he accepted was not a "sufficient surety." By requiring security in advance the justice can bypass this sometimes difficult determination of the sufficiency of the surety. Yet it is surely this very determination that is required of the justice of the peace. To facilitate his decision he can examine the sureties under oath.[14] An affidavit of justification by a surety is now normally required for cases of property bail, except when the amount of bail is low. In addition, there are certain statutory provisions which are designed to discourage an inadequate surety from entering into a recognizance. If a surety signs a recognizance and is not able to satisfy the judgment in the event the accused absconds, the surety is liable under s. 679 of the Code to be sentenced by a County Court Judge to any period of imprisonment which the Judge "considers proper in the circumstances."

The sections of the Code prohibiting indemnification of the surety[15] and giving the surety extraordinary powers of seizing and surrendering the accused[16] support the view that bail as presently envisaged in the Code is a matter of supervision rather than simply a question of money. If the law were concerned only with money then there would be no need to prevent indemnification of the surety. Magistrates in Toronto set bail at a certain sum without caring whether the sum is advanced by the accused or by a surety. It is inconsistent with this practice to prohibit indemnification; if magistrates are not to be concerned with who is to take the risk of loss, why should there be any prohibition against indemnification?

The Canadian Bill of Rights provides, as a guide to interpretation, that no person shall be deprived of "the right to reasonable bail without just cause."[17] There have been no cases reported under this section and it is uncertain what, if anything, it adds to the existing law. The section, however, raises the interesting question: can bail be said to be reasonable

[14]See Armour, "Bail in Criminal Cases" (1927) 47 C.C.C.1 at p. 12: "And if it be doubtful whether the sureties are sufficient to answer for the amount of the bail the Justice may examine them on their oaths and require them to justify on oath before him as to their sufficiency." See also Archbold, *Criminal Pleading Evidence and Practice* (35th ed., 1962) § 205: "the proposed bail may be examined upon oath as to his means. . . ;" Jackson, *The Machinery of Justice in England* (4th ed., 1964) at pp. 133–34: "A proposed surety may . . . be questioned about his means by the justices, or the police may be asked to inquire into the apparent standing of the person."

[15]Criminal Code, s. 119.

[16]*Ibid.* ss. 673 and 674. See also s. 672.

[17]Stat. Can. 1960, c. 44, s. 2(f). Cf. *R.* v. *Collins* (1962) 38 C.R. 169 (Man. C.A.).

if the accused cannot raise it?[18] The day is probably not far distant when the United States Supreme Court will hold that it is unconstitutional to set bail at a sum which the accused cannot raise. Freed and Wald state: "Some have suggested that requiring monetary bail an accused cannot post may be 'excessive' by definition, in violation of the Eighth Amendment. Others believe that to condition release on a price that some can pay and others cannot, discriminates between rich and poor so as to amount to a denial of the 'equal protection of the laws.' These arguments coupled with [certain Supreme Court decisions[19]] have provoked the suggestion that monetary bail may at some future date be found unconstitutional when applied to a man without money."[20]

Not only is the present practice contrary to that envisaged by the Code, but also the Ontario Bail Act,[21] in permitting a lien to be placed on property used by a surety, is inconsistent with the Code which, as we have seen, does not contemplate the creation of a property interest in the Crown in advance of forfeiture of the recognizance. Section 1 of the Act provides that in cases in which a person has been committed for trial and is admitted to bail, the Crown attorney shall, and, in any other case in which a person is admitted to bail, the Crown attorney may, send a certificate of lien to the Sheriff of the county in which the land mentioned is situate. The effect of making this entry is, in the words of the Act, to give the Crown "a lien against the surety's property mentioned in the certificate of lien for an amount equal to the amount for which he offered himself as a surety as shown in the certificate of lien."[22] The inconsistency between the Code and provincial legislation makes it arguable that The Bail Act is unconstitutional as an interference with

[18]See the English case of *Ex parte Thomas* [1956] *Crim. L. Rev.* 119.

[19]*Griffin* v. *Illinois* (1956) 351 U.S. 12; *Coppedge* v. *United States* (1962) 369 U.S. 438; *Gideon* v. *Wainwright* (1963) 372 U.S. 335; *Hardy* v. *United States* (1964) 375 U.S. 277; see also *Bandy* v. *United States* (1960) 81 S. Ct. 197; (1961) 82 S. Ct. 11.

[20]*Bail in the United States: 1964* at p. 74.

[21]R.S.O. 1960, c. 28. The Act was first introduced in 1957 following a report by an interdepartmental government committee which was to consider problems connected with bail. Their report has not been made public, but it apparently concentrated on the question of "straw" bail. No other province appears to have similar provisions.

[22]S. 4. The Act goes on to say (s. 7): "As soon as a surety is discharged, the lien is discharged, and the Crown attorney shall deliver or transmit a certificate of discharge (Form 2) to the sheriff to whom the certificate of lien was delivered or transmitted." These sections clearly indicate that the intent of the section was to create a lien which was to prevent the owner from dealing with the property until the lien was discharged. If the only intent was to create a lien after default, then there would be no necessity for delivering the certificate of lien at the time the accused is admitted to bail.

the authority of the federal government to legislate on criminal procedure.[23] The Crown's lien should not arise until the accused fails to appear. If the Act were so limited its constitutional validity would be clearer. The Crown would be able to protect its interest in the accused's property between the time the accused absconds and the time the writ of *fieri facias* is sent to the sheriff.

In England it is clear that only a potential debt is created by the surety entering into a recognizance. Dr. R. M. Jackson states: "Bail in our courts rests on recognisances, which are really promises; there are no deposits of money or the pledging of property or bondsmen."[24] The following comments were made recently concerning the practice in England: "In this country, once bail has been determined, with or without sureties, recognisances are entered into and the accused is free until he returns to face his trial. No money changes hands, whatever the amount at which bail is set. Only if the accused fails to appear for his trial does the question of estreating bail arise. It is only then that forfeiture to the Crown of the sum shown in the recognisance or any lesser sum is in point."[25] The point is made by Sybille Bedford in *The Faces of Justice* which contains the following account of a proceeding in a London magistrates' court: "The defendant is asked whether he wants an adjournment to see a solicitor, and he decides he does. 'Sixty pounds,' says the magistrate after what must have been a lightening calculation, for bail must be both large enough and not prohibitive. It need not be put down in cash."[26] This has long been the English practice. In 1824, Petersdorff, in his treatise on bail stated: "The bail are not liable as in civil cases to stand in the place of their principal, in the event of his non-appearance and non-conformity with the condition of the recognizance; but are only bound in a certain specified sum, which then becomes forfeited, and attaches upon their lands, tenements, and personal property."[27] The surety in England need only be "possessed of property equal to the responsibility incurred."[28] It is true that as a rule only "householders" are accepted,[29] but this is far different from insisting

[23]There are numerous cases bearing on the constitutional invalidity of provincial legislation which interferes with the federal power over criminal law and procedure. See, e.g., *R. v. Badman* (1956) 116 C.C.C. 212 (B.C.C.A.); *Toronto v. The King* [1932] A.C. 98 (P.C.); *A.G. Que. v. A.G. Can.* [1945] S.C.R. 600; *Re Bence* (1954) 108 C.C.C. 373 (B.C.S.C.).

[24]*Op. cit. supra* note 14, at p. 133.

[25]Mostyn, *op. cit. supra* note 5, at p. 801.

[26]Sybille Bedford, *The Faces of Justice* (New York, 1961) at p. 41.

[27]Petersdorff, *op. cit. supra* note 11, at p. 510.

[28]*Ibid.* at pp. 505–6.

[29]See Archbold, *op. cit. supra* note 14, § 205; Egan, "Bail in Criminal Law" [1959] *Crim. L. Rev.* 705.

upon "homeowners" and, in any event, it is not an absolute rule. Archbold states: "They are usually householders; but it is for the magistrate or judge to act upon his discretion as to the sufficiency of the bail. . . ."[30]

It is interesting to note that, in North America, when the word "bail" is used, one thinks of a sum of money;[31] when English writers, for example, Petersdorff in the above quotation, use the word "bail" they are normally referring to the surety. In England, the leading criminal practice treatise, Archbold, *Criminal Pleading Evidence and Practice*, states: "Bail are sureties taken by a person duly authorized, for the appearance of an accused person at a certain day and place, to answer and be justified by law."[32]

A recent Home Office Study, *Time Spent Awaiting Trial* (1960), discussed in chapter 7, presents convincing statistical proof that security in advance is not a part of the English practice. It was pointed out in chapter 7 that out of 1,934 cases examined, only 26 (1 per cent) were in custody because of inability to raise bail, i.e., to find acceptable sureties. The amounts required also demonstrate that the sureties' obligation is probably more a formality than a sizable financial responsibility. For example, in 95 per cent of the cases which were tried summarily and in which the accused was released on bail, the sureties' recognizance was for a sum under £50.[33] An accused in England is rarely kept in custody: he usually can find sureties willing to enter into an obligation to pay this small sum if he absconds but, if he cannot, he often is released on his own recognizance.

In Canada we have combined the American practice of requiring security in advance with the English prohibition against professional bondsmen or indemnification in any form. Thus the practice in Canada adopts the most restrictive features of both the English and the American systems.

The fundamental aim of any reform, therefore, must be to eliminate the requirement of security in advance. By simply reverting to the original concept of bail, many of the ills of the system would be cured. It is obvious that it is far, far easier for an accused to find a surety who will undertake to pay, say, $500 if the accused absconds, than it is to find a surety who has $500 cash or property available to be tied up in advance as security. Even persons who are worth substantial sums of money may have difficulty in raising ready cash on short notice.

[30]Archbold, *op. cit. supra* note 14, § 205.
[31]See, e.g., Sutherland, Cressey, *Principles of Criminology* (6th ed.) at p. 358: " 'Bail' is the name for the financial security which is pledged. . . ."
[32]Archbold, *op. cit. supra* note 14, § 201.
[33]See *supra* chapter 7, Table XXII.

It might be tempting to leave the provisions of the Code as they now are: after all, they do not envisage security in advance by the surety. However, it is obvious that the present practice of requiring security in advance is so much a part of the practice in Toronto (and, it is believed, in most other areas in Canada)[34] that the best means of changing it is a clear legislative statement that security in advance by a surety shall *not* be required. It is, of course, possible for this change in philosophy to be brought about by judicial decision, but so few cases are brought to a higher court on a question of bail that it might be some time before such a decision would be possible, even if the higher courts were willing so to hold.

There would be little point, however, in a complete reversion to reliance on the supervision of sureties. Apart from the difficulties faced by many accused persons in today's large urban centres in obtaining sureties, it is impractical to expect that sureties will, in fact, supervise the movements of the accused and will track him down if he absconds. The practice of generally not estreating the sureties' recognizance is a tacit acknowledgment by the courts of this fact. In earlier periods it was understandable that total reliance was placed on the surety: not only were communities smaller and more closely knit, but also there was no alternative solution—there were no police forces or efficient means of communication if the accused absconded and there was no provision for a penalty if he was apprehended. Today the supervision and apprehension of the accused can best be left to the police. Having the surety undertake supervision is therefore only of secondary importance. The formality involved in having the recognizance signed by the sureties and the accused is ultimately more important than supervision by the sureties. Little harm can result in a recognizance in a modest sum by a surety; if hardship and delay result, however, sureties should not be required. The concept of suretyship has probably been retained in

---

[34]It is interesting to note that when the present Criminal Code was being discussed in Parliament in 1954, the then Minister of Justice, the Honourable Stuart Garson stated, "As I understand the practice of applying for and securing a bail order, it is that counsel for the accused would make an application under the clause we are now considering [s. 465], of course after it is passed. The nature of the offence with which the accused is charged would be disclosed to the court, and the accused's counsel would urge the judge to admit his client to bail of so much. Perhaps crown counsel might agree with that sum. In many cases they do. But if the offence was a particularly serious one crown counsel might oppose the amount suggested by the accused's counsel, and then as between the two contending viewpoints the judge, exercising his judicial discretion in the matter, would have to make up his mind as to what he thought was a fair amount at which to set bail under all the circumstances, one of which could be the accused's financial resources." Parliamentary Debates, House of Commons, 1954, at p. 2840.

England for formal and traditional reasons rather than for practical necessity.[35] As mentioned above, in 95 per cent of the cases in the Home Office Study, which were tried summarily, the recognizance entered into was for a sum under £50 and in many cases only the accused entered into the recognizance.[36]

Steps are presently being taken in the United States to encourage the use of release on one's own recognizance. The Manhattan Bail Project, discussed in chapter 4, provides the machinery for encouraging courts to release accused persons without security. The accused's roots in the community are examined before his appearance in court by an official of the Project and the court is then informed whether the accused is recommended for release without security. Similar projects have been undertaken in other cities throughout the United States with the active support of the Department of Justice.[37] These projects, however, appear to operate only for the "good risks." The requirement of security in advance still operates in the vast majority of cases.

In many cases there is no necessity of requiring a recognizance from the accused because he obviously will appear in court. Although there is no statutory provision for not requiring a recognizance, it is often not demanded. It would be desirable to legalize the procedure by a provision similar to the proposed United States Federal Rule 46.1: "The commissioner or court or judge or justice may release defendant without bail upon his written agreement to appear at a specified time and place and upon such conditions as may be prescribed to insure his appearance."[38]

III. Establishing Proper Criteria for Withholding Bail

Although appearance for trial is the primary consideration in the setting of bail it is not the only criterion in deciding whether bail should

[35]There is some indication that the supervision of the surety was not always taken seriously in early Canadian history. See Riddell, *Upper Canada Sketches* (1922) at p. 90, note 13, where it is pointed out that common bail was a "solemn farce": two alleged but mythical bondsmen, John Doe and Richard Roe, or John Denn and Richard Fenn, became sureties for the appearance of the defendant. See also the interesting account of a duelling case on p. 27 in which the accused was released pending trial on a charge of murder.

[36]See Fitzgerald, *Criminal Law and Punishment* (1962) at p. 179; Bedford, *op. cit. supra* note 26, at p. 41; Devlin, *The Criminal Prosecution in England* (1960) at p. 73.

[37]The Department of Justice co-sponsored, along with the Vera Foundation (which implemented the Manhatten Bail Project), the National Conference on Bail and Criminal Justice held in Washington in May 1964.

[38]*Second Preliminary Draft of Proposed Amendments to the Rules of Criminal Procedure before the United States District Courts,* 1964.

be granted or denied.[39] No attempt will be made to analyse in detail the cases reported in which the courts have permitted accused persons to be kept in custody without bail. It is assumed here that, to a certain extent, this practice is permissible in Ontario;[40] it is clearly so in England.[41] It is important that the practice, if permissible, be carefully controlled because of the harmful consequences of custody and the possible misuse of inarticulated, vague criteria. This study does not argue that all persons should be released pending trial. It does, however, argue strenuously for definite, clear, and unequivocal criteria to be used in denying bail. There are strong indications that the police would welcome them. The *Report of the Ontario Police Commission on Organized Crime*, dated January 31, 1964, stated: "It is recommended that discussions take place between federal and provincial authorities to establish a statutory provision governing circumstances in which bail may be denied."[42]

[39]See, e.g., *Ex parte Fortier* (1902) 6 C.C.C. 191 (Que. C.A.); *R. v. Cooperbloom* (1924) 43 C.C.C. 394 (Ont. S.C.); *R. v. Lepicki* (1925) 44 C.C.C. 263 at p. 265 (Man. K.B.); *R. v. Greig* (1914) 23 C.C.C. 352 (Sask. Dist. Ct.); see generally, *infra*, note 44.

[40]Even for offences which were misdemeanours at common law: see, e.g., *R. v. Russell* (1919) 32 C.C.C. 66 (Man. K.B.); cf. *Ex parte Fortier* (1902) 6 C.C.C. 191 (Que. C.A.). Bail was refused in *Re N.* (1945) 19 M.P.R. 149 because it was thought that the accused might be a danger to the public because he was a sexual offender and had a serious communicable disease. See also the cases cited in note 45 *infra*. As a rule bail is normally not granted in murder cases. See generally, *Tremeear's Criminal Code* (5th ed., 1944) at p. 793. In *R. v. Jackson* (1959) 31 C.R. 368 at p. 372 (Man. Q.B.) Hall C.J.Q.B. stated: "There are cases (other than murder) in which bail may rightfully be refused but they are few and far between."

[41]See, e.g., *R. v. Guest* [1961] 3 All E.R. 1118 (even for misdemeanours); *R. v. Phillips* (1922) 128 L.T. 113 and cases cited therein. See generally, Archbold, *op. cit. supra* note 14, § 202. Cases which discuss denial of bail because of the danger of repetition are set out in note 43 *infra*. See also Bedford, *op. cit. supra* note 26, at pp. 43–44. It may well be that more persons are being kept in custody in England at the present time than appears to be desirable. One suspects that bail is sometimes denied too freely. See generally, for the number of persons tried in the superior courts who were denied bail, the *Report of the Interdepartmental Committee on the Business of the Criminal Courts*, 1961, Cmnd. 1289 at pp. 4–5 which showed that, of all persons tried in the superior courts, 40 per cent were kept in custody pending the higher court hearing and 60 per cent were released on bail. Of those who pleaded not guilty, 30 per cent were kept in custody pending the hearing and 70 per cent were released on bail, 18 per cent of those who pleaded not guilty after being kept in custody were acquitted. See generally, Mostyn, *op. cit. supra* note 5. English Courts have, perhaps, departed somewhat from the philosophy expressed in the *Report of the Committee on the Detention in Custody of Prisoners Committed for Trial in England and Wales*, 1921, Cmd. 1574 at p. 7: "Magistrates have ample power to admit prisoners to bail, but we feel we cannot too strongly express our view that, except in cases of the most serious character, or cases where there is cogent reason to believe the prisoner will escape, this power cannot be too freely used."

[42]At p. 73c. Cf. p. 89 where a group of Crown attorneys recommended to the

The most troublesome ground often used for denying release is that concerning the risk of repetition by the accused. In England, following the *Phillips* case in 1947, this criterion for denying bail is now well recognized,[43] although not fully accepted by all legal authorities.[44] In Ontario it is the practice and may also be the law.[45] The danger is readily apparent: the very concept presumes that the accused is guilty of the crime with which he is presently charged. Deprivation of liberty for this reason can easily be abused. Further, it is not really a sound method of assuming jurisdiction over the accused. If an accused in fact commits offences while awaiting trial he can be dealt with by law in the same manner as any other alleged offender. Why should an accused be deprived of his liberty in this very important period before trial because of something he may do in the future? As Denning M.R. has observed: "It would be contrary to all principle for a man to be punished, not for what he has already done but for what he may hereafter do."[46] If

---

Commission "that the Criminal Code be amended to set out grounds where bail may be *granted.*" (Italics mine.) Note the subtle change in approach.

[43]See *R. v. Phillips* (1947) 32 Crim. App. R. 47 at p. 49 in which the Court (*per* Atkinson J.) stated: "They wish magistrates who release on bail young housebreakers, such as this applicant, to know that in nineteen cases out of twenty it is a mistake." See also *Re Whitehouse* [1951] 1 K.B. 673 (Div. Ct.) *sub nom. H.M. Postmaster-General* v. *Whitehouse* (1951) 35 Crim. App. R. 8; *R. v. Gentry* (1955) 39 Crim. App. R. 1951 (C.C.A.); *R. v. Wharton* [1955] *Crim. L. Rev.* 565 (C.C.A.); Home Office Circular No. 132/1955 (Sept. 8, 1955); "Bail and Bad Character" (1956) 106 *The Law Journal* 22. See generally, Foote, "Introduction: The Comparative Study of Conditional Release" (1960) 108 *U. Pa. L. Rev.* 290 at pp. 295–96.

[44]Archbold, *op. cit. supra* note 14, § 203 maintains the traditional rule that "the proper test of whether bail should be granted or refused is whether it is probable that the defendant will appear to take his trial. *Re Robinson*, 23 L.J.Q.B. 286; *R. v. Scaife*, 10 L.J.M.C. 144." The *Phillips* line of cases are dealt with by stating simply: "It is not usual to grant bail . . . where the prisoner has a bad criminal record. . . ." See also *R. v. Rose* (1898) 18 Cox C.C. 717 at p. 719 (Cr. Ca. Res.) *per* Lord Russell C.J.: "It cannot be too strongly impressed on the magistracy of the country that bail is not to be withheld as a punishment, but that the requirements as to bail are merely to secure the attendance of the prisoner at the trial."

[45]The cases are conflicting. See, approving *Phillips*, *R. v. McKinney* [1963] 40 C.R. 137 (Sask. Q.B.); *R. v. Travers and McGuire* (1963) 42 C.R. 32 (Que. Q.B.); *R. v. Vickers and Fletcher* (1948) 93 C.C.C. 342 (B.C. Co. Ct.); *R. v. Wing* [1964] 3 C.C.C. 102 (B.C. Co. Ct.); cf. *R. v. Samuelson and Peyton* (1953) 17 C.R. 395 (Newf. S.C.); *Re Johnson's Bail Application* (1958) 122 C.C.C. 144 (Sask. Q.B.); *R. v. Henderson* (1963) 45 W.W.R. 55 (Alberta S.C.).

[46]*Everett* v. *Ribbands* [1952] 2 Q.B. 198 at p. 206 (C.A.). See also *Williamson* v. *United States* (1950) 184 F. 2d 280 (2d Cir.) *per* Jackson J. at p. 282: "Imprisonment to protect society from predicted but unconsummated offences is so unprecedented in this country and so fraught with danger of excesses and injustice that I am loath to resort to it. . . ." The federal constitution and that of the great majority of the states have a constitutional provision guaranteeing bail as a matter of right in all non-capital cases. See Foote, *op. cit. supra* note 43, at p. 291.

preventive detention were really justified in these cases it would be even more justified after the accused was convicted. No one would deny that some persons on bail commit offences, but there is no evidence to suggest that the danger is significantly higher before trial than after release from prison.[47] A term in prison, particularly a very short one, would appear to do very little to decrease the likelihood that the accused will commit a further offence. Yet it is very rare for an application for preventive detention to be made under Part XXI of the Code to have the accused declared an habitual criminal or a dangerous sexual offender. One wonders why the heavy burden of justifying preventive detention at the time of the trial should not also be carried with respect to preventive detention before trial.

Legislation should set out the criteria which can be used to determine in what cases an accused can be deprived of release pending trial. The onus of establishing, by proper evidence either under oath or by affidavit, the necessity for denial of bail should be on the Crown.[48] The court denying bail should also be required to give its reasons for doing so.[49] Some of the possible criteria that could be used to deny bail (although denial of bail should not follow simply as a matter of course in such cases) are: a previous conviction for skipping bail; a previous conviction for an indictable offence committed while awaiting trial for an indictable offence; the bringing of a subsequent charge for an indictable offence alleged to have been committed while the accused was already on bail awaiting trial for an indictable offence; and a serious risk of intimidation of witnesses.[50] To guard against the possibility that the police will bring an unfounded charge in order to have the accused placed in custody, the police should be required to introduce at least *prima facie* evidence of guilt at the bail hearing. Further, if there is a serious risk that the accused will abscond he should, of course, not be released pending his trial.

Allowing a complete denial of bail increases the importance of decreasing the time spent awaiting trial, a problem that has only been

[47]Cf. The Toronto *Globe and Mail*, Dec. 20, 1963, where Metropolitan Toronto Police Chief Mackey is reported to have stated that "criminals often commit crimes while free on bail. . . ."

[48]Williams, *The Reform of the Law* (1951) at p. 189.

[49]*Ibid.*

[50]See the *Report of the Ontario Police Commission on Organized Crime*, dated January 31, 1964, at pp. 122–23, referring to the denial of bail because of the danger of intimidation of witnesses. Such a criterion can easily be abused. See Devlin, *op. cit. supra* note 36, at p. 80. In any event the accused can be charged with intimidation or assault. See the American Law Institute's *Code of Criminal Procedure* (1930) § 70 for well-considered criteria for denying bail.

touched on in this study. Its solution requires a complete re-assessment of the present inadequate court facilities.

IV. ADDITIONAL CHANGES REQUIRED IN THE BAIL SYSTEM

Where it is felt necessary to provide some measure of control over the accused when not in custody pending trial, certain techniques, not presently used, could be employed. A position midway between total custody and complete release without effective supervision would undoubtedly influence the courts to release more persons. The Code should specifically permit the Courts to impose conditions in the accused's recognizance.[51] At the present time the only condition stated in the Code is appearance at trial, and it appears reasonably clear that the imposition of a condition not envisaged by the Code would not be binding on the accused.[52] One condition, for example, which might occasionally be employed, is periodic reporting by the accused to the police or probation officers. The police would thus have reasonable notice if the accused absconded. Other conditions might be that the accused reside at a certain address, notify the police of any change of address, remain on the premises after a certain time at night, or even, in appropriate cases, during both day and night. A further condition, which might be appropriate if there were a risk that the accused would flee abroad, would be the surrender of the accused's passport. This practice is often resorted to in England and can effectively be followed without legislation simply by refusing to release the accused until his passport is surrendered. A step which would be desirable in all cases, but in particular in cases where the remand is for more than a week, is for the court to mail to the accused a card stating the time when, and the court in which, he is to appear.[53]

If security in advance is not eliminated from the bail system, it is

[51]See generally, on the imposition of conditions, note, "Conditions of Bail" (1961) 125 J.P. 787; Egan, *op. cit. supra* note 29, at p. 707; Devlin, *op. cit. supra* note 36, at p. 74. The proposed United States Federal Criminal Rules will specifically permit the imposition of conditions. See the *Second Preliminary Draft of Proposed Amendments to the Rules of Criminal Procedure before the United States District Courts*, Rule 46(d): "the court . . . may authorize the release of the defendant without security upon such conditions as may be prescribed to insure his appearance."

[52]If a collateral undertaking were given and not honoured, this might be a factor taken into account by the magistrate in cancelling bail. Even when used in this manner, it would be preferable if legislative backing were given to the imposition of conditions in any form.

[53]See the *Report of the Attorney General's Committee on Poverty and the Administration of Federal Criminal Justice* (1963) at p. 78.

imperative that steps be taken to eliminate the unnecessary delay and hardship caused by certain of the present rules. These are discussed in chapter 7, where it is suggested that there is no reason why a justice of the peace, in order to eliminate delay in releasing the accused, should not accept a cheque from a surety or from the accused in appropriate cases, or why an accused should not be able to use his own real property as security, or why an accused's spouse cannot use property held jointly. At present these procedures are not permitted.

A further change which is clearly necessary, whether or not security in advance is the accepted rule, is to permit certain non-judicial officers to accept bail which has already been set by a judicial officer.[54] In England a rule provides: "Where a magistrates' court having jurisdiction to take a recognisance from any person has fixed the amount in which he and his sureties, if any, are to be bound, the recognisances may be entered into before any justice of the peace, or before the clerk of any magistrates' court, or before any police officer not below the rank of inspector, or before the officer in charge of any police station or, if the person to be bound is in a prison or other place of detention, before the governor or keeper of the prison or place."[55]

Regardless of what else is done with the bail system one obvious change must be made: the magistrate deciding the bail must have sufficient knowledge on which to base an intelligent decision. The system in Toronto depends mainly on speculation, the view of the police, and the magistrate's ability to judge the likelihood of the accused appearing for trial merely from his looks in court. The large mass of cases in the Toronto Magistrates' Courts makes a sound bail assessment almost impossible at present. As the American National Commission on Law Observance and Enforcement observed in 1931: "in more pioneer and rural days, the court or court's advisers were sufficiently acquainted with the few persons brought into court to know, with a fair degree of accuracy, whether they would be dependable or whether they need be detained or put on bail. With the tremendous mass of cases brought into court in the modern metropolitan community, this personal knowledge is no longer possible, and the attempt to substitute uninformed, casual, and arbitrary decisions has made the bail system the failure that it is."[56] A system similar to that first used by the Vera Foundation in New York, described in chapter 4, should be adopted here. Independent officials, perhaps law students, could, before the accused's appearance in court,

[54]See chapter 3, note 32, and chapter 7, note 20.
[55]Magistrates' Courts Rules, 1952, Rule 68 (1).
[56]*Report on Prosecution* (1931) at p. 89 *et seq.*

collect the relevant information on his background and ties in the community. In much the same way that probation officers now present presentence reports to assist the magistrate in imposing sentence, the information could then be presented to the magistrate with a recommendation of what might be desirable in the circumstances. Even in smaller communities this technique would be helpful. At the present time magistrates who will eventually try the case either delve into the accused's background or they do not. Either approach is undesirable because the latter leaves the magistrate uninformed, the former, possibly, prejudiced.[57] If an independent person makes an investigation and recommendation, some of the material prejudicial to the accused but not relevant to the decision for bail would not come before the magistrate. It would, of course, also be desirable to have counsel available to the accused at this stage.[58]

To sum up, the accused should be released, if he is to be released at all in the particular case, on his own recognizance or, in appropriate cases, with recognizances by sureties in reasonable amounts, recoverable if the accused fails to appear. Failure to raise a certain sum of money should never be the reason for the accused remaining in custody, however. Financial security in advance must be eliminated from our release practices before trial. The real deterrents against absconding should be vigilance of search, certainty of recapture, and eventual prosecution for the principal offence as well as for the accused's failure to appear for his trial.

[57]See *R. v. Hoggard* [1964] 2 C.C.C. 302 (Alta. S.C.).

[58]For a general discussion on this point see the writer's study dated September 1964 "Legal Aid: Working Papers Prepared for the Joint Committee on Legal Aid for Ontario." See also Williams, *op. cit. supra* note 48, at pp. 189–90: "All undefended persons should have the benefit of legal assistance on the question of bail. The moment bail is refused, the presiding magistrate should ensure that there is a lawyer to represent the interests of the defendant and use his best efforts to secure bail for him."

Cases

Statutes

Index